Acting Companies and their Plays in Shakespeare's London

ALSO AVAILABLE

Acting Companies and their Plays in Shakespeare's London

Siobhan Keenan

BLOOMSBURY
LONDON • NEW DELHI • NEW YORK • SYDNEY

Bloomsbury Arden Shakespeare

An imprint of Bloomsbury Publishing Plc

50 Bedford Square	1385 Broadway
London	New York
WC1B 3DP	NY 10018
UK	USA

www.bloomsbury.com

Bloomsbury is a registered trade mark of Bloomsbury Publishing Plc

British Library Cataloguing-in-Publication Data
A catalogue record for this book is available from the British Library.

ISBN: HB: 978-1-4081-4667-5
PB: 978-1-4081-4663-7
ePDF: 978-1-4725-7568-5
ePub: 978-1-4725-7567-8

Library of Congress Cataloging-in-Publication Data
A catalog record for this book is available from the Library of Congress.

Typeset by Fakenham Prepress Solutions, Fakenham, Norfolk NR21 8NN
Printed and bound in India

For Sally-Beth MacLean

CONTENTS

ACKNOWLEDGEMENTS

For assistance and permission to quote from manuscripts held in their collections I would like to thank the following: The British Library Board; Calista Lucy and the Governors of Dulwich College; The Trustees of Lambeth Palace Library; The National Archives; Manuscripts and Special Collections at the University of Nottingham; and Somerset Archives and Local Studies Service. I am also very grateful to the following scholars and colleagues, each of whom kindly looked at and commented on extracts from this book during its composition: Nicola Boyle, Gabriel Egan, Sally-Beth MacLean, Tiffany Stern, Suzanne Westfall and Charles Whitney. Any faults or errors that remain are, of course, my own. The completion of this book has been assisted by a period of research leave granted by my Vice-Chancellor (Professor Dominic Shellard) and De Montfort University for which I express my thanks. I have also appreciated the support that I have received during the writing of the book from Arden and Margaret Bartley especially. My final and greatest debt of gratitude is, as always, to my husband David Morley and my sons, Gabriel and Edward, for their support and encouragement.

TEXTUAL NOTE

All quotations from Shakespeare are from the *Shakespeare: Complete Works*, revised edition, edited by Richard Proudfoot, Ann Thompson and David Scott Kastan (London, 2011), unless otherwise stated. Similarly, all quotations from the diary of Philip Henslowe are from the second edition of *Henslowe's Diary*, edited by R. A. Foakes (Cambridge, 2002), unless otherwise stated. Quotations from textual editions printed prior to 1700 have been cited from the facsimiles of those editions accessible via the subscription service Early English Books Online (http://eebo.chadwyck.com). When quoting directly from manuscripts and early printed texts the original spelling and punctuation is retained, as are contractions. Unless otherwise specified, the dates given for literary works cited in the text are their dates of publication.

ABBREVIATIONS

BL	British Library
ELR	*English Literary Renaissance*
ET	*Early Theatre*
HLQ	*Huntington Library Quarterly*
MLR	*Modern Language Review*
MP	*Modern Philology*
MRDE	*Medieval and Renaissance Drama in England*
MS	Manuscript
ODNB	*Oxford Dictionary of National Biography*
PMLA	*Publications of the Modern Language Association*
REED	Records of Early English Drama
RES	*Review of English Studies*
RORD	*Research Opportunities in Renaissance Drama*
SEL	*Studies in English Literature, 1500–1900*
SP	State Papers
SQ	*Shakespeare Quarterly*
SS	*Shakespeare Survey*
SSt	*Shakespeare Studies*
TN	*Theatre Notebook*
TNA	The National Archives
TRI	*Theatre Research International*
TS	*Theatre Survey*
UTQ	*University of Toronto Quarterly*
v	verso (left page)
YES	*Yearbook of English Studies*

Introduction

The Tudor and Stuart eras saw a revolution in English theatre. This included the establishment of the first permanent playhouses in London, the gradual secularization and professionalization of theatre and the establishment of a repertory system in which there were daily performances of different plays which saw more than a thousand plays performed publicly between the accession of Elizabeth I (1559) and parliament's closure of the theatres in 1642. Although the London playhouses and players were not without their detractors (see p. 115), by the end of the sixteenth century theatre in London was a thriving business. At the centre of this transformation of the English stage were the period's acting companies.

Acting companies and their playwrights: The research context

Some of the major histories of the English Renaissance stage produced in the early and mid-twentieth century – such as E. K. Chambers's *The Elizabethan Stage* (1923) and G. E. Bentley's *The Jacobean and Caroline Stage* (1941–68) – offered brief accounts of its leading acting companies, and Bentley was an early advocate of the value of studying playwrights such as Shakespeare in the context of 'the London commercial theatre and the organized professional acting troupe'; but recent years have seen a marked increase of scholarly interest in acting companies as central to English Renaissance theatre history.[1] This has included Andrew Gurr's seminal survey of the troupes active in Shakespearean London, *The Shakespearian*

Playing Companies (Oxford, 1996); studies which explore specific aspects of the history of acting companies such as Jerzy Limon's *Gentlemen of a Company: English Players in Central and Eastern Europe, 1590–1660* (Cambridge, 1985), Willem Schrickx's *Foreign Envoys and Travelling Players in the Age of Shakespeare and Jonson* (Wetteren, 1986), my own *Travelling Players in Shakespeare's England* (Basingstoke, 2002) and Roslyn L. Knutson's *Playing Companies and Commerce in Shakespeare's Time* (Cambridge, 2001); works which explore particular types of acting company such as Michael Shapiro's *Children of the Revels: The Boy Companies of Shakespeare's Time and Their Plays* (New York, 1977) and Edel Lamb's *Performing Childhood in the Early Modern Theatre: The Children's Playing Companies* (Basingstoke, 2008); and a series of company-specific studies, including W. Reavley Gair's *The Children of Paul's: The Story of a Theatre Company, 1553–1608* (Cambridge, 1982), Roslyn L. Knutson's *The Repertory of Shakespeare's Company, 1594–1613* (Fayetteville, 1991), Scott McMillin and Sally-Beth MacLean's *The Queen's Men and Their Plays* (Cambridge, 1998), Mary Bly's *Queer Virgins and Virgin Queans on the Early Modern Stage* (Oxford, 2000) (about the Children of the King's Revels), Andrew Gurr's *The Shakespeare Company, 1584–1642* (Cambridge, 2004) and *Shakespeare's Opposites: The Admiral's Company, 1594–1625* (Cambridge, 2009), Lucy Munro's *Children of the Queen's Revels: A Jacobean Theatre Repertory* (Cambridge, 2005), *Locating the Queen's Men, 1583–1603: Material Practices and Conditions of Playing* (Farnham, 2009), edited by Helen Ostovich, Holger Schott Syme and Andrew Griffin, Bart van Es's *Shakespeare in Company* (Oxford, 2013) and Lawrence Manley and Sally-Beth MacLean's forthcoming history of Lord Strange's Men.

Part of the explanation for the widening scholarly interest in acting companies and their plays is to be found in the pioneering work of individual theatre historians such as Andrew Gurr, William Ingram, Roslyn Knutson, Scott

McMillin and Sally-Beth MacLean. MacLean and her collabo-rator McMillin have been important advocates for further study of troupes and their repertories, too, explicitly stating in the preface to their ground-breaking study of the Queen's Men that their 'underlying agenda is to suggest that a new approach to Elizabethan drama can be opened by centring on the acting companies instead of the playwrights'. Perhaps most radically, McMillin and MacLean make the case for seeing playing companies as active agents in shaping the plays that were produced for them, arguing that troupes like the Queen's Men 'were responsible for the plays they performed and can be evaluated according to that responsibility'.[2]

Another explanation for the growth of interest in acting companies is arguably to be found in the increasing evidence about acting companies made available in recent decades thanks to the efforts of scholars involved in the Records of Early English Drama (REED) project based at the University of Toronto. This project, founded in 1975, aims 'to locate, transcribe, and edit historical surviving documentary evidence of drama, secular music, and other communal entertainment and ceremony from the Middle Ages until 1642'.[3] The work of the project is on-going but it has already published more than 27 volumes covering numerous English counties and some of early England's major cities (including Bristol, Ecclesiastical London, Norwich and York). As Tom Rutter notes, studying acting companies and their repertories provides a new and illuminating way 'of synthesizing the findings of theatre historians', including those yielded by the REED project. It also 'arguably reflects the priorities of early modern playgoers ..., for whom the names of dramatists may not have been paramount'.[4]

Lucy Munro links the recent interest in acting companies to 'the influence of post-structuralist uncertainty regarding the place of the author', an 'uncertainty' fostered in the late twentieth century by the work of French theorists such as Roland Barthes, Michel Foucault and Jacques Derrida.[5] If the focus on acting companies is indeed partly a response to the thinking of such post-structural theorists, it is a rather belated one, with many late twentieth and early twenty-first-century scholars coming to reject the 'death' of the author (heralded by Barthes) and to 'accept the "return" of the author to the production and transmission of literary texts', as Grace Ioppolo notes.[6] Indeed, one might equally link the new interest in acting companies to the heightened concern with historical context, fostered by critical movements such as new historicism and cultural materialism which came to prominence in the 1980s. Certainly, those engaged in the study of acting companies and their repertories have often championed such research because of what it can teach us about the general (and specific) cultural context(s) in, and through which, plays were created and disseminated during this ground-breaking era. Thus, in his landmark history of the major English Renaissance acting companies, Andrew Gurr observes that his 'ultimate justification ... is not the companies' history as an end in itself, but that of supplying a fuller context for the plays'.[7]

At the same time, a number of scholars working on acting companies have seen their research as emphasizing the collaborative nature of play production, something which they know other scholars may find disconcerting. In her study of the short-lived Children of the King's Revels (based at the Whitefriars Theatre), Mary Bly writes of scholars' tendency 'to resist imputing strong control to a theatrical company' and acknowledges that reading the Whitefriars plays 'together ... for similarities' implicitly challenges 'the idea of the sovereign author'.[8] In similar fashion, Lucy Munro's study of the Children of the Queen's Revels considers 'the input of all those involved in the production and dissemination of plays: dramatists, actors, shareholders, playhouse functionaries, patrons, audiences and publishers' and it leads her to argue for a 'model of collaborative authority over dramatic production'.[9]

Although most scholars of Renaissance drama have welcomed the turn to acting company history and repertory studies, neither is unproblematic. The incomplete nature of the surviving evidence hampers our ability to reconstruct the history of the period's acting companies, and we face similar difficulties when seeking to reconstruct company repertories: we do not necessarily have full records of the plays bought or owned by individual acting troupes, and not all of the known plays have survived. This makes it difficult to generalize about individual troupe repertories. These problems are particularly acute when we are looking at the Elizabethan stage, as many of the plays written before the 1590s have been lost and which companies performed the extant plays is not always certain. Questions have been raised, too, about how we might establish or measure the influence of acting companies on the plays in their repertories and about troupes' alleged cultivation of 'house' styles. These are questions Roslyn Knutson tackles in a recent essay, when she discusses the difficulty of distinguishing between evidence of 'company ownership and company influence' on plays, the dangers of presupposing that acting companies had a house style and the challenge of knowing how much the 'style' of a company's plays is 'the result of the dramatists' sense of identity rather than that of the company'.[10] Those engaged in repertory study and company-based analyses of drama have generally wanted to make the case for the influence of troupes upon the plays that they owned, but even some of those involved in such research have recognized the difficulty of proving such influence, as is reflected in Mary Bly's review of Lucy Munro's *Children of the Queen's Revels*. Munro focuses on an individual company and makes the case for its role in shaping its repertory, but Bly remains unconvinced by Munro's reading of the troupe's plays in these terms, mainly because she does not think Munro makes clear enough how the troupe's repertory was distinctive, noting that 'without much reference to other repertories as ballast to her argument about the Queen's Revels, the question of whether the company has a relevant, creative influence on its plays is stated, not proved' and that such wider contextualization of the repertory is necessary to really make the case, that 'the Queen's Revels' plays are best viewed together, and that their similarities to each other grow from production and performance not from wider theatrical influences'.[11]

Other scholars have been concerned that the focus on acting companies has led to an over-statement of the extent to which English Renaissance playwriting was collaborative. Jeffrey Knapp, for example, challenges the recent tendency to see 'dramatists and actors as equivalently collaborative' and Gabriel Egan rejects the similar fashion for describing authorship and authority over play texts as dispersed, arguing instead for the key role of playwrights in shaping plays.[12] At least some of the theatre historians working on acting companies and playwriting in this era have actively embraced what Mary Bly describes as the 'substitution of authorship' whereby creative authority over plays is seen to be shared.[13] But other theatre historians have explicitly sought to counter fears about the potential displacement of authors. In 2001 Scott McMillin argued that 'the most important advance that could be made just now in Elizabethan drama studies' would be achieved by 'taking the companies as the organizing units of dramatic production', yet he also insisted that 'this does not mean neglecting playwrights' but rather 'reading their plays more fully than we have been trained to do'.[14] Similarly, in his recent study of Shakespeare's company, although Andrew Gurr acknowledges the Chamberlain's/King's Men's control over the plays that it bought he is careful to state that he still sees the 'most potent shaping factor in the repertory' as being 'the individual aspiration of the writers, and the personal views they put into their raw material'.[15]

Reconciling an interest in the agency of playing companies with a recognition of the role and importance of individual playwrights (and Shakespeare in particular) has, in fact, been a problem for many of those working on acting companies and their plays, as Tom Rutter acknowledges when he observes that 'to a striking extent, the discourse of repertory studies seems to be one that Shakespeare is called upon to authorize, even as it seeks to move him to the margins'.[16] Given the importance of the Shakespeare industry and the power of his name to sell books this is perhaps no surprise but it also shows the difficulty of weighing up the respective contributions and influence on English Renaissance plays of playwrights and the players for whom they wrote.

Nonetheless, few would disagree that the recent spate of work on acting companies and their plays has 'demonstrated that reading the repertories of individual playing companies with the plays grouped together can yield fresh insights into the companies, their plays, and the general theatre history of the period concerned', as David Nicol argues.[17] Such work has also offered a useful 'framework' for understanding 'the many early modern plays that, because of widespread practices such as anonymous publication and collaborative writing and rewriting of plays, do not straightforwardly fit into a more author-centred approach', as Tom Rutter notes. He is arguably right, too, when he observes that 'any fears (or hopes) that an emphasis on acting companies and their repertories might mean the elimination, or at least marginalization, of authors, critically speaking, have proved premature'. Most scholars continue to be interested in the works of individual playwrights as well as in the companies for whom they wrote.[18]

As more evidence about the Renaissance theatre world continues to be uncovered as a result of the efforts of scholars involved in projects such as REED, there are likely to be further opportunities for company-based research. Indeed, although there have been studies of some of the major Elizabethan and Stuart acting companies, the stories of many of the era's other lesser or shorter-lived troupes have yet to be explored in the same depth. Likewise, there is more to be done when it comes to looking at the work of competing companies and their repertories in tandem. Already it is clear that the relationship between acting companies and playwrights was a key element in the shape and development of drama in this period. Further histories of the English Renaissance stage's playing companies (and of the interplay between them and their playwrights) promise to yield valuable insights into the workings of the world of English Renaissance theatre and its plays.

Building on recent research in this field, *Acting Companies and their Plays in Shakespeare's London* explores how the needs, practices, resources and pressures on acting companies and playwrights informed not only the performance and publication of contemporary dramas but playwrights' writing practices. In doing so it aims to enhance our understanding of surviving Renaissance plays and our appreciation of the multiple factors which fostered and shaped the theatre of Renaissance England. Each of the following chapters focuses on one significant factor influencing the work of Renaissance playwrights and players. Chapter 1 looks at the chief factor affecting most playwrights – the nature and composition of the acting companies for whom they wrote their plays – exploring what we know about the history, traditions and customary working practices of Renaissance English acting companies and their significance for playwrights. Chapter 2 looks more specifically at the relationships between acting companies and playwrights and the evidence about how playwrights worked in this innovative period, using the evidence preserved in sources such as the *Diary* of theatre manager Philip Henslowe and manuscript playbooks showing signs of theatrical use. Chapter 3 focuses on what we know about Renaissance staging, acting, the physical design and facilities of London's outdoor and indoor theatrical spaces and the involvement of playwrights in staging preparations; and it considers the ways in which the pragmatics of contemporary performance shaped the writing and staging of plays in the theatre. Chapter 4 looks at the diverse audiences before whom playing companies performed at the open-air and indoor playhouses and on tour, and the extent to which the nature of these audiences informed the plays written for them by the era's playwrights. The final chapter considers the importance and possible influence of royal and noble patrons on acting companies and their repertories; and the Epilogue reflects on what *Acting Companies* reveals overall about the relationship between

England's Renaissance players, playwrights and their plays in this exciting theatrical era.

In paying such close attention to the contexts in which playwrights and playing companies worked, *Acting Companies* accepts the premise that the practices of playwrights and performers were influenced by the world within which they lived but it does not assume that playwrights and their plays were simply the products of these circumstances. On the contrary, this book is underpinned by the belief that playwrights were the chief artistic force in the creation of the plays eventually performed on the Renaissance stage and that the individual playwright was both 'something more than a product of the text and something less than its exclusive producer', as David Scott Kastan observes of Shakespeare. Like Kastan, I would argue that we do not have to choose between seeing playwrights either as 'unfettered by history or language' or as 'a mere epiphenomenon of one or the other', and that it is 'more sensible … to recognize Shakespeare's agency' and the agency of other playwrights 'within the conditions of possibility for writers' of their time.[19] *Acting Companies* explores these conditions, accepting that how writers wrote their plays was shaped (but not wholly determined) by the theatrical world and the companies for which they catered, as well as their own artistic wishes.

1

The acting companies

Post-hast. *Lett's make vp a company of Players,*
For we can all sing and say,
And so (with practice) soone may learne to play.[1]

The custom of actors joining together to perform as companies
was a well-established tradition by the time that John Marston
wrote *Histrio-mastix* around 1599. Sometimes patronized
by elite individuals (such as gentlemen, nobles and royalty)
and sometimes travelling under the names of local towns and
villages, England's earliest acting companies were touring
players. Without permanent places to perform these travelling
troupes were accustomed to performing in a variety of
spaces from market-places and town-halls to monasteries and
country houses; a fortunate few were also invited to perform
at court. By the mid-sixteenth century acting companies were
of two main types: adult companies and boy companies.
Both types of troupe were exclusively male as women did not
perform professionally until the Restoration era. England's
Renaissance acting companies occupied the new theatres
created in Elizabethan London and bought and performed
the period's plays: their story lies at the heart of the history of
drama in this era.

The boy companies

The earliest boy (or children's) acting companies emerged from the grammar and choral schools of Tudor London and the tradition of pupils performing plays as a way of developing their rhetorical and oratorical skills. Companies of pupils from the most highly esteemed London schools began to receive invitations to perform at court from the early sixteenth century. At this point the companies usually consisted of 12 to 14 boys aged between 10 and 15, overseen by a school or choral master. Before performing at court it was usual for the boys to perform a rehearsal in front of court officials. By the late sixteenth century these rehearsals had become a popular event, with increasing numbers of courtiers choosing to attend them and to offer the boys and their master rewards. Here was a clear commercial opportunity and in the 1570s two choral masters acted upon it. In 1575 Sebastian Westcote, Master of the Children of St Paul's, created a temporary indoor playhouse in the precincts of St Paul's Cathedral and started to exercise his boys in playing weekly before paying audiences. His example was quickly followed by Richard Farrant, deputy to the Master of the Children of the Chapel Royal (William Hunnis). In 1576 Farrant created a playhouse for the Chapel boys in the buttery of the former Blackfriars Monastery in London. Neither venture lasted especially long: the groups appear to have merged after Wescote's death in 1582 (possibly under the patronage of the Earl of Oxford); the Children of the Chapel had lost the lease on their Blackfriars space by 1584; and both troupes seem to have stopped performing by 1590.[2] Nonetheless, they had set a precedent for commercial performances by boy companies and for the use of indoor theatres in London.

Boys using the names of the choral schools were to resume public playing around the turn of the century. The Children of St Paul's seem to have been playing again in their playhouse by 1599; and a company calling itself 'the Children of the

Chappell' appears to have been performing at the Second Blackfriars Playhouse (created by James Burbage) from some time in 1600 when Burbage's sons sub-let the property to scrivener and would-be theatrical impresario, Henry Evans. Evans appears to have gone into partnership with Nathanial Giles (Master of the Chapel at Windsor) to create the new company, possibly having gained a taste for theatrical management through his involvement with the first group of Chapel Children in 1584.[3]

The Chapel troupe set up by Evans with Giles appears to have been slightly different from those which had gone before it, in that it does not seem to have consisted wholly of choristers. As John Astington notes, 'one or two' of the boys 'were singers' but the troupe 'also included boys recruited from grammar schools'.[4] Giles soon found himself in trouble when the father of one of the boys that he and Evans had impressed (or taken up), using Giles's authority to recruit choristers, brought a case against Giles in the court of Star Chamber (1601). According to Henry Clifton, his son Thomas had been recruited for the choir but then trained for playing, and he listed a number of other boys impressed on similarly false grounds, including Nathan Field, who was to become one of the Jacobean stage's most famous actors.[5] This trouble seems to have led to Giles returning to his duties as Master at Windsor and to Evans putting his son-in-law Alexander Hawkins in his place as manager of the troupe; Evans also brought in two new financiers to help oversee the players: Edward Kirkham (Yeoman of the Revels) and Thomas Kendall (a haberdasher). But the original pair's implicit plan to create a specifically theatrical boy troupe was to come to fruition in 1604 with the obtaining of a patent for a new acting troupe at the Blackfriars: the troupe was named as the Children of the Queen's Revels and Alexander Hawkins, Thomas Kendall, Edward Kirkham and Robert Payne were cited as those responsible for the company.[6] Unlike the earlier boys' troupes which were made up of choristers overseen by a master, this new company was effectively a professional troupe, supervised by a group of adult entrepreneurs and made up of specially recruited boys, rather than trainee choristers moonlighting as players. There is also reason to think that this commercial boy troupe – like those which came later – was made up of older boys than those traditionally found in the choral or school-boy companies. Nathan Field, for example, was about 13 when he was first recruited to join the Children of the Chapel Royal in 1600–1 but 17 when the Children of the Queen's Revels received their patent in 1604 and about 23 when he became one of the members of a new troupe of Children of the Queen's Revels in 1610.

The boy companies appear to have enjoyed considerable success during their second phase of public performing, not only briefly rivalling the adult companies in reputation but securing plays from most of the leading playwrights of the day (including Ben Jonson, John Marston and Thomas Middleton). The boys became renowned for their performance of satire and for their association with generic innovation. As Michael Shapiro notes, the boy companies could not match the adult companies in terms of the number of plays that they performed; instead they 'claimed ... to offer new *types* of play'.[7] But the careers of the revived troupes were not to be much longer-lived than those of their earlier Elizabethan counterparts. The Children of Paul's may have stopped playing at their playhouse as early as 1606 and the Children of the Queen's Revels were officially 'dissolved' in 1608 after they staged a pair of plays which reportedly satirized first the French royal family and then James I. A third publicly playing boy company – the Children of the King's Revels – based at a new playhouse in the Whitefriars also proved short-lived (1607–8), perhaps being set up when the Children of Paul's closed the doors of their playhouse, but seemingly ceasing activity with the closing of the theatres as a result of plague in 1608.[8]

The story of the Jacobean boy companies did not end in 1608. When the theatres reopened in London in 1610 a new troupe calling itself the Children of the Queen's Revels was established by patent. Possibly set up with the support, and perhaps even at the instigation, of the Master of the Revels, the troupe appears to have performed at court as early as the Christmas season of 1608–9 and subsequently took up residence at the Whitefriars Theatre (following the departure of the Children of the King's Revels).[9] Although there were connections between the two incarnations of the Children of the Queen's Revels (including the continued membership of Nathan Field), Richard Dutton argues that the troupe set up in 1609 was a new enterprise and that the '*dis*continuities with the Children of the Blackfriars were at least as marked as the continuities'.[10] The new troupe was to continue at the Whitefriars Theatre until 1613 when it merged with the newest of the adult companies, the Lady Elizabeth's Men. By this time the Revels troupe appears to have consisted of at least six young men as well as boys, including Field (then aged 25 or 26) and to have numbered around 14 or 15 players. After 1613 there were to be no commercial boy companies in London until the Caroline era, although there is evidence of youth troupes active on tour, including companies calling themselves the Children of the Queen's Revels and the King's Revels, which could mean that some members of these troupes took to the road rather than joining the companies which superseded them in London.[11]

The next stage in the history of boy companies on the commercial London stage dates from 1629 when one-time player Richard Gunnell built the Salisbury Court Playhouse and established a company there of 14 youths. As Andrew Gurr reports the 'object was, ostensibly, "to train and bring up certain boys in the quality of playing not only with intent to be a supply of able actors to his Majesty's servants of the Black Friars"' but for '"the solace of his Royal Majesty when his Majesty should please to see them"'.[12] The Children of the Queen's Revels has been seen as an 'apprentice-based' troupe, implicitly training up-and-coming young actors, but with Gunnell's venture this became an overt purpose of the newly formed troupe.[13] In arguing that the chief aim of the new company was to train future actors for the royal company, Gunnell might simply have been finding an acceptable justification for the creation of a new troupe, but it is also possible that he was responding to a real demand in a theatre world in which there were, as yet, no acting schools from which future players might be recruited. Whatever the true motives for the establishment of the Salisbury Court troupe, it set a renewed precedent for youth-based companies, which fellow actor-cum-theatre owner, Christopher Beeston, was to follow in 1637. Beeston, who owned the Cockpit Playhouse, had played host to the newly formed Queen Henrietta's Men from 1626 until 1636 when plague closed the London playhouses. Beeston appears to have taken the opportunity of the prolonged closure to secure a new troupe for his theatre, setting up another youth company, possibly at the command of the Master of the Revels. This new troupe performed at court on 7 and 14 February 1637 (as 'Beeston's Boys') and Beeston received a patent on 21 February 1637 appointing him as 'Govvernor of the new Company of the Kinges & Queenes boyes'.[14] Implicitly, Beeston was to assume a role rather like that of the early masters in the school-boy troupes, acting as a teacher and authority figure over its members. Beeston's son William was to assume the same role as governor after Christopher's death, later testifying that he had been responsible for taking 'prentices and covenant servants to instruct them in the quality of acting, and fitting them for the stage'.[15] Like the adult companies, however, these late boy companies were to have their careers cut short by the closing of the theatres in 1642 and there appears to be no evidence of the youth companies playing after this date: boy companies were to be a phenomenon confined to the Renaissance stage.

Adult companies

Most of the acting companies active commercially in and beyond Renaissance London were adult troupes, mainly made up of men, although it was usual for such companies to include two or more boy apprentice players, too, who would be responsible for performing the female roles in the company's plays. Early Elizabethan companies were comparatively small, often consisting of between six and eight adult players. By the late sixteenth century the average size of adult troupes was much larger. In 1594 Shakespeare's company the Lord Chamberlain's Men consisted of a core of eight adults, while in 1634 the infant Prince Charles's company reportedly consisted of a core of 11 adults.[16] Occasional records of troupe sizes on tour offer confirmation that they typically numbered between 14 and 20 players in total. The troupe of Lady Elizabeth's players who visited Coventry in 1615 included 14 players and a company using the same name included 20 players when it visited Plymouth in 1617–18.[17] Contemporary plays are clearly written with these averages in mind, too, most calling for a cast of around 16 actors.[18]

Traditionally, adult troupes travelled under the name of an elite patron, but these patrons were not usually directly involved in the day-to-day organization or financing of the companies (see p. 170). On the contrary, most acting companies were effectively actor-collectives. Actors did not have their own guild, as did musicians, but the emergent profession appears to have been 'guild-like' in some of its working practices (such as its use of apprenticeship).[19] Most troupes consisted of three categories of player: sharers, hired men and boy apprentices. The sharers were the adult men who formed the core of the company. They were the people who would be named on company patents, who invested collectively in the playing stock of the troupe and shared company decisions and who usually played the major roles in company productions. The model for the actors' shared investment in the property of the troupe was the contemporary joint-stock company, 'a form of investment increasingly popular in London during Elizabeth's reign'.[20] Having shared the investment and accompanying financial risk, actor-sharers subsequently shared jointly in the company's profits, receiving a cut of the receipts of each performance, rather than a weekly wage. If a sharer chose to leave a company he could expect to be compensated for his share. Thus, Richard Jones and Robert Shaw apparently received 50 pounds when they left the Admiral's Men in 1602.[21] If a sharer died, it appears to have become customary, likewise, for the player's next of kin to receive some compensation. Charles Massey of the Lord Admiral's Men alludes to these emergent traditions in a letter to Philip Henslowe (c. 1613), describing how it is agreed between his company that if any one leaves with 'the consent of his fellows, he is to receive three score and ten pounds' and 'if any one die his widow or friends whom he appoints it to receive fifty pounds'.[22]

The number of sharers in professional acting companies seems to have varied during the Renaissance from as few as six in the 1560s to as many as twelve later in the era. At the turn of the century the average seems to have been eight with both the Lord Chamberlain's and Lord Admiral's Men's troupes apparently consisting of this number of sharers in 1594.[23] Just as companies differed slightly in size so the value of company shares appears to have varied somewhat between companies and across the period. In 1592 a share in the Queen's players seems to have cost about 80 pounds, while a share in young Prince Charles's company in 1634 appears to have cost 100 pounds.[24] While we have no detailed records of individual players' earnings, we know that it became possible for at least some players to retire comfortably on 'the proceeds of a career in the theatre, as Shakespeare did' and contemporary records include some indicators of average earnings.[25] Philip Henslowe's records at the Rose Theatre suggest that in 1598 sharers in the Lord Admiral's Men earned between 7 and 26 shillings a week; while Andrew Gurr estimates that in 1599 the 'total annual income' for a sharer in the Lord

Chamberlain's Men 'would have been over £60' and thus more than a pound a week.[26] Such earnings compared very favourably with the average earnings of other skilled artisans. According to a 1588 proclamation regulating London wages, most 'workmen, journeymen' and 'hired servants' were expected to earn between 4 and 6 pounds a year (with meat and drink) and up to nearly 9 pounds, if food and drink were not included.[27] The figures for the Lord Admiral's and the Lord Chamberlain's/King's Men suggest that sharers could earn much more than this. Sharers' incomes were even greater if they were also shareholders in the playhouses used by their companies (as was true of a number of the King's Men), as the players then received a share not only of the actors' takings but of the playhouse owners' share of the gallery receipts. In the case of the King's Men, E. K. Chambers suggests that this could have meant earning an extra 40 to 50 pounds a year.[28]

Hired men were bound to troupes on a temporary basis. They included 'minor actors, musicians, prompters or book holders, stagekeepers, wardrobe keepers or tiremen' and gatherers (who collected the playhouse entrance fees).[29] Such hired men received a weekly wage. According to Stephen Gosson (1579) hired players could earn as much as 6 shillings a week. By the end of the century this had seemingly increased with Philip Henslowe agreeing to pay William Kendall 10 shillings a week in London and 5 shillings a week 'in yᵉ Cuntrie' when he bound him as a hired player for two years in 1597.[30]

The boy members of the adult companies were effectively apprentice players and varied in age from around 13 to 22. In the early years of the London playhouses it seems to have been usual for such boys to be bound as covenant servants to one of the members of the company. David Mateer recently discovered that Richard Perkins, for example, was bound as a servant to Edward Alleyn for three years in 1596.[31] Later it became more usual for boys to be bound formally as apprentices. Actors did not have their own guild, as noted above, but the fact that many players were formally trained and freed in other professions meant that they were able to bind apprentices to that trade, even when they planned to exercise and train their apprentices exclusively for the stage, as David Kathman's pioneering research has shown. The 'first evidence of a professional player binding apprentices who can clearly be traced on the stage' is John Heminges of the King's Men, who was freed as a grocer in 1587. Between 1595 and 1628 Heminges bound ten apprentices, most of whom 'ended up as actors with the Chamberlain's/King's Men', with one of them 'explicitly' stating 'that he had been trained in "l'arte d'une Stageplayer"' during his apprenticeship'.[32] Whether the boys were paid and, if so, how much, is less clear and may have depended on the nature of their bond with their master. Bound servants might expect some payment, whereas apprentices did not usually receive wages, but just their food, lodging and training.

The superficially democratic model of company management that prevailed in the adult companies in the mid-Elizabethan era was modified over time, with some troupes coming to be dominated by their star players, as seems to have been true of Edward Alleyn and the Lord Admiral's Men. It also became increasingly usual for troupes to appoint one or two sharers to take responsibility for the administration and finances of the company. John Heminges appears to have assumed this administrative role in the King's Men, with John Lowin and Joseph Taylor taking over from him on his retirement.[33] Later, at least some players, playwrights and theatre-owners sought to assume more extensive managerial powers over individual acting companies and/or the theatre spaces that they used. In the case of those who were primarily theatre landlords this appears to have been, in part, a response to the greater financial risks that they faced and their desire to exercise more control over their investments. This second model of company management, whereby playhouse owners or company leaders sought to control the activities of individual acting troupes, is often described as impresario- or manager-led. Two of the most famous examples of such impresarios are Philip Henslowe and Christopher Beeston. Having started off as a theatrical landlord and later a banker for Elizabethan companies such as the Lord Admiral's Men, Philip Henslowe (joint owner of the Rose, Fortune and Hope Theatres) appears to have sought more control over the acting companies he hosted, binding players to play at his playhouses in the late 1590s (usually for three years), and later becoming involved in the buying of playing clothes, properties and playbooks as well as the hiring and firing of hired men for troupes such as Lady Elizabeth's Men. As Bernard Beckerman notes, by 'gradually making actors and writers responsible to him rather than to the company, he took the first step toward genuine management'.[34] Similarly, having begun his career as an actor and having served as the informal business manager of Queen Anne's Men, Christopher Beeston later became a playhouse owner and appears to have exercised considerable control over which companies played at his playhouses and what they performed.

Whereas some theatre impresarios started primarily as financial investors in playhouses or acting companies (as did Henslowe), others (like Beeston) became managers having started out, or while still, serving as theatre practitioners. Part of the success, and the long theatrical life, enjoyed by Shakespeare's company derived from the fact that leading members of the troupe became joint shareholders in the playhouses that they used (the Globe from 1599 and the Blackfriars from 1610). Owning the spaces and/or the ground leases of the plots that they used all but guaranteed them access to London venues and meant that they benefited as landlords as well as players from the profits of performance. While the King's Men's shared ownership of their playing spaces was partly forced upon the original investors (the Burbages) by the financial difficulties they faced when they wanted to rebuild the Theatre as the Globe in 1599, it proved a very successful model and gave the Lord Chamberlain's/King's Men unique control over the means of commercial dramatic production. A similar desire for commercial control and regular employment seems to have motivated the consortium of playwrights that invested in the new children's company established at the Whitefriars (c. 1607–8): the Children of the King's Revels.[35]

Part of the explanation for the emergence of theatrical entrepreneurs and would-be managers of players as well as theatres lies in the growing commercial success of theatre in London which made playhouses an increasingly viable investment and playing companies an asset potentially worth controlling. For similar reasons the number of people associated with and involved in the London theatre industry expanded rapidly in the early seventeenth century. This is reflected not only in the emergence of a large support industry of hired musicians, costumiers and the like but in the growing number of men and boys identified as actors in contemporary records. According to William Ingram we 'know the names of close to a thousand people in Shakespeare's day who, at one time or another in their lives, were said to be stage players'.[36] We know rather less about how and why this growing body of people entered the theatrical profession. In 1582 Stephen Gosson claimed that 'most of the Players' came to the theatre by one of three routes having been 'eyther men of occupations, which they haue forsaken to lyue by playing, or common minstrels, or trayned vp from theire childhoode to this abominable exercise'.[37] Gosson's account of the origins of Elizabethan London's players is borne out, to some extent, by what we know about the backgrounds of London's professional players. Many were freed in other trades; others were the sons of actors (or minstrels); and some started their careers as boy apprentices with the adult troupes. But this still does not explain precisely how or why so many men and boys came to take up the 'quality' of stage players. While the growing money associated with the London playhouses provides one explanation for the entry of contemporaries into the theatre, in other cases the decision to make a career of acting appears to have been borne out of a taste for the stage and/or a family tradition of acting (as seems to be true of Richard Burbage, son of actor and early playhouse owner, James Burbage). Other performers appear to have been recruited on the road and/or from provincial troupes. Michael Bowyer, for example, who went on to become a famous player on the Caroline stage appears to have started his acting career with a provincial troupe led by an otherwise unknown actor called William Hovell.[38]

Finding a way in to the theatrical profession was not the only challenge for those keen to become actors on the London stage. Although there were acting companies that lasted for many years, there were many more that enjoyed only brief careers in London and there was a regular traffic of actors between companies in and beyond the metropolis, as troupes vied for the few authorized playing venues and faced plague-induced playhouse closures and, later, periodic impresario-led reorganizations and relocations. Older, more established companies like the Lord Chamberlain's/King's Men and the Lord Admiral's/Palgrave's Men competed with, and occasionally poached players from, newer acting companies such as the Duke of York's players and Lady Elizabeth's players, and vice versa. In 1611 the new troupe of Lady Elizabeth's Men included two young men who had previously worked with the King's Men (William Ecclestone and John Rice) and later lost a series of players to the royal company, including Robert Benfield, Ecclestone and Nathan Field.[39] Newer companies only tended to thrive, in fact, if they 'took over the assets of a previous company', as when Queen Henrietta's Men inherited the Cockpit Theatre in 1626 and many of the plays previously performed there by the Lady Elizabeth's Men: the new royal troupe went on to play successfully at the same playhouse for the next ten years.[40] The difference between the long, comparatively stable careers of companies like the Lord Chamberlain's/King's Men and the much shorter and unstable careers of other troupes has led some scholars such as Andrew Gurr and Bart van Es to characterize the period's acting troupes in terms of 'strong and weak companies'.[41] But one might equally distinguish between the period's troupes in terms of the usual and the exceptional. In their longevity and sustained commercial success

Shakespeare's company and, to a lesser extent, the company which started life as the Lord Admiral's Men were all but unique; and even the Lord Admiral's company eventually foundered after being weakened by the loss of its playhouse and most of its playing stock following a fire in 1621.

The pressures faced by acting companies and the fact that the different troupes active in London were in inevitable competition as they performed daily has led some scholars to characterize the relations between the leading companies in terms of fierce rivalry. Much has been made, for instance, of the alleged animus between Richard Burbage and the Lord Chamberlain's Men at James Burbage's Theatre and Edward Alleyn and the Lord Admiral's Men at Henslowe's Rose after an alleged dispute between Alleyn and Burbage senior. But more recent research by scholars such as Roslyn Knutson has encouraged us to re-examine such assumptions, drawing attention to the close connections within and between acting companies, not least because it was not uncommon for actors to move between troupes. That acting companies were not always fierce rivals and that there was some fluidity in the make-up of troupes would seem to be borne out by contemporary evidence of players collaborating with each other on occasion. In 1594 Philip Henslowe recorded a series of receipts for performances at the theatre in Newington Butts between 3 and 13 June by 'my Lord Admeralle men & my Lorde Chamberlen men'. Although Henslowe could be describing a shared but alternating residency, he might equally be alluding to a temporary collaboration between the troupes.[42] In either case, the players' shared use of the Newington Butts Theatre points to their familiarity with each other and a readiness to work alongside each other when necessary.

Evidence of the bonds that existed between, as well as within, acting companies of the day is, likewise, afforded by the letters that players exchanged with each other and fellow members of the theatre world. We know from Philip Henslowe's gossipy letters to Edward Alleyn, while on tour, that players took an interest in each other, Henslowe famously passing on the news of the Earl of Pembroke's players' troubles to Alleyn after he asked about them in September 1593.[43] Henslowe's papers contain further evidence of the web of connections linking those in the theatre world, including numerous personal letters from actors and playwrights, at least some of which point to close friendships. Actor and playwright Nathan Field, for example, wrote a number of affectionate letters to Henslowe during his time with Lady Elizabeth's players, addressing Henslowe as 'Father Hinchlow' in one letter and signing another as his 'louing and obedient Son'.[44] Likewise, there is evidence of players from different playing companies writing to and assisting each other, as in 1581 when Thomas Bayly (one of the Earl of Shrewsbury's players) wrote from Sheffield to Thomas Bandewine (one of the Earl of Leicester's players) to ask for 'more play texts', as Barbara D. Palmer records. Given such evidence, one can see why Roslyn Knutson might conclude that 'commerce among the playing companies was built on patterns of fraternity' as well as rivalry.[45]

A related issue that has prompted similarly lively debate in recent years is the question of the extent to which different Renaissance acting companies had distinctive company styles. In their pioneering study of the Queen's Men Scott McMillin and Sally-Beth MacLean argue that each acting company will have needed to develop 'its own style, its own textual procedures, its own sense of purpose, and its own impact on audiences and other acting companies'. They go on to outline what they see as some of the distinctive features of the Queen's Men's style, including the troupe's favouring of what they term the 'medley' mode and their privileging of the visual so that the focus in performances was 'on objects, costumes, the gestures of the actors, and patterns of stage movement'.[46] On the other hand, scholars such as Roslyn Knutson have suggested that, in terms of repertory at least, the acting companies regularly duplicated and imitated each other's offerings so that by the Caroline era 'the early modern English playing companies and their repertories were blended into slight variations of one another'.[47] That there were limits to how distinctive the plays written for any individual company could be might also be suggested by the fact that plays passed between companies as well as spaces.

Making a home in the metropolis: Public playing and acting companies in Shakespeare's London

The story of acting companies in Shakespeare's London is partly a story of growing professionalization and commercialization but it is also one of increasingly tight regulation. In 1559 Elizabeth I issued a proclamation insisting that all public play performances be licensed either by two lieutenants or by two Justices of the Peace 'within that part of the shire where any shall be played'.[48] This was to be the first of a series of legislative changes which were to impact upon the development of theatrical culture in England. The next significant changes occurred in 1572 when the regulations on players were further tightened with a proclamation calling for the execution of the statutes against unlawful retainers and a new Act for the Punishment of Vagabonds and for Relief of the Poor and Impotent. While the former forbade lords from giving their livery to anyone other than their household servants, the latter act stated that players could only perform legally if they had a royal or noble patron or the authorization of two Justices of the Peace.[49] It was the issuing of these two edicts in 1572 which appears to have led the players of the Earl of Leicester to write to him seeking his authorization for their playing and which, subsequently, led to the same troupe obtaining 'the first written patent for a playing company ever to be allocated by the government' in 1574.[50] The regulative 'net' was further tightened in 1598 when the Act for the Punishment of Vagabonds was revised to remove the power to license players from Justices of the Peace. When James I came to the throne in 1603 the power to patronize players was limited yet again, being officially confined to the Master of the Revels and the royal family, although not everyone chose to heed this change.

Despite the growing restrictions on those allowed to perform, especially in London, theatre thrived in the late Elizabethan capital. Scholars such as William Ingram suspect that this is no coincidence. Although the tighter regulations limited the number of acting companies officially allowed to perform, the Elizabethan legislation and the court's intervention in theatrical culture also served to protect those companies that were licensed.[51] By the 1570s and the opening of the first open-air playhouses there were thus a number of noblemen's acting companies active in the capital and at court, including the Earl of Leicester's Men, the Earl of Warwick's and the Earl of Sussex's players. At the same time the first indoor playhouses were being set up and used for 'private' performances by boy troupes (see p. 12). These same companies were those invited to perform at the Elizabethan court, their performances in London justified by the players and the court as preparation for their royal duties. Indeed, it is possible that the opening of several playhouses during the 1570s was partly a response to, and tolerated because of, the Revels Office's increasing reliance on the commercial playing companies for the court's seasonal entertainments.[52]

The English Renaissance court and the Privy Council have often been seen as champions of the players, defending them at various points against the city's attempts to limit their activities in London, but there is reason to believe that at least some courtiers were similarly keen to control theatrical activity in and beyond the metropolis. This has been seen as one of the possible motives for the formation of a dedicated royal playing company in 1583: the Queen's Men. The troupe that Edmund Tilney, the Master of the Revels, assembled was much larger than earlier acting troupes, consisting of 12 actors cherry-picked from the leading troupes of the day. There is no official record of why Tilney was asked to form the company.

Andrew Gurr wonders if the idea of setting up a new royal company may have started with the Lord Admiral, Charles Howard, while Scott McMillin and Sally-Beth MacLean argue that it was most likely the idea of Elizabeth's Principal Secretary, Sir Francis Walsingham and Robert Dudley, the Earl of Leicester.[53] Likewise, while the formation of the royal troupe could be seen as reflecting a desire to cater for Elizabeth's interest in drama and as a politic way of promoting her power and views, McMillin and MacLean also read it as an act of control, arguing in their ground-breaking history of the troupe that the 'central government was not protecting the theatre so much as reducing and gaining control over it'.[54] Whatever the motives that underpinned it, the troupe's creation temporarily disrupted the activities of the other leading companies in London, with several losing key players to the royal troupe.

During the 1580s the Queen's Men went on to become the country's 'best known and most widely travelled professional company'. They also became one of the first Elizabethan companies to run more than one branch, apparently dividing into two groups as early as their first summer tour in 1583. Despite (or perhaps because of) the royal company's success on the road, the Queen's Men never seem to have developed a firm foothold in London and disappear from the metropolitan records by 1589.[55] Plague closures, patrons' deaths and company collapses meant that the late 1580s and early 1590s were a period of instability for most troupes. Indeed, no company would establish a firm base at any of the London theatres until the 1590s. In 1594, when the playhouses reopened after prolonged plague closure, the newly formed Lord Chamberlain's Men and the Lord Admiral's Men were licensed to perform at the Theatre and the Rose, respectively. Officially, no other playing companies or playing spaces were licensed for performance in London from this date. The establishment of what Andrew Gurr terms a 'duopoly' has been seen as a fresh government attempt to regulate the theatre industry while guaranteeing the availability of theatrical entertainment for the queen during the holiday seasons. Indeed, Gurr (who believes that the impetus for the formation of the two new companies came from their powerful patrons) thinks that the 'duopoly' was deliberately modelled on 'the original Queen's Men's monopoly of eleven years before'.[56]

Other scholars have questioned the extent to which the Lord Chamberlain and Lord Admiral wished (or expected) to limit theatre in London to their two companies.[57] Either way, if this was their aim they were not wholly successful as the 1594 order did not prevent the creation of new playhouses, the continued use of other theatres such as the Curtain, or the emergence of new companies in the 1590s. In 1595 Francis Langley opened a new open-air theatre on the Bankside (the Swan) and in 1597 established a new company there (the Earl of Pembroke's Men), poaching a number of Lord Admiral's Men in the process; and in 1599 the Earl of Derby's players began playing at the newly improved playhouse at the Boar's Head, with the Earl of Worcester's players later taking their place at that playhouse (1601). The proliferation of playhouses and playing companies in the capital probably explains why on 19 July 1598 the Privy Council felt obliged to restate that only the Lord Admiral's and the Lord Chamberlain's players were authorized to perform in London and why on 22 June 1600 they issued an order licensing only the Lord Admiral's at their new playhouse, the Fortune, and the Lord Chamberlain's at the Globe. Nonetheless, there were three – rather than two – adult companies officially active in the capital when King James acceded to the throne (1603), the Earl of Worcester's men having been accepted as a third troupe by the Privy Council in 1602.[58]

With the accession of the new monarch, patronage of the leading companies officially passed into the hands of the royal family, the Lord Chamberlain's Men becoming King James's players, Worcester's Men becoming Queen Anne's players and the Lord Admiral's players becoming Prince Henry's players. The two boy companies active at the indoor theatres appear to have been exempt from the need to have a royal licence, at least initially, perhaps because it was traditionally claimed that their indoor performances were 'private'. In the following decade the number of acting companies active in the capital was further swelled by the creation of additional royal companies, so that there were six royal troupes by 1611, with the formation of the Duke of York's Men (for Prince Charles) in 1610, the licensing of the Blackfriars Children as the Children of the Queen's Revels (in 1604 and again in 1610) and the establishment of Lady Elizabeth's Men for the King's daughter in 1611. However, there were not enough available or suitable playhouses in the capital to sustain this many companies and the average number of troupes active at any one time in the early Stuart capital later stabilized at four. On the eve of James I's death in 1625, the following companies were active in the capital: the King's Men at the Globe and Blackfriars, the Palsgrave's players (previously Prince Henry's Men) at the Fortune, Prince Charles's Men at the Red Bull and Lady Elizabeth's Men at the Cockpit.[59]

For the two leading companies, the King's Men and the Palsgrave's Men, the Jacobean era was a period of comparative stability, as both made London their home and enjoyed a continuous existence (despite their name changes) from 1594 until 1625. It was also a period of consolidation more broadly, as the playhouses and their daily performances became an accepted part of London life. On the other hand, the lesser royal companies and the children's acting companies struggled to sustain themselves in London, especially with so few playing spaces being available and it being difficult to obtain permission to create new theatres. For these players, theatrical life in the capital continued to be characterized by instability, many companies only enjoying short periods of playing at particular London playhouses before being obliged to move playhouse, to leave the capital and/or to merge with each other, as will be demonstrated when we trace the eventful history of Lady Elizabeth's Men below. The long theatrical life, comparative stability and sustained success of the King's

Men and the Palsgrave's Men in London appear to have been the exception, rather than the rule.

1625 was to be another year of theatrical shake-ups and changes, the death of James I and a long plague closure prompting a fresh round of company reorganizations. The King's Men survived the death of their patron, their patronage passing to the new king, Charles I, but the other companies that restarted in the Caroline era were 'a mix' of troupes 'with new patrons and new groupings without patrons'.[60] At the Cockpit, Christopher Beeston hosted a new group under the patronage of Charles I's queen, Henrietta Maria; at the Fortune the Palsgrave's players appear to have merged with Lady Elizabeth's Men to become the King and Queen of Bohemia's players; a fourth company of players resumed playing at the Red Bull but without acquiring a named patron. In 1629 a fifth company was added to those playing in London when Richard Gunnell set up a fresh troupe of young players at the Salisbury Court Theatre. Like the Red Bull troupe, the Salisbury Court players did not perform under a specific patron's name but rather as a 'King's Revels' company. The fact that the latter pair of companies were not assigned to a specific royal family member might partly default from the fact that there were fewer royals available to act as patrons in 1626, but it also seems to reflect the diminishing importance of named patrons as the Revels Office gradually opted for a system of annual licences for acting companies.

The next set of reorganizations in the London theatre scene appear to have been precipitated by the formation of the last of the named royal companies, a second troupe of Prince Charles's Men, in 1631 for the son of King Charles. The newly formed company (assembled partly from the King and Queen of Bohemia's players) took up residence initially at the Salisbury Court Theatre, while the King's Revels troupe that had been using that space moved to the Fortune Theatre, following its vacating by the Bohemia players. Like their contemporaries, the new Prince Charles's troupe was not to remain indefinitely at their first theatre, moving in 1634 to the Red Bull, while the Red Bull troupe moved to the Fortune, and the King's Revels company went back to the Salisbury Court Theatre.[61]

A severe and sustained plague outbreak in 1636 closed the London playhouses and prompted the next round of company changes, Christopher Beeston setting up a new youth troupe (the King and Queen's Young Men) at the Cockpit. This displaced the previous occupants (Queen Henrietta's Men) who moved to Salisbury Court, perhaps merging with or absorbing members of the company there (the King's Revels) whose name then disappears from the records. The final set of company moves appears to have occurred in 1640 when Prince Charles's players (at the Red Bull) and the Revels company (at the Fortune) swapped playhouses, as mentioned above. As Andrew Gurr notes, it is often unclear what 'determined the shifts of company between one kind of playhouse and another' or who instigated such moves in the Caroline era. G. E. Bentley thought that such relocations were evidence that the companies involved were 'weaker' than troupes such as the King's Men, but, as he notes, almost all of the 'Jacobean and Caroline companies changed theatres, often more than once'.[62]

Despite the regular movements of companies between playhouses and some fluidity in the make-up and names of the companies in Caroline London, the era as a whole was one of considerable stability for the industry. From 1629 until the eve of the civil war and the closure of the playhouses, London playgoers could generally count on being able to see plays in five different playhouses, even if the resident companies at each theatre changed roughly every three years. London playing became a year-round occupation for the players, too, as it became less common for the leading metropolitan companies and players to leave London. From the mid-Jacobean era, at least, some of the royal companies appear to have adopted the system employed by the famous Queen's Men, dividing into more than one troupe, one specializing in London playing and the other (or others) specializing in touring, using licences issued by the Master of the Revels.[63] Gilbert Reason appears to have been responsible for running a touring group of Prince Charles's players from 1610 when he was named in the patent for the new troupe, and Ellis Guest seems to have run a similar company for Lady Elizabeth's Men in the late years of James's reign. As in earlier periods, there is evidence of wily players using 'duplicates' of official company patents to run unsanctioned touring companies under royal names, too.[64]

While the evolution of specialized metropolitan and touring companies is, on one level, evidence of the growing maturity of the professional theatre industry, it was a development which was to have a profound effect on the future development of English theatre. The early professional stage grew out of the traditions of touring theatre and was shaped by its practices, especially the need for plays to be adaptable for different spaces and audiences. This fostered a dramaturgy that made little use of large properties, scenery or elaborate special effects. Once the players no longer needed to think about being able to take plays on tour, they and their playwrights were free to consider the use of larger, more complex stage furniture and to develop plays more specifically tailored for specific venues and audiences. Arguably, these are precisely the kinds of innovation one begins to see in the Caroline theatre and that were to be realized more fully on the Restoration stage, as English theatre became less portable and increasingly site and audience specific.

Lady Elizabeth's men: A case study

1611–16

Licensed by royal patent on 27 April 1611, the company of Lady Elizabeth's players was the last royal troupe to be created in the Jacobean era, taking as its nominal patron

James I's daughter, Lady Elizabeth (1596–1662); its career was to be fast-changing and eventful, falling into two main phases in London, from 1611 to 1615–16 and 1622 to 1625. Study of the troupe's career has much to tell us not only about its struggles for survival but about the challenges faced by many acting companies as they sought to make London their home in the Renaissance. The 1611 patent which created the new troupe licensed John Townsend and Joseph Moore 'with the rest of theire Companie, to vse and exercise the Arte and qualitie of playing Comedies, histories, Enterludes, Morralls, pastorals, stage playes, and such other like'.[65] The troupe possibly started its life on the road, but the players appear to have been back in London by the end of the summer when the troupe's leading members, John Townsend and Joseph Moore, co-signed a duplicate bond with theatre-owner Philip Henslowe (29 August 1611), along with 11 other players: William Barksted, Thomas Basse, William Carpenter, William Eccleston, Alexander Foster, Giles Gary, Robert Hamlen, Thomas Hunt, John Rice, Joseph Taylor and Francis Wambus.[66] Unfortunately, the accompanying articles of agreement between Henslowe and the players have been lost but it seems likely that the agreement related to the provision of a playing space for the troupe in London. Some of the new company's members were recruited from other London troupes and thus already had valuable experience of professional playing. William Barksted was previously a member of the Children of the Queen's Revels; William Ecclestone had worked with the King's Men as a hired man from 1609; Giles Gary (or Carey) may also have come to the new troupe from the Children of the Queen's Revels; John Rice had been a boy-apprentice with the King's Men; and Joseph Taylor had been one of the founder members of the Duke of York's players in 1610.[67] Other members may have been new to the London theatre scene and the troupe was generally quite youthful. In 1611 Barksted, Ecclestone and Rice were all around the age of 21; Taylor was probably 25; and Basse was probably 26.[68] Joining a new acting company was a risk, and how and why the players named in the 1611 bond came to be members of the new Lady Elizabeth's company is not known. The special permission Taylor received to leave the Duke of York's Men for the new troupe could suggest that he, at least, was officially head-hunted. This could have been true of the troupe's other experienced actors, too. Either way, young but experienced recruits to the company such as William Ecclestone and John Rice are likely to have been motivated to join the new company, despite the gamble involved, by a desire to become sharers in an adult company.

Whether Lady Elizabeth's players started performing immediately in the capital after the 1611 agreement is unclear. Henslowe's Rose Theatre had closed by this time and the Fortune was being used by Prince Henry's players. It is possible that Henslowe arranged for the troupe to perform temporarily at the Curtain or the Swan Playhouses. There is certainly evidence to suggest that the Swan was 'in use continuously from 1611 to 1615', as Roberta Brinkley notes, and the company was responsible for performing the only extant play known to have been performed at the playhouse: Middleton's *A Chaste Maid in Cheapside*.[69] Whether or not the troupe had taken up residence at the Swan in late 1611 the company – or one branch of it – was within travelling distance of London in the early months of 1612 since they were invited to perform at court three times: on 19 January, 25 February and 11 March. Only one of the plays performed by the troupe is named, the players staging *The Proud Maid's Tragedy* on their second visit to court.[70] This is the earliest record of a named play performance by the company. Unfortunately, the play does not appear to have survived, unless its title was another name for Beaumont and Fletcher's *The Maid's Tragedy*. The troupe was back at court later that year performing on 20 October 1612 and, again, on 25 February 1613 and 1 March 1613. The play performed by the company in October is unnamed but they performed plays recorded as 'Cockle de moye' on 25 February and 'Raymond Duke of Lyons' on 1 March.[71] While the latter play appears to be lost, the former title is thought to be an alternative name for Marston's *The Dutch Courtesan* (performed c. 1604 by the Children of the Queen's Revels). The fact that Lady Elizabeth's Men appear to have been performing a play originally written for the Children of the Revels seems to confirm what other sources suggest – that Lady Elizabeth's players merged with the Children of the Queen's Revels in early 1613. In a later draft list of grievances against Henslowe compiled by members of Lady Elizabeth's players (c. 1615) they claimed that this merger occurred in March 1613, Henslowe 'joining companies with Mr Rosseter' (one of the leaders of the Children's troupe). As part of the new arrangements, Henslowe also persuaded the company

> that they should enter bonds to play with him for three years at such house and houses as he shall appoint, and to allow him half galleries for the said house and houses, and the other half galleries towards his debt of £126, and other such moneys as he should lay out for play apparel.[72]

The troupe's performance of one of the boys' plays at court on 25 February suggests that the merger had already occurred.

It is not clear why the two troupes amalgamated or who instigated the merger, although the players later implied that Henslowe was the initiator of these events. Part of the explanation for joining the troupes might be found in the comparatively small size of the children's troupe and/or the fact that its members were no longer boys, strictly speaking, many being in their early twenties. It might also have been a pragmatic response to the limited playing spaces available in London and a way for Lady Elizabeth's players to gain a more desirable indoor playing venue, as the Children of the Queen's Revels were at this time based in the Whitefriars Theatre. R. A. Foakes wonders whether the troupes might even have amalgamated 'with the intention of using Whitefriars as a winter playhouse, and the Swan as a summer house, in emulation of the King's Men at Blackfriars and the Globe'.[73] If this idea was in the minds of the players and/or their investor-managers, it was not an experiment that could last long, the lease on the Whitefriars expiring in 1614. But, if Lady Elizabeth's Men did perform at the Whitefriars Playhouse, even briefly, it would make them the first adult troupe to imitate the King's Men in their use of an indoor theatre in London.

The troupe's performance of Middleton's *Chaste Maid in Cheapside* at the Swan might post-date its merger with the Children of the Revels, too, the amalgamated company's larger than usual number of boy or youth players perhaps explaining or making possible the play's large cast of nearly 20 women.[74] Two cast lists found in the 1679 edition of Beaumont and Fletcher's plays might, likewise, date from this period: one is for Beaumont and Fletcher's *The Coxcomb*, a play originally written for the Children of the Queen's Revels but inherited by the Lady Elizabeth's players; the other is for *The Honest Man's Fortune*, co-written by Nathan Field with Fletcher and Massinger. The cast list for *The Coxcomb* names Field, Joseph Taylor, Giles Gary, Emanuel Read, Richard Allen, Hugh Atawell, Robert Benfield and William Barksted. The cast list for *The Honest Man's Fortune* lists Field, Taylor, Benfield, William Ecclestone, Read and Thomas Basse.[75] If these performances were, indeed, staged by the amalgamated company around 1613 it would suggest that at least five youths passed from the Children of the Queen's Revels to the new company: Field, Read, Allen, Atawell and Benfield. If *The Coxcomb* cast list relates to an earlier performance by the Children of the Queen's Revels rather than by the enlarged Lady Elizabeth's, however, it would suggest that Taylor, as well as Barksted and Gary, was a member of the boy company before joining Lady Elizabeth's Men in 1611. Robert Baxter may have been another actor to move from the Children's troupe to Lady Elizabeth's Men, if he is the 'Baxter' mentioned as a fellow of the company in the later complaint by the players.[76] Such connections might explain why Henslowe and Rosseter, and the remaining members of the Children of the Revels, would consider a merger with Lady Elizabeth's Men in 1613. In some respects it was just a continuation of the traffic in players already established between the companies. Brandon Centerwall goes even further and suggests that the boy company effectively took 'over the Lady Elizabeth's Men' instead of continuing to serve as a 'feeder' troupe.[77] But the newly organized troupe does not seem to have absorbed all the players previously associated with the two companies. The leading players of the original 1611 Lady Elizabeth's Men – John Townsend and Joseph Moore – seem to have formed a touring branch of the company instead, obtaining a patent to travel as Lady Elizabeth's Men, dated 31 May 1613. In March 1615 the pair visited Coventry with this patent along with five other men and seven boys.[78] Although the list of actors who visited Coventry includes other known players such as William Perry none of them is known to have been previously connected with the London branch of Lady Elizabeth's Men. It is possible that Townsend and Moore joined an existing touring branch of the company or that they lent their name to another group of touring actors, as there is evidence of players playing provincially under Lady Elizabeth's name every year between 1611 and 1616.[79] That the association of the men and boys listed in Coventry with Lady Elizabeth's Men (and Townsend and Moore) was opportunistic and temporary might find some confirmation in the fact that many of the same players later toured with William Perry under a different name.[80]

Whatever the precise auspices of the merger, back in London, Lady Elizabeth's company proved the chief beneficiary, not only gaining a fresh supply of young, talented players, but temporary access to the boys' theatre and (it seems) many of their plays which included works by fashionable writers such as Beaumont, Fletcher and Jonson and a mix of tragedies, comedies and – the Children's most innovative offering – tragicomedies.[81] During the Christmas season the troupe performed one of these inherited plays at court, reviving Jonson, Chapman and Marston's *Eastward Ho* there (25 January 1614).[82] But the amalgamated metropolitan company was not to enjoy a settled life in London. It had

lost at least one of its early members by the end of the year
(William Ecclestone having returned to the King's Men) and,
according to the players' later complaints, Henslowe 'broke'
the company in March 1614 and made up a new troupe of
Lady Elizabeth's players. An agreement signed between Philip
Henslowe, Jacob Meade and Nathan Field (on behalf of his
company of players) probably dates from this period and
indicates that Field had taken on the role of company leader,
probably in the absence of Townsend and Moore who had
taken to the road with a touring troupe of Lady Elizabeth's
Men. Under the terms of the agreement Henslowe and Meade
bound themselves 'during the space of three years at all
times ... at ... their own proper costs and charges' to 'find
and provide a sufficient house or houses' for Field and his
company 'to play in'.[83]

It is with the re-formed Lady Elizabeth's in mind that
Henslowe and his latest business partner, waterman Jacob
Meade commissioned the construction of a new playhouse:
the dual-purpose open-air theatre, the Hope, which is thought
to have opened in autumn 1614.[84] The plan was to alternate
between playing and bear baiting and the theatre was fitted
with a demountable stage to make this possible. The bears
and the players did not prove happy companions. Indeed,
Lady Elizabeth's players are one of the few troupes of players
thought to have performed there, apparently staging Jonson's
Bartholomew Fair at the Hope on 31 October 1614 before
taking it to court the next day (see pp. 120–1). Jonson may
have offered to write for the company and/or been approached
by them partly because of his experience of writing for the
Children of the Queen's Revels and his intimacy not just with
Henslowe but with members of the amalgamated company
such as Field, whom he is reported to have taught and to
whom Jonson jokingly alludes in the play.[85]

During this third phase of the company's existence in
London there is also evidence of Henslowe's increasingly
active role in the day-to-day business of the troupe. As well as
being their landlord and financier, it is clear that Henslowe was

becoming involved in decisions about company membership, not only reputedly reforming the troupe in March 1614 but taking responsibility for contracting new players to work with the company. Troupe members later alluded to Henslowe's bringing in of Robert Pallant and Robert Dawes, for example, in mid-1614.[86] Pallant was probably known to Henslowe from his associations with Lord Strange's Men and the Lord Admiral's Men, while Dawes was an old associate of Joseph Taylor, having been one of the original sharers in the Duke of York's players.[87] That Henslowe sought to exercise control of these new additions to the troupe would seem to be confirmed by the nature of the agreement signed by Dawes (7 April 1614), which bound Dawes to Henslowe and Meade (rather than Lady Elizabeth's Men) for three years, even though Henslowe later expected the company to pay Dawes's wages.[88] Henslowe's papers also show him commissioning plays, apparently in his own right, rather than simply on behalf of, or in the name of, the company. These include a number of letters and bonds from playwright Robert Daborne between 17 April 1613 and July 1614 that allude to plays he was writing for Henslowe, some of which might have been offered to Lady Elizabeth's players including *Machiavel and the Devil* (17 April 1613), *The Arraignment of London* (5 June 1613), *The Bellman of London* (23 August 1613), *The Owl* (10 December 1613) and *The She Saint* (28 March 1614).[89] Unfortunately, none of these plays appears to have survived. Like Jonson, Daborne had earlier connections with members of Lady Elizabeth's Men, having been one of the patentees of the Children of the Queen's Revels in 1610, which might explain why he approached Henslowe and why he might have offered plays to Lady Elizabeth's Men.[90]

Fresh evidence of Henslowe's growing power over the acting companies he invested in and hosted at his playhouses and of the potential fragility of professional acting companies in the Renaissance is afforded by events alleged to have taken place in early 1615 and the next major reorganization of Lady Elizabeth's Men. This is the year from which the draft Articles of Grievance and Oppression against Henslowe, drawn up by members of Lady Elizabeth's Men, are thought to date. According to the disgruntled players, Henslowe had again broken up the troupe in February 1615, releasing the hired men, selling their playing gear to another troupe and retaining their playbooks and 'other properties' in his own hands. By their account, Henslowe's actions were motivated by his fear of the players' growing financial independence. Indeed, they claimed that he said as much, reportedly declaring: 'Should these fellows come out of my debt, I should have no rule with them.'[91] If the latter accusation is true, it would seem that Henslowe deliberately chose to keep players and companies in his debt as a way of securing their residence at his playhouses and of exercising greater control over their activities. After Henslowe's early experiences at the Rose and knowing the difficulties of keeping companies at his theatres, it is perhaps not surprising that Henslowe should have sought to ensure greater stability for his investments, especially once he could no longer rely on the kinds of personal ties that linked him and his son-in-law, Edward Alleyn, the leader of the Lord Admiral's Men.

That Lady Elizabeth's Men were temporarily inactive by March 1615 following the debâcle with Henslowe would seem to be confirmed by the fact that no one from the company attended when the Privy Council summoned the 'leading representatives' of the London playing companies to see them on 29 March 1615.[92] But the company and its players did not disappear entirely. Rather they appear to have made arrangements to work with Prince Charles's players (previously the Duke of York's Men), the next newest adult company and Joseph Taylor's old troupe. Whether it was a complete merger or simply a temporary collaboration of the two companies, at this stage, is unclear. Like most of the new acting companies set up in Jacobean London the greatest challenge facing Lady Elizabeth's Men and Prince Charles's was that of securing a settled London playing venue. Henslowe's dispute with Lady Elizabeth's men and their seemingly enforced departure from the Hope Theatre may partly explain why on 3 June 1615 Philip Rosseter and three partners secured permission for the use of a new theatre created 'within the Precinct of the Blacke ffryers' in a building called Porter's Hall (owned by the father of playwright Robert Daborne). The new playhouse itself was to be partly funded by Philip Henslowe and, later, Edward Alleyn.[93] According to the 1615 patent the theatre was intended for three troupes: 'the Children of the Revels for the tyme being of the Queenes Maiestie and for the Prince's Players and for the ladie Elizabeth's players'.[94] Whether Rosseter and his colleagues envisaged the playhouse being used by an amalgamation of the three named companies or its shared but independent use by the three troupes is uncertain. Work on the playhouse had begun by the end of the summer as the Lord Mayor attempted to halt it on 26 September 1615. Despite this disruption, work on the playhouse appears to have continued subsequently and it is possible that the playhouse even opened briefly in 1616, being used by Lady Elizabeth's Men and Prince Charles's Men for a joint performance of Field's *Amends for Ladies*. Certainly, when Field's play was published in 1618 it appeared with a title page which claimed that it had been 'acted at the BlackFryers, both by the Princes Servants, and the Lady Elizabeth's'. The only other theatre in the Blackfriars was that used by the King's Men so, unless this is an error, it implies that the two companies used the Porter's Hall Playhouse.[95] Either way, Lady Elizabeth's Men's second bid to establish itself at an indoor playhouse failed when a royal order was given for the new theatre to be pulled down.[96]

If Lady Elizabeth's Men and Prince Charles's players had not already merged formally in London late in 1614 or early 1615, it seems that they had done so by early 1616 when a group of players, made of up actors from Lady Elizabeth's and Prince Charles's players, entered into a new agreement with Henslowe's partner, Jacob Meade and Edward Alleyn (Henslowe having died in January 1616). The agreement (20 March 1616) was signed by William Rowley, Robert

Pallant, Joseph Taylor, Robert Hamlen, John Newton, Hugh Ottewell, William Barksted, Thomas Hobbs, Anthony Smyth and William Fenn.[97] Pallant, Taylor, Hamlen, Ottewell and Barksted all appear to have come from Lady Elizabeth's company, while the remainder of the players came from the Prince's troupe. This amalgamated company appears to have performed briefly at the Hope Playhouse under the name of Prince Charles. During this period of reorganization, other Lady Elizabeth's players left the company to join new troupes (Field and Benfield joined the King's Men, for example, and Basse and Reade joined Queen Anne's players); other company members, including the troupe's original leaders, John Townsend and Joseph Moore, appear to have stayed in the country with a touring branch of Lady Elizabeth's Men.

Those players who chose to continue with Lady Elizabeth's Men on tour, rather than joining Prince Charles's players in London, were potentially assisted by the Lord Chamberlain's decision to send one of its members Joseph Moore around the country in 1616 with a letter intended to suppress unauthorized companies of players touring with false or duplicate royal patents and naming players said to be guilty of doing this: Thomas Swynerton and Martin Slaughter (as Queen's players); William Perry (with the Children of the Queen's Revels); Gilbert Reason (as the Prince's player); and Charles Marshall, Humphrey Jeffs and William Parr (as the Palsgrave's company).[98] There is no mention in this letter of Lady Elizabeth's players, although it is likely that at least some of her players were involved in similar activities. This has led James Marino to suggest that the Lord Chamberlain was effectively clearing the field for Lady Elizabeth's Men, with the idea that they might sustain themselves by touring while the other licensed royal companies were theoretically confined to performing in the capital.[99]

Between 1616 and 1622 when the next London-based incarnation of the troupe was to be launched, there is no evidence of a company under the name of Lady Elizabeth's players performing commercially in London. This suggests that the London branch of the company was dissolved and that those players who continued to act under Lady Elizabeth's name went on tour. That there continued to be a touring branch of the troupe is confirmed by the fact that Lady Elizabeth's players were invited to perform at court in 1617, and the troupe (led by Townsend and Moore) was rewarded in the same year for 'acting three several playes before his Ma^tye in his Jorney towards Scotland', an indication that the touring company still enjoyed some prestige.[100] Lady Elizabeth's players also appear regularly in provincial records between 1615 and 1622.[101] Around this time Henry Herbert, Master of the Revels, appears to have instituted a new system of annual licences for touring, Lady Elizabeth's Men securing one such licence on 20 March 1617. Given Joseph Moore's role in policing the activities of unauthorized touring players in 1616 it is perhaps unsurprising that he and his fellow Lady Elizabeth's Men appear to have been careful to obtain authorization for their provincial activities, although this does not seem to have prevented them from dividing on occasion and running the kind of illegal duplicate companies the Lord Chamberlain had sought to suppress in 1616. In 1620 Norwich was seemingly visited by two troupes of Lady Elizabeth's Men. The second, led by Francis Wambus, arrived on 22 April. Asked about the absence of Joseph Moore (who was named on the company patent Wambus presented, dated 20 March 1617), Wambus claimed that Moore 'ys one of their Company but he hath not played with them this last yeare'. Yet only two months earlier on 8 February 1620 the same Mayors' Court Books record that 'This day Ioseph Moore & others brought a patent Teste 27° Aprilis Anno Nono Iacobi authorizing them to play &c And they haue leaue to play till Satterday next.'[102] Although it is possible that the player claiming to be Moore in February was not Moore, it seems more likely that we are looking at two separate troupes of players touring under Lady Elizabeth's name, one led by Wambus using the 1617 licence and one led by Moore using the troupe's original patent (27 April 1611). The apparent success of Lady Elizabeth's players on tour between 1616 and 1622 may have played a part in the eventual relaunch of a company of Lady Elizabeth's players in the capital, keeping alive their patron's name and a core of players who might be called on again in the capital. This is certainly how James Marino reads the troupe's story, arguing that 'six years in the country was enough to repair the Lady Elizabeth's Men's fortunes' allowing Moore, and perhaps others from the troupe, to return to London in 1622 and to take over at the Cockpit from the troupe they made way for in London in 1616: Prince Charles's players.[103]

We do not have many plays from this first extended chapter in the history of Lady Elizabeth's players in London, but what we know points to a company keen to distinguish itself and to capitalize on the traditions associated with the early seventeenth-century boy troupes from which its membership was partly drawn and with one of which it was to merge. In fact, those plays that survive may all post-date the company's amalgamation with the Children of the Revels: Middleton's *A Chaste Maid in Cheapside*, Field and Fletcher and Massinger's *Honest Man's Fortune* and Jonson's *Bartholomew Fair*. At this point (1613–14), it would seem that Lady Elizabeth's Men were following in the footsteps of the boy companies and specializing in London-centred city comedy and tragicomedy. In the case of Jonson and Middleton the incorporation of especially large casts of women was perhaps a way of taking advantage of the larger than usual number of youths in the troupe, while the fact that Middleton's and Jonson's plays are 'in their different ways important and ground-breaking comedies' suggests that the newly merged company perhaps sought to emulate the Jacobean boy companies' reputation for innovative versions of familiar genres.[104] In this respect, the troupe's new plays complemented those inherited from the Children of the Revels which included Marston's *The Dutch Courtesan*, Beaumont and Fletcher's *The Coxcomb*, John Cooke's *Greene's Tu Quoque*, Thomas Dekker's *Match Me in London*, Field's *Amends for Ladies* and Jonson, Chapman and Marston's *Eastward Ho*, all of which were comedies or tragicomedies. They acquired at least one tragedy, too: Beaumont and Fletcher's *Cupid's Revenge*. Like the Jacobean boy companies Lady Elizabeth's Men did not confine their repertory to comedy and tragicomedy. The earliest known play performed by the troupe was a tragedy (*Proud Maid's Tragedy*) and the lost play that they performed at court on 1 March 1613, *Raymond, Duke of Lyons*, was probably a history or tragedy. Only the titles survive of the plays Robert Daborne wrote for Henslowe between late 1613 and 1614, some of which might have been resold to the troupe, but their titles point to a similar mix of genres being potentially available to them. At least two appear to have been city plays (*The Arraignment of London* and *The Bellman of London*); one was a tragedy (*Machiavell and the Devil*); the genre of the other two plays Daborne mentions (*The Owl* and *The She Saint*) is uncertain, although the latter would seem to be another play focused on women.

1622–5

The company of Lady Elizabeth's players that took up residence at Christopher Beeston's Cockpit Theatre in 1622 appears to have been largely new in its membership. The first evidence of the new London-based company appears in the office books of the Master of the Revels and is the entry recording the licensing of *The Changeling* for performance by the troupe (7 May 1622). Elsewhere Sir Henry Herbert listed the chief players as being 'Christopher Beeston, Joseph More, Eliard Swanson, Andrew Cane, Curtis Grevill, William Shurlock, Anthony Turner'.[105] With the exception of Moore, these players appear to have been new to Lady Elizabeth's Men. Beeston started his playing career as an apprentice to Augustine Phillips of the King's Men, later joining the Queen's players (1603) and becoming a theatre investor and manager in 1616 when he built the Cockpit Playhouse. Whether he acted after this date and thus with the new Lady Elizabeth's in 1622 is not clear. Elliart Swanston was presumably a newer actor, first appearing in the London records in 1622 with the newly established Lady Elizabeth's Men, but going on to be a leading player with the King's Men and thus presumably talented. Andrew Cane is also unknown as a player before 1622 in London, having originally trained and continuing to practise as a goldsmith, but he went on to become one of the Caroline stage's most famous clowns and the leader of the new Prince Charles's players in 1631. Curtis Greville is, likewise, unknown before 1622. Like Swanston, he was later recruited to the King's Men but appears to have taken only modest roles and finished his career with the King's Revels troupe. William Sherlock may have started his acting career as Beeston's apprentice which probably explains his inclusion when the new troupe of Lady Elizabeth's Men was set up at Beeston's theatre in 1622. Anthony Turner, another actor unknown before 1622, may also have been brought in by Beeston, remaining at the Cockpit after the departure of Lady Elizabeth's players in 1625.[106] For Beeston to oust Prince Charles's players in favour of a company of largely unknown players would seem surprising and it may be that at least some of the actors were Beeston protégés, had performed with other London companies (perhaps as hired men), and/or that they were brought in to London by Moore, having cut their teeth as actors with one of the travelling branches of Lady Elizabeth's Men. Either way, with a guaranteed playing space and the backing of an entrepreneur with a stock of plays and playing gear, the newly constituted Lady Elizabeth's Men was well placed to succeed in London and seems to have thrived. As well as securing performances at court in 1623–4 and 1624–5, the company helped to put the Cockpit on the map, contributing to its growing reputation in London.[107]

Part of the troupe's success appears to have derived from the fact that its repertory mixed old plays and revivals with a wave of exciting new dramas. Sir Henry Herbert licensed 14 plays for the company between May 1622 and 11 February 1625: Middleton and William Rowley's *The Changeling* (7 May

1622); *The Black Lady* (10 May 1622); *The Valiant Scholar* (3 June 1622); *The Spanish Gypsy* (9 July 1623) (attributed on publication to Middleton and Rowley but thought to be written by Dekker and Ford); a revival of Dekker's *Match Me in London* (21 August 1623); Henry Shirley's *The Martyred Soldier* (23 August 1623); William Bonen's *The Cra... Merchant or Come to my Country House* (12 September 1623); Massinger's *The Bondman* (3 December 1623); Dekker and Ford's *The Sun's Darling* (3 March 1624); Massinger's *The Renegado* (17 April 1624); Heywood's *The Captives* (3 September 1624); Robert Davenport's *The City Nightcap* (14 October 1624); Massinger's *The Parliament of Love* (3 November 1624) and James Shirley's *Love Tricks or the School of Compliment* (11 February 1625). Like the troupe's earlier repertory, most of the company's new plays were tragicomedies or comedies, although their new works also included one masque-like play (*The Sun's Darling*), perhaps with an eye to courtly tastes, and at least one tragedy (*The Changeling*).[108] Evidence of the troupe on tour yields the title of another apparently new play and an interest in political drama. In 1624 Francis Wambus and a touring group of Lady Elizabeth's players found themselves in trouble in Norwich when they advertised a performance of a play called *The Spanish Contract*, despite having been denied permission to perform in the city.[109] The play does not appear to survive or to have been licensed, but the contemporary context would suggest that it was a topical political drama, which dealt with James's recent, controversial attempt to match Prince Charles with the Spanish Infanta, like Middleton's *A Game at Chess* which premiered at the Globe later that summer. The prospect of a Spanish match had been widely opposed in England but was especially controversial because of Spain's involvement in the Netherlands and in the deposition of Lady Elizabeth's husband, Frederick, as King of Bohemia. A play opposed to the Spanish match and possibly supportive of the case for English intervention to support the King of Bohemia would have been especially politically charged as performed by Lady Elizabeth's players.

Herbert named only seven players in his list of chief actors at the Cockpit in 1622. These were probably the 'sharers' in the revamped company but the troupe's surviving plays make clear that the troupe was considerably larger than this, with the largest scenes in some of the plays written for the troupe requiring up to 20 performers and between three and six boys for female roles.[110] The Cockpit Theatre used by the company was comparatively small, but it is thought to have been fitted with much the same features as the other outdoor and indoor playhouses, including a stage backed by a tiring house fitted with two side doors, a central opening and an upper playing area.[111] Those plays written specifically for the troupe while it performed at the Cockpit tend to confirm these assumptions: almost all of them allude to the use of two doors and several call for action above; at least one of the plays incorporates a discovery scene, possibly requiring a large opening in the tiring house (*The Renegado*); one play suggests that the tiring house may have been fitted with at least one window (*The Spanish Gypsy*); and another calls for use of the below-stage area and a trap door in the stage (*The Renegado*).[112] Evidence of the new company's (or Beeston's) ambition is arguably found in the fact that the troupe bought plays both from well-established writers such as Heywood, Middleton and Rowley, and from up-and-coming writers such as Ford, Massinger and Shirley. The company's new plays share some other features which might be seen as shaping the 'style' of the new company's repertory. As well as being dominated by comedy and tragicomedy, almost all of the plays use continental or foreign settings and demonstrate 'a more or less gentlemanly concern for questions of honour and love', as Andrew Gurr observes.[113] In this respect the troupe's repertory can be seen as reflecting the growing fashion for plays focused on women in this period and as anticipating the Caroline vogue for tragicomedy and plays about love and honour fostered by the Caroline court.

Despite their success, the career of the new Lady Elizabeth's Men was to be cut short in 1625 when a serious outbreak of plague closed the London theatres for many months. As on so many previous occasions this interruption of business was to prove a catalyst for changes in the London theatre world. When the theatres were finally reopened six of the seven known members of the troupe had joined new companies. Two of the actors stayed at the Cockpit with Beeston (Sherlock and Turner) as Beeston played host to a new royal company: Queen Henrietta's Men. Andrew Cane had joined the Palsgrave's players even before the plague closure and Elliart Swanston and Curtis Greville followed the example of earlier members of Lady Elizabeth's Men, joining the King's Men.[114] The fact that many of the troupe's plays stayed at the Cockpit and were revived by Queen Henrietta's Men (including *The Renegado*, *The Spanish Gypsy*, *The Changeling* and *The School of Compliment*) suggests that Christopher Beeston may have owned the company's plays, thus emulating the example of Henslowe in the later stages of his career as a theatre impresario.

Other players from the Cockpit company may have headed to the Fortune Theatre with Cane to join the Palsgrave's Men who became known as the King and Queen of Bohemia's players, performing there from 1626 up until 1631.[115] On 30 June 1628 a group of men (including Joseph Moore and Alexander Foster from the 1611 Lady Elizabeth's troupe) were sworn as 'the Queen of Bohemia's players' and Grooms of the Chamber but there is no evidence of this troupe performing independently in London and the King and Queen of Bohemia's company seems to have dissolved by 1631 or 1632, being displaced during the company reorganizations that followed the creation of the new Prince Charles's company. There may have been no independent company of Lady Elizabeth's players in the Caroline capital, but at least one group (and possibly more) continued to tour under Lady Elizabeth's name in the provinces, still led by Joseph Moore and including two other early members of the troupe, John Townsend and Alexander Foster.[116] A second company led by sometime member of the touring troupe, Ellis Guest, also appears to have operated in the early Caroline provinces, although at least one of its hosts had doubts about its right to do so. In July 1630 the Walmesley family's steward records a payment to 'a sorte of Players which tearmet them selfes the lady Elizabethes players for playing one night' at Dunkenhalgh (Lancashire), other references suggesting that the troupe hosted on this occasion was that led by Guest.[117] No records of players calling themselves Lady Elizabeth's or the Queen of Bohemia's players have been found after 1632 so far, although some of the players who had been in her companies continued to be active in and beyond London in other acting companies, including Ellis Guest, Joseph Moore, John Townsend and William Perry.[118]

Conclusions

Lady Elizabeth's Men are not as well known as the King's Men but, in some respects, their chequered history has more to tell us about the life of an average acting company in Renaissance London. Theirs is a story of firsts and innovations, too. As well as being responsible for performing the only play explicitly described as having been performed at the Swan Theatre (Middleton's *A Chaste Maid in Cheapside*) the company was the first to perform at Henslowe's dual-purpose playhouse, the Hope (1614) and is thought to have been the first adult troupe to follow the example of the King's Men by performing at an indoor theatre (the Whitefriars). The fact that the company performed in so many venues is telling, however, in that it demonstrates the importance of gaining a secure playing place in the capital. In the troupe's two main phases of existence in London, Lady Elizabeth's Men were not able to do this and this was one of the reasons that it did not enjoy a lasting career in the capital. At the same time, the fact that the players were able to adapt to a variety of venues reminds us of the essential versatility of players in this period, first learned and honed by the experience of touring. It also reinforces the fluidity of the London theatrical market. The playhouses of Renaissance London became a settled feature of London life but the companies using them rarely enjoyed the same stability. In this respect, the life of the Lord Chamberlain's/King's Men was virtually unique. No other company enjoyed a continuous existence from 1594 to 1642 or enjoyed the long residency that they did at the Globe and the Blackfriars. For many actors and acting companies, life was a 'hand-to-mouth business characterized by low levels of investment and considerable instability for the individuals involved'.[119] If this was what it was to be part of a weak company, nearly all of the period's acting companies were weak for some if not for much of their lives. The most successful company in Renaissance London – the King's Men – succeeded not just because it had royal patronage or a genius as its resident writer (though both no doubt helped). It was also because, uniquely, members of the acting company owned the theatres that they used and thus could guarantee the availability of those playhouses for the troupe's use. For most of the other acting companies of the day, life was far less secure, even if some of the theatrical successes were as great and the profits sometimes as generous.

2

Playwrights and playwriting

Mr Dawborne and I haue spent a great deale
of time in conference about this plot, wch will
make as beneficiall a play as hath come these
seauen yeares.

LETTER FROM NATHAN FIELD TO THEATRE OWNER, PHILIP
HENSLOWE, C. 1613.[1]

The creation of permanent playhouses in late Elizabethan
London and the establishment of daily playing created a huge
demand for new plays which led to an explosion in playwriting
in English and the emergence of the professional playwright.
G. E. Bentley estimates that around 900 plays were written
for the commercial theatre between 1580 and 1642, and
we know the names of more than 250 English Renaissance
playwrights. Not all of those who wrote plays wished to be, or
succeeded in becoming, professional playwrights. Some, like
Walter Mountfort, author of *The Launching of the Mary*, are
only known to have written one play; others enjoyed longer,
more productive careers, most of the plays for the commercial
stage being written by a group of around 40 playwrights.[2] It is
these pioneering individuals – the first people to make a living

wholly or partly from playwriting in England – that are the focus of this chapter.

Playwrights and playing companies

Whereas the earliest playwrights for the professional stage often appear to have been actors-turned-writers it became increasingly common in the late sixteenth century to employ the services of dedicated playwrights. As early as 2 June 1572 we find players Lawrence and John Dutton allegedly contracting Rowland Broughton to write 18 plays for their acting company over a period of two and a half years. Broughton, who is identified in the legal records as a gentleman, is otherwise unknown but seems to have been hired specifically as a writer rather than an actor. Perhaps unsurprisingly, Broughton does not seem to have been able to satisfy the demanding terms of this contract. Indeed, it is this apparent failure and the complaint it prompted against him that preserves our only evidence of his contract for plays with the Duttons, the contract itself having been lost.[3]

Some of the new generation of playwrights were university educated (such as Christopher Marlowe and Thomas Heywood), others, like Shakespeare and Ben Jonson, were products of the English grammar-school system, putting their humanist training in classical literature and rhetoric to innovative use within the emerging market of the theatre. Most of the known playwrights were of middling stock, although more elite figures (such as Sir John Suckling) and humbler individuals (such as Richard Brome who started his career as Ben Jonson's servant) are known to have written plays for the professional players, too.

Most of those regularly active as playwrights in late-sixteenth-century London worked on a freelance basis. In a bid to produce plays more quickly and to corner the market it also became common for writers to team up and to write collaboratively for companies such as those hosted by Philip Henslowe at the Rose and Fortune Theatres. Indeed, it has sometimes been argued that most dramatic writing in the period was collaborative.[4] The importance of collaboration in the 1590s is borne out by Henslowe's *Diary*. As Bentley notes, 'nearly two-thirds of the plays' that Henslowe bought on behalf of players were 'the work of more than one man'.[5] Whether collaborative writing was as common in the repertories of all the London companies is less clear and there is some reason to believe that collaboration was an innovation of the late-sixteenth-century theatre world that became less common in the early seventeenth century, as company play stocks grew and the demand for new plays eased.[6]

Whereas most of the successful playwrights from the period worked for several acting companies during the course of their careers, some acting companies and playwrights established longer-lived relationships with each other. Perhaps most famously, Shakespeare became the Lord Chamberlain's Men's resident playwright. It is not clear if Shakespeare ever had a formal contract with the company as a playwright but, so far as we know, he did not write for any other acting company after he joined the troupe in 1594. After Shakespeare's death, the troupe seems to have been keen to continue the custom of having at least one regular playwright, much the same role being taken in turn by John Fletcher, Philip Massinger and James Shirley.

The Lord Chamberlain's players' chief rivals in the 1590s – the Lord Admiral's Men – do not seem to have employed a resident playwright in the same way but they do seem to have cultivated the services of a regular stable of writers and there is evidence to suggest that Philip Henslowe sought to bind at least some of these writers more closely to the companies that he hosted. On 28 February 1598 Henslowe records a payment of 40 shillings to Henry Porter in earnest of his play *The Merry Women of Abingdon* and notes that 'for the Resayte of that money he gaue me his faythfulle promysse that I shold haue all*e* the boockes w*c*ʰ he writte ether him sellfe or wᵗʰ any other'. Similarly, Henslowe records a payment of 3 pounds to Henry Chettle (25 March 1602) at the wish of the Lord Admiral's Men, 'at the sealleynge of h Chettells band to writte for them'.[7]

There are only two other known cases where playwrights appear to have been formally contracted to write plays for an individual company over an agreed period of time. The first is the contract allegedly made between the Dutton brothers and Rowland Broughton (1572) and a pair of contracts between Richard Brome and the Revels players of Salisbury Court Theatre, the first of which (20 July 1635) required that Brome write three plays a year for the company for three years, while the second (August 1638) required him to work exclusively for the troupe, writing three plays a year for them for the next seven years.[8] The fact that there are so few records of formal contracts and that playwrights often wrote for several acting companies, sometimes at the same time, might mean that such formalized, exclusive arrangements were not common, as Eleanor Collins notes.[9]

In either case, it seems fairly clear that in the late sixteenth century playwrights could hawk around with their plays as Nathan Field feared Robert Daborne would in 1613 (see p. 53). That playwrights might be ready to pit one company against another would seem to be borne out by some of the fascinating letters written by Daborne to Philip Henslowe. In one letter (14 October 1613) begging for an advance Daborne suggests that the King's Men are ready to 'pay it' back to Henslowe in return for taking the papers of Daborne's latest play. In a similar letter written shortly afterwards (29 October 1613) Daborne again alludes to the King's Men's interest in his play, writing 'I hav bin twise to speak wth y[u] both for the sheet I told y[u] off as also to know y[r] determination for the company wheather y[u] purpose they shall haue the play' or not; 'they cald vpon me I fear bycause the Kings men hav givn out they shall hav it'.[10]

Some playwrights may have been less scrupulous actually selling plays to more than one company. This is certainly what the anonymous author of *The Defence of Conny Catching* (1592) accused Robert Greene of doing with his play *Orlando Furioso*: 'Aske the Queens Players, if you sold them not Orlando Furioso for twenty Nobles, and when they were in the country, sold the same Play to the Lord Admirals men for as much more'.[11] Similarly, there is evidence of acting companies allegedly buying plays promised to other troupes and of companies luring playwrights away from the service of their competitors. According to Brome, this is what happened to him in 1635. Prior to signing his first contract with the Revels Company at Salisbury Court he had been writing for Prince Charles's Men at the Red Bull. By his account, the Revels troupe 'did intice and *Inveagle this d*efend^t *to depart* and leave the company of the Red Bull players'. Likewise, the Revels players complained that Brome had been subsequently encouraged to break his contract with them 'throughe the perswasions and inticement' of the Cockpit's manager, William Beeston.[12]

The case involving Brome confirms the competitive nature of the relationship between English Renaissance acting companies, but there is little evidence to suggest that their relations were routinely antagonistic. On the contrary, playwrights and players often seem to have worked amicably with each other. Robert Daborne's letters to Philip Henslowe reveal that he had an intimate knowledge of the business of the acting companies associated with Henslowe. In a letter dated 8 May 1613, for instance, Daborne writes to Henslowe about a play that he is working on for one of Henslowe's troupes promising that it will be ready 'vpon ye neck of this new play they ar now studying'. There is also evidence of his being friends with players and acting as an intermediary between them and Henslowe. In one letter to Henslowe (28 March 1613) after making his usual plea for money, Daborne alludes to the discontent of one of the players, Robert Pallant, writing 'm^r Pallat is much discontented wth your neglect Of him I would I knew y^r mynd to give him answer'.[13]

Just as some scholars have assumed that relations between playwrights and companies were vexed, so it has been argued that relations between fellow playwrights were fraught. Playwrights were undoubtedly in competition with each other and it is clear that there was sometimes tension between them, as demonstrated at the turn of the seventeenth century by the so-called Poets' War which saw playwrights such as Jonson, Marston and Dekker engaged in a battle of wits as they disputed about the social function of drama.[14] Sometimes the disputes were more personal, as when John Day killed fellow playwright Henry Porter in June 1599.[15] On the other hand, the widespread evidence of collaborative playwriting in the period and the fact that some writing teams worked together for whole seasons and on numerous plays suggests that playwrights were not always at odds with each other or desperate to work alone. At least some writers, including one of the era's most influential playwrights, John Fletcher, appear to have '*preferred* to collaborate', as Gordon McMullan points out.[16]

Similarly, although proven playwrights were in demand and enjoyed considerable independence, they could not ignore the wishes or needs of the actors to whom they sold their plays. If they did not persuade their employers of the potential value of their work there was no guarantee that their plays would be bought or that they would be employed again. Playwrights needed to take account of the actors for whom they were writing (potentially including their acting strengths as well as cast size), the specific requests that they might make, the staging resources likely to be available to the players, as well as audience tastes and theatrical fashions. Playwrights were the main artistic force behind the plays written for the English Renaissance stage but they were also its servants, their writing shaped by the theatrical world in which they worked.

The business of writing

If the records of Philip Henslowe are representative, it would seem that the average payment for a completed play in the 1590s was between 5 and 7 pounds, rising to around 20

pounds in the early seventeenth century.[17] Although writing a
new play might take several months, Henslowe's records show
that playwrights could work with great speed, sometimes
producing new plays within a matter of days. The rapid
production of new plays, combined with the fact that their
authors were working for money, could easily lead to the
conclusion that playwriting was essentially mercenary, but
contemporary evidence suggests that for many playwrights
writing was not solely about making money. Many of the
letters Robert Daborne sent to Philip Henslowe are concerned
with procuring loans or advances on plays, and thus superficially preoccupied with money, but they also afford evidence
of the artistic effort and attention which Daborne brought to
his work. On 25 June 1613, for instance, Daborne describes
his work on his current tragedy, reporting how he has taken
'extraordinary paynes wth the end & altered one other
scean in the third act which they haue now in parts'.[18] While
Daborne might be overstating the 'pains' he is taking with the
play as an excuse for potential tardiness with its completion,
the fact that he writes of altering a section of the play that
he has already submitted is suggestive of an author keen to
perfect his work, rather than a hack simply churning out
sheets of dialogue. If Daborne's example is representative
(and it might well be), it seems that playwriting could be a
commercial *and* a creative activity, at least for its writers, and
that working fast and for money did not necessarily mean
working without care.

Once a play was sold to a company it was no longer the
writer's property, although authors may have occasionally
received a bonus once the play was performed.[19] Later, it
seems to have become customary for playwrights to receive
the profits from one of the early performances of the play,
too. An entitlement to the 'Benefitte of one dayes proffittee'
of each new play formed part of Richard Brome's first
contract with the Revels players in 1635.[20] Playwrights could
not look forward to 'royalties', but the money to be earned
from writing plays was potentially good: Henry Chettle and

Thomas Dekker 'averaged about £25 a year' between 1598 and 1603, for example. Such an income compared favourably with the earnings to be made in other careers open to literate young men such as the Church and teaching, clerics and schoolmasters generally earning between 10 and 15 pounds annually.[21] But the life of the playwright was vulnerable: the theatres were sometimes closed for prolonged periods as a result of plague, acting companies could break up suddenly and there was never any secure promise of future employment for those who worked freelance.

In many cases it seems that writers approached acting companies, sometimes with complete plays but more often with a proposal for a play. In some cases, the proposal took the form of a 'plot' outline (or scenario), summarizing the story of the play and the characters scene by scene. Few of these documents survive, but there are several contemporary allusions to the writing and sharing of such 'plots' with acting companies.[22] In other cases, playwrights might present part of the written-up play as well as or instead of a 'plot'. On 4 April 1601 Lord Admiral's player, Samuel Rowley wrote to Philip Henslowe that he had heard five 'sheets of a play of the Conqueste of the Indes'; persuaded that it would be 'a verye good play' he requested that Henslowe deliver the writers 40 shillings 'In earnest of It & take the papers Into yo[r] hands'.[23] Once a play was ready in its entirety the playwright(s) might arrange to read it to the company and/or the company might read it collectively.[24]

How usual it was for playing companies to approach playwrights with specific requests for plays is less clear. One possible example of such a commission is *Keep the Widow Waking,* a Red Bull play (1624) reportedly written by John Ford, John Webster, Thomas Dekker and William Rowley, and based on a recent murder case in London in which a son was alleged to have killed his mother. The play became part of a lawsuit subsequently brought by one of the relatives, Benjamin Garfield, 'accusing a number of people of slandering his mother-in-law'. When interviewed about the play, Dekker described how he, Webster, Rowley and Ford 'did make and contrive the same upon the instructions given them by one Ralph Savage' (apparently on behalf of the Red Bull players).[25]

Further information about the ways in which playwrights worked is preserved in Henslowe's *Diary* which includes not only advance payments to playwrights but serial payments to playwrights as they worked on individual plays. In the case of plays written collaboratively these payments are sometimes made to different members of the writing team at different times and for differing amounts. The payments preserved in the *Diary* relating to a lost play, *Richard Coerdelion's Funeral*, between 13 and 26 June 1598, are typical in this respect: the *Diary* records nine payments relating to the play of varying amounts (from 5 to 30 shillings) to four different playwrights; only one of the payments (on 17 June 1598) is listed as a collective payment (to Chettle, Wilson and Munday).[26] That the amount of money playwrights received for their work on collaboratively written plays was not necessarily the same may reflect the fact that the division of work was not always equal. How such divisions were made is not documented, although there is reason to believe that some writers specialized in writing particular kinds of scene or act. Cyrus Hoy, for example, argues that Philip Massinger was often tasked with writing 'the opening and closing scenes of a play'.[27]

Playwrights seem to have been responsible for forming their own collaborative teams, as was Robert Daborne in 1613, reporting in one of his letters to Henslowe (5 June 1613) that he had given Cyril Tourneur 'an act of ye Arreignment of London to write'.[28] Like Daborne and Tourneur, most playwrights also appear to have worked on their apportioned parts separately. Hence, in the added crowd scene in the collaboratively revised *The Book of Sir Thomas More* written in Hand D (often believed to be Shakespeare's hand) the writer names some of the speakers simply as 'other', possibly because he did not know to whom the parts should be assigned, leaving it to one of the other revisers to name the speakers.[29]

The plays

Plays were generally written in ink on a series of paper sheets which might be submitted in instalments to the acting company or its representative. On 29 October 1613 Robert Daborne mentioned having sent Henslowe '3 sheets' of the play he was working on; while earlier that year he was contracted to write a tragedy about *Machiavel and the Devil*, he and Henslowe agreeing that he should receive six pounds in earnest of its writing on 17 April, a further four pounds 'vpon delivery in of 3 acts' and 'ten pounds vpon delivery in of yᵉ last scean'.[30] As the latter example suggests, plays were usually divided into acts, the final payment for a play usually being made when the final scene was submitted. The practice of submitting plays in instalments potentially allowed players to offer (and playwrights to seek) feedback on a play before its completion. An anecdote later told by Gerald Langbaine suggests that John Fletcher may have solicited players' input in precisely this way (if unwisely in his view), reporting that, ''twas generally Mr. *Fletcher*'s practice, after he had finish'd Three Acts of a Play to shew them to the Actors, and when they had agreed on Terms, he huddled up the two last without that care that behoov'd him'.[31]

Thus far none of the 18 surviving manuscript plays thought to be associated with the English Renaissance theatre world has been definitively identified as the papers a playwright originally submitted to an acting company (although it is possible that some of the extant manuscripts could have this provenance).[32] The correspondence of Robert Daborne suggests that it was customary for the text supplied to be what Daborne termed 'fair' rather than 'foul' in its presentation.[33] Much ink has been spilt about what Daborne was describing when he distinguished between 'fair' and 'foul' papers. W. W. Greg used the phrase 'foul papers' to refer to the author's final draft in 'contradistinction to the fair copy made for theatrical purposes', whereas Paul Werstine argues that the phrase refers to a manuscript 'that is to be or is being or has been fair-copied' and Tiffany Stern's research suggests that it might refer to the author's plot scenario.[34] In the absence of Daborne's 'fair' and 'foul' papers we cannot be sure which (if any) of these interpretations of Daborne's terms is accurate, but the playwright's consistent preference for the submission of 'fair' copies of his works implies that acting companies expected to receive a readable copy of the author's (or authors') play.

Those plays which survive in theatrically annotated manuscripts afford an insight into their usual presentation. By the late sixteenth century it had clearly become customary for plays to be divided into five acts, for example, in keeping with classical precedents and it was usual for the dialogue to be written in a contemporary type of handwriting called secretary hand, while act and scene divisions and stage directions were usually written in italic script. The speech prefixes (identifying the speakers) were generally abbreviated and appeared in the left-hand margin, while the dialogue was written in the middle of the page and stage directions were either centred (as at the start of a scene) or written in the right or left margin. There were established ways of structuring the action of plays, too. Thus, it was common for writers to combine a main plot and a sub-plot, the sub-plot often being used either to mirror or to contrast with the action of the main plot. Similarly, it was common to alternate between scenes of main and sub-plot action or between different styles, as for example between 'high' scenes featuring elite characters and 'low' scenes featuring lowly born figures.[35]

Linguistically, the plays of the Renaissance stage were more varied than those that preceded them, contemporary playwrights employing their usual training in classical rhetoric and literature to develop new forms of dramatic speech. Whereas medieval and early-sixteenth-century plays were usually written in short rhyming couplets, and early Elizabethan plays were often composed in rhyming 'fourteeners' (with 14 syllables), late-sixteenth and early-seventeenth-century dramatic writing was to be much more varied and rhetorically complex. One of the first great innovations was the use of blank verse (unrhymed iambic pentameter). Its first recorded use for drama was in Thomas Norton and Thomas Sackville's *Gorboduc*, a topical British tragedy written for performance at the Inner Temple in 1561–2, but Marlowe was the writer who pioneered its use on the public stage with his ground-breaking tragedy *Tamburlaine the Great*. Blank verse was especially well suited to serious subject matter as it avoided the jingling, potentially comic, effects of rhyming couplets; but it was also to prove an important verse form because it fostered the development of more realistic characterization, allowing characters to speak more naturalistically, not least because its rhythm is very close to that of spoken English. Some playwrights experimented with the use of prose, too. John Lyly became famous for his elaborate euphuistic prose – a highly artificial prose style which makes extensive use of parallelism, antithesis and complex figures of speech – while other playwrights such as Shakespeare mixed verse and prose, occasionally distinguishing between characters or moods through alternations between the two modes.

Generically, English Renaissance dramatists were indebted both to earlier English dramatic forms (such as Medieval morality and mystery plays) and to classical comedy and tragedy, but they generally turned for their material to the new wealth of literature made available by the sixteenth-century print revolution. Especially popular sources included the series of English histories published in the sixteenth century – works such as Raphael Holinshed's *Chronicles of England, Scotland, and Ireland* (1577, 1587) – and the risqué Italian novellas of writers such as Matteo Bandello and Gerald Cinthio with their multiple tales of love, lust and intrigue. As the theatre business thrived, playwrights also imitated each other. Thomas Kyd's *The Spanish Tragedy* started a late Elizabethan vogue for revenge tragedies, while the success of George Chapman's *A Humorous Day's Mirth* inspired a wave of so-called 'Humours' comedies in the late 1590s.[36] In fact, the leading acting companies regularly duplicated each other's plays and genres that were successful in their own repertories and the repertories of their competitors. This is not to say that there were no differences between the repertories of plays owned by the leading acting companies. One of the specialities of Shakespeare's company in the 1590s was romantic comedy, a sub-genre that their main rivals, the Lord Admiral's players, generally seem to have avoided.[37] Likewise, although there was clearly pressure to follow established fashions and conventions, playwrights were not afraid to innovate on occasion, as demonstrated by the pioneering of new types of play. For playwrights, and the companies for whom they wrote, the trick was offering audiences plays (and a repertory) that combined the popular and the new, familiarity and novelty both being proven ways of drawing and keeping audiences.

The writing and performance of new plays (and, occasionally, of new types of play) was one of the key ways in which writers and acting companies sought to distinguish themselves from their competitors. This was presumably one of the reasons that the leading London companies continued to buy new plays (if at a much slower rate) in the Jacobean and Caroline eras when they could have relied on their large back catalogues of plays. One of the other guaranteed (if more risky) ways to draw large audiences was to perform plays which addressed topical issues, even if the censorship to which plays were subject meant that playwrights were frequently obliged to engage with such matters indirectly. One common technique was to set the action of plays in the past or elsewhere. But playwrights were sometimes bolder, representing topical events and individuals more directly. This is apparent if we consider some of the plays bought by the King's Men such as Fletcher and Massinger's 1619 play about the downfall and execution of Dutch statesman Sir John Van Olden Barnavelt, written and performed only months after the events which it dramatizes.

One of the more contentious questions relating to company playing repertories is the extent to which the different Renaissance troupes cultivated distinctive 'house' styles to

which would-be or subsequent playwrights were expected to
conform. The work done by scholars such as Scott McMillin
and Sally-Beth MacLean on the Queen's Men and by Mary
Bly on the Children of the King's Revels, suggests that some
companies did, indeed, develop distinctive performance styles
and repertories.[38] Bly, for example, notes the predominance
in the Children's repertory of 'romantic comedies graced by
punning and desirous virgins' and links the 'homogeneity'
of the troupe's plays to the close collaboration between its
playwrights and to the audience for which the troupe sought
to cater, based at it was in a theatre in Renaissance London's
red-light district.[39] On the other hand, Roslyn Knutson's
research on company repertories leads her to conclude that the
major playing companies were performing essentially similar
repertories of plays from the late 1590s onwards.[40] The fact
that playwrights often wrote for several companies without
necessarily changing their writing style significantly and that
plays (and players) moved between companies might also
seem to undermine the case for the development of consistent
or long-lived 'house' styles. Indeed, it might be more appropriate to speak of acting companies fostering occasional
dramatic and staging specialities, rather than developing
wholly distinctive company repertories and performance
practices, such as the Lord Admiral's Men's special line in
'disguise' plays during Edward Alleyn's career with them
or the Lord Chamberlain's Men's distinctive repertory of
romantic comedies in the 1590s.[41] In other respects, each of
these companies' repertories overlapped with those of their
competitors.

Preparing plays for the stage

Once a writer's papers were submitted to an acting company
they became the property of that troupe and company staff
generally presided over the play's preparation for the stage.
By the early seventeenth century these preparations appear

to have been overseen by a figure known as the book-holder. One of the first jobs for the book-holder was the forwarding of a copy of the play to the Master of the Revels to secure his licence for its performance. Only five manuscript plays survive which carry the licence of the Master (or his deputy): Middleton's *The Second Maiden's Tragedy* (31 October 1611) (BL, Lansdowne MS 807, ff.29–56) (scribal copy); Field and Fletcher and Massinger's *The Honest Man's Fortune* (re-allowed 8 February 1624) (Victoria & Albert Museum, Dyce MS 9) (scribal copy); Massinger's *Believe As You List* (6 May 1631) (BL, Egerton MS 2828) (authorial copy); Walter Mountfort's *The Launching of the Mary* (27 June 1633) (BL, Egerton MS 1994, ff.317–49) (authorial copy); Henry Glapthorne's *The Lady Mother* (15 October 1635) (BL, Egerton MS 1994, ff.186–211) (scribal copy). These examples suggest that sometimes the book-holder forwarded an authorial copy of the play and, in other cases – perhaps where the manuscript was harder to read – he forwarded a copy prepared by himself or a scribe.

The readying of plays for performance is likely to have generated a series of further documents. Some Elizabethan companies appear to have produced a theatrical 'plot': a document listing the entrances of characters scene by scene and sometimes also recording information about required properties and sound effects, exits and some or all of the actors' names. Seven of these 'plots' are extant today: six are preserved in manuscript form; the seventh (*I Tamar Cam*) survives in a printed transcription in the *Variorum Shakespeare* of 1803. Four of the plots are preserved in full. Three are found in BL, Additional MS 10449: *The Dead Man's Fortune* (f.1), *Frederick and Basilea* f.2), *The Battle of Alcazar* (f.3) and a fourth is at Dulwich College, *The Seven Deadly Sins, Part 2* (MS XIX); and three plots survive as fragments: *Fortune's Tennis* and *Troilus and Cressida* in BL, Additional MS 10449 (ff.4–5) and *I Tamar Cam*. Although the extant plots all share a similar presentation (being written on folio-sized paper and divided into two columns, subdivided into boxes) scholars have disagreed about their theatrical function. W. W. Greg and Tiffany Stern argue that plots were akin to the modern-day 'call-list', whereas David Bradley suggests that their main purpose was 'to count the actors' and 'to construct a framework for the correct making-out of their acting scrolls'.[42] In either case, it is clear that the 'plots' were documents intended to assist with the management of performances.

Other documents likely to have been prepared at an early stage are the cast list, recording which actors were to play which parts and information about any doubling of roles, and the actors' parts, for actors were not given whole copies of the play: they worked just with copies of their own speeches and then only if those speeches were sizable.[43] There is one extant part from the professional English Renaissance stage – for the role of Orlando in Greene's *Orlando Furioso*[44]– but contemporary allusions and the evidence of amateur theatre in the era suggest that the preparation of such parts was customary. Orlando's part is thought to be in a scribal hand but the scribe left some gaps in his transcription most of which appear to have been filled in by the probable actor of the part, Edward Alleyn, raising the possibility that actors may have contributed to the writing and revision of their roles.[45]

As well as preparing the parts, the book-holder is thought to have been the person usually responsible for marking up at least one copy of the play for use in the theatre. Although this copy of the play or 'book' is sometimes referred to as a 'promptbook' there has been some debate about whether the book-holder acted as a prompter. Similarly, whether the copy used to direct performances was the same as that first submitted to the company by the playwright(s) and then to the Master of the Revels has been a matter of dispute. A. W. Pollard famously suggested that the author's papers were generally passed to the Master of the Revels for licensing and then to the book-holder for use in the theatre (the so-called 'continuous copy' theory). William B. Long made a similar case in the late twentieth century, suggesting that players rarely copied out or modified authors' papers unless there were problems with their manuscripts.[46] However, the varied nature and provenance of the surviving playbooks which show signs of preparation for theatrical use suggests that this was not necessarily the case and that one or more copies might be made of a play, including one for the Master and one for theatrical use, as Gabriel Egan points out.[47] Those manuscripts which show signs of being marked up for performance by one or more adaptors suggest that they were mainly concerned with the back-stage management of performances, generally only adding notes for large properties, sound effects and act breaks, often in the left margin. Occasionally, adaptors also add actors' names and directions for the readying of actors in advance of their entrances.

The stage adaptor whose hand can be seen at work in the manuscript of Massinger's *Believe As You List* annotates the text in several ways: he adds some stage directions and moves others to the left margin; he deletes Massinger's scene references but marks the act breaks more clearly; he adds some missing speech-prefixes; he corrects a casting problem in 2.1 where Massinger has confused two characters (Demetrius and Calistus); and he adds the names of some of the actors.[48] Some of the added directions are examples of readying directions, occurring some time before the entrance of the relevant actor or the need for the specified property. In Act 4 the entry of Antiochus (apparently played by Joseph Taylor) from below the stage is prepared for well in advance, the adaptor adding the following readying direction on f.18v (ll.1825–31): 'Gascoine: & / Hubert / below: / ready to open / the Trap / doore for / Mr Taylor'. This is followed by a later readying direction for Antiochus (Taylor): 'Antiochus / ready: vnder / the stage' (f.19, ll.1877–9).[49]

Several of the extant manuscript playbooks also show signs of being cut and revised for performance by the stage adaptor and/or other theatrical personnel, including *The Tragedy of Sir John Van Olden Barnavelt* (BL, Additional MS 18653) and *The Captives* (BL, Egerton MS 1994, ff.52–73). Indeed, it is common to find multiple hands at work in these manuscripts. The same is true of at least one of the printed plays seemingly marked up for theatrical use: the printed quarto of *The Two Merry Milke-Maids* (1620) has been annotated and cut by at least two stage adaptors.[50] Interestingly, when the stage adaptor (and others) wished to mark text for omission they generally did so by putting a vertical line in the margin next to the text, rather than by scoring it through, so that such text remained available for reintroduction.[51] But perhaps what is most fascinating about the surviving theatrical play 'books' is the general lightness of the adaptors' markings and the fact that they do not always resolve staging problems posed by the manuscripts in which they appear.[52] This may sometimes be a sign that we are dealing with an intermediate copy of the play, but it could also mean that much was left to the actors (including their exits and the carrying on of small properties). Given that some of the surviving theatrical 'plots' duplicate the kind of information found in the playbooks apparently marked up for performance it might also be the case that companies either used a theatrical 'plot' to manage performances or a marked-up playbook but not both, as Tiffany Stern suggests.[53]

Censorship

Drama in Renaissance England was subject to two licensing systems: licensing for performance and for print. From 1581 the person responsible for licensing plays for performance was the Master of the Revels. Initially players were expected to perform their plays before the Master; later it became customary to present him with a manuscript of the play. The Master could choose to ban a play outright, but it was more common for him to mark up for revision any scenes, lines or phrases he thought unacceptable. Often this marking took the form of ink or pencil lines and/or crosses in the left margin next to the offending text; more rarely the Master might cross out text, sometimes inserting alternative text or a note about the kind of revision expected. Famously, Sir Edmund Tilney called upon the authors of *The Book of Sir Thomas More* to leave out the scene of 'insurrection wholy and the Cause ther off and begin with Sir Thomas Moore att the mayors session with a report afterwards off his good service one being Shrive off London'.[54] In some cases, the Master would read through a play more than once, marking up the text initially with pencil and then going through it again with ink to confirm which lines or sections he wanted revised. In some cases, this appears to have involved having second thoughts about what needed to be changed. In the manuscript of *The Tragedy of Sir John Van Olden Barnavelt* (1619), for example, Sir George Buc appears to have erased some of the pencil crosses that he initially marked on the manuscript.[55] It does not seem to have been usual for the Master to ask to see a play following its post-censorship revision, although it may have become customary under Sir Henry Herbert for companies to provide the Master with a copy of the plays that he licensed, Herbert writing in a 1633 note that the 'Master ought to have copies of their new playes left with him, that he may be able to shew what he hath allowed or disallowed'.[56]

Plays most often faced censorship prior to performance when they satirized or alluded to living individuals or if they addressed politically, morally or ecclesiastically sensitive subject matter. This is reflected not only in Tilney's censorship of *The Book of Sir Thomas More* but in the kind of censorship evidenced in later manuscripts such as *Barnavelt* in which Sir George Buc carefully censors the play's representation of living royal, Prince Maurice of Orange, writing alongside the scene in which the Prince is prevented from entering the Dutch Council Rooms 'I like not this: neith[r] / do I think y[e] pr. was / thus disgracefully vsed. / besides he is to much / presented'.[57] After 1606 and the passing of the Act to Restrain Abuses of Players playwrights could also expect the censor to delete any oaths (swearing by deities) found in the plays they submitted to him.[58] Yet what the surviving manuscripts reveal collectively is the extent to which consecutive Masters sought to work with, rather than against, players and playwrights to render their texts acceptable for performance. Given the Master's increasing reliance on professional players for the annual entertainments he oversaw at court and the money he garnered from licensing plays for performance, it was clearly in his interest to ensure the livelihoods of the leading companies. Some members of the Revels Office had an even more direct interest in the playing companies whose plays they scrutinized. William Blagrave (deputy to Herbert) was an investor, for example, in the Salisbury Court Theatre.[59] Scholars such as Richard Dutton are thus no doubt right when they describe the Master as usually being 'as much a friend of the actors as their overlord'.[60]

Confirmation that the Master was seen as an adviser as much as a prescriber of what playwrights and acting companies could stage might be found in the way that they responded to the Master's suggestions. Censorship sometimes resulted in the playwright or other playhouse personnel making significant changes to the play; but writers and players did not necessarily follow the Master's recommendations to the letter. This seems to be true of *The Book of Sir Thomas More* where the play's revisers appear to have chosen to adapt, rather than to omit, the scene of the insurrection which Tilney had ordered to be cut.[61]

The licensing system for printed plays was managed separately from the licensing of drama for performance. The authority for the former was concentrated from 1586 in the hands of the Archbishop of Canterbury and the Bishop of London. No play could be printed legally in England without their prior approval. Like the Master of the Revels, the press censors had the right to ban or to ask for corrections to any work that they deemed to be libellous, seditious, offensive or in any other way unacceptable. Evidence of plays being censored prior to publication is generally indirect. Often it is only the existence of differing contemporary versions or editions of a play that points to the possibility of censorship having occurred before its printing. Perhaps most famously, the on-stage deposition of Richard II by Henry Bolingbroke (4.1.162–318) in Shakespeare's *Richard II* appears in the 1608 edition of the play but not in the earlier Elizabethan editions (1597, 1598). The fact that controversial parallels were drawn by contemporaries between Richard II and Elizabeth I has led at least some scholars, such as Andrew Gurr, to conclude that the deposition scene 'was deleted from the early printed quartos as an act of censorship'.[62] On the other hand, the difficulty of proving that censorship occurred, in the absence of direct evidence, is reflected in the fact that not all scholars have been persuaded by this argument, noting that the extra lines could be a later composition.[63]

Play texts were not necessarily only subject to censorship by the official censor. The extant playbooks which show signs of theatrical use also include examples of what appear to be unofficial censorship by authors and/or other theatrical personnel. Thus, the cutting of a section of dialogue alluding to the Dutch and their controversial massacre of English traders at Amboyna (1623) in the manuscript of Mountfort's *The Launching of the Mary* (ff.329–30, ll.1076–125) is in keeping with Sir Henry Herbert's marking of two earlier allusions to Amboyna for omission (see f.320, ll.98, 111–12), but appears to be the work of the author, rather than the censor.[64] Given what they knew about the censorship regime to which plays were subject, it is, likewise, possible that writers effectively self-censored when writing, avoiding material that was likely to provoke the Master of the Revels' ire or finding subtle ways to address more dangerous material. As mentioned above (p. 65), this might include setting the action of your play in the past or in another country or the use of indirect modes of expression such as allegory and coded allusions to address current affairs. The need to be wary did not leave writers artistically hamstrung, however, nor did it prevent playwrights from tackling controversial material, as is demonstrated by the case of Middleton's *A Game at Chess* (1624) which commented allegorically on recent relations between England and Spain (see pp. 183–5).

Revision

As the example of the different early printed editions of *Richard II* highlights, plays written for the English Renaissance stage sometimes survive in different versions in print and/or manuscript. Some of these differences may be the result of censorship; others may be a consequence of errors (for example, of transcription or typesetting); but at least some appear to be the result of deliberate revision either by the author, other playwrights and/or theatrical personnel. Revisions might happen at various points in a play's life and could have more than one source. Sometimes playwrights revised as they wrote. They might continue to revise plays as they copied them out for submission to acting companies and/or individual readers. We see this in the manuscript of Massinger's *Believe As You List* (BL, Egerton MS 2828) which includes examples of Massinger composing and making small changes while writing out the fair copy of his play, as on f.10v (ll.792–3) where he varies the phrasing used: 'our faedaries, our strength ~~at sea superior~~ vpon the sea / exceeding theirs'. Some of the licenced manuscript playbooks show signs of being revised by their authors post-censorship, too, including Glapthorne's *The Lady Mother* (BL, Egerton MS 1994, ff.186r–211r) and Mountfort's *The Launching of the Mary* (BL, Egerton MS 1994, ff.317–49).[65] As scholars such as Grace Ioppolo have noted, such evidence challenges the traditional 'linear' model of play transmission, suggesting that the playwright's part in his plays did not necessarily end with his submission of his papers to a troupe.[66]

Just as a playwright might revise a play right up to (and even after) its sale to an acting company, so, too, it appears to have been customary for plays to be revised as companies readied them for performance. Indeed, contemporary manuscript plays associated with theatrical use sometimes show evidence of being revised by stage adaptors, censors and other unidentified theatrical personnel as well as, and sometimes instead of, their authors. There is, for instance, evidence of three hands at work in the manuscript of Fletcher and Massinger's *Tragedy of Sir John Van Olden Barnavelt* (BL, Additional MS 18653), that of the scribe, the censor and the stage adaptor, but no evidence of the hands of Fletcher and Massinger participating in the revisions and annotations found in the manuscript.[67] Although this does not mean that the playwrights could not have been consulted about the play's revision, it is clear that the work on the manuscript submitted to the censor was left to others.

As well as adding information such as missing entrances and stage directions for sound effects and large properties, it is common to find company adaptors marking plays for cutting, often to streamline the action or to reduce the casting demands a text posed. Andrew Gurr argues that such cutting was probably common practice, with 'performance almost always' meaning 'a text trimmed and modified in various degrees of substantiality, out of' what Gurr terms 'the maximal playscript', meaning the full, licenced text.[68] That performed texts were often shorter than those which survive in print would seem to find confirmation in some of the statements which preface printed editions of public plays, several of which comment on the fact that the printed play contains material cut during performances. The 1600 quarto of Jonson's *Every Man Out of His Humour* is typical describing it as 'Containing more than hath been Publickely Spoken or Acted'.[69] Some of the cuts (and changes) made to plays may have arisen during or as a result of rehearsal, but the fact that proposed cuts to play texts were often indicated in the manuscripts by a line in the left margin (rather than by their deletion) meant that it was possible for such material to be reintroduced in later productions and/or printed editions of a play. Such a policy is suggestive of a business in which people knew that it was wise to keep your options open and to be thrifty with the material that you had.

If scholars such as Tiffany Stern are correct, further revisions to a play might follow on from the play's first performance in response to audience feedback.[70] We know from Henslowe's *Diary* that acting companies sometimes commissioned writers to revise plays for court performances and revivals, too, as appears to have occurred when the Lord Admiral's Men paid Thomas Dekker for 'alterynge' his lost play, *Phaeton*, 'for the courte' (1600) and when the troupe paid for revisions to *The Spanish Tragedy* and *Dr Faustus* prior to their revival in 1601 and 1602 respectively. In the latter cases the revisers were not the original authors but Jonson (in the case of *The Spanish Tragedy*) and William Bird and Samuel Rowley (in the case of *Faustus*).[71] There is also evidence to suggest that playwrights themselves occasionally chose to revise their plays post-performance. One well-known example is that of Jonson. When he published *Sejanus* in 1605 he chose to remove the work of a collaborator and replace it with his own writing.[72] Similarly, Jonson chose to revise *Every Man in His Humour* after its first publication so that the text of the play included in the 1616 Folio edition of his *Works* differs from the 1601 edition in a variety of ways (including the relocation of the play's setting from Florence to London).

In the case of *Every Man in His Humour* we know that the differences between the early printed editions are the result of authorial revision. In other instances, the origins of the differences found between early printed play editions are less certain. Similarly, although the changes made in extant manuscript playbooks are sometimes clearly authorial (being, for instance, in the author's hand) in other cases there is more ambiguity about their origin. For instance, several of the changes made to the manuscript of *Sir John Van Olden Barnavelt* post-censorship appear to be scribal in origin, as the play's editor Trevor Howard-Hill notes: 'some changes, like Crane's replacement of "a fresh whore" by "a kind wench" (line 206)' and the 'deletion of "vpon my soule" (line 2425) occur in circumstances which suggest that no one other than the scribe himself was responsible for them'.[73] Although these could be rewrites authorized by the playwrights, the fact that they are in the scribe's hand means that we cannot rule out the possibility that they are scribal compositions, just as we cannot be sure that Massinger wrote the prologue and epilogue in the manuscript of *Believe As You List* (BL, Egerton MS 2828, ff.28v, 29) because they are not in Massinger's hand (as is the rest of the manuscript) but in the hand of the stage adaptor.

John Kerrigan suggests that play revision took two main forms in the Renaissance: when

> one man of the theatre overhauled another's play, he cut, inserted and substituted sizeable pieces of text without altering the details of his precursor's dialogue. Revising authors, by contrast, though they sometimes worked just with large textual fractions, tended to tinker, introducing small additions, small cuts and indifferent single-word substitutions.[74]

The evidence afforded by manuscript playbooks and printed plays is arguably less clear-cut. Textual revisions (large and small) were sometimes made not only by authors but by the censor and other theatrical personnel. In the case of the manuscript playbooks, it is sometimes possible to be reasonably clear about who was responsible for at least some of the textual changes to a revised text. Where we only have printed texts it is much harder to assign responsibility for textual variations, including what might appear to be artistically motivated revisions of the kind generally associated with authors.

Plays and/in print

Few plays in English were printed before the 1580s, but just as the professional theatre thrived in late-sixteenth-century London so, too, did the book trade and at least some publishers chose to invest in play publication. The number of new playhouse plays published increased steadily from the 1580s, Peter Blayney's research showing that 96 new plays were published between 1583 and 1602, 115 between 1603 and 1622 and 160 between 1623 and 1642. Despite this growth in publication, Blayney controversially argues that plays were not generally in great demand or very profitable for publishers, but this conclusion has been challenged more recently by Alan B. Farmer and Zachary Lesser who argue that plays were 'more popular than Blayney contends', noting that 'in their peak years, professional plays made up 6.2 percent of the overall speculative market' so that even if they were 'not the dominant segment, playbooks were hardly marginal' to the London book trade.[75]

Before publication, a play would go through a number of processes. First, the publisher had to obtain a licence to print the play. He/She then needed to get permission to print the play from the Stationers' Company. He/She then might also pay to have his/her right to publish the play entered in the Stationers' Register (later this would become mandatory). Most plays were printed as small 'quarto' editions (roughly A5 size), costing around 6 pence each unbound, and so-called because each of the sheets they were printed on had been folded twice to make four leaves. Later, some playwrights such as Jonson published large folio editions of their works (printed on sheets of paper folded only once). These books were larger and more expensive than quartos, their format being traditionally associated with prestigious forms of literature such as the Bible. The 1616 Jonson Folio cost between 9 and 10 shillings unbound and 13 to 14 shillings bound.[76]

Although some publishers may have been motivated to publish drama by an interest in the genre, most are likely to have seen play publication as another form of speculative investment. The flourishing of the professional theatres and the audiences their plays drew were probably what encouraged some publishers to risk such an investment. It could prove lucrative, especially if the play went into a second edition, it being far cheaper to produce the subsequent edition. Why the playing companies who owned the period's commercial plays chose to publish some of the works from their repertory is less clear. Traditionally, it was assumed that acting companies were reluctant to see their plays printed as this potentially diminished the value of the performed play and made the texts available to competitors. That such anxieties existed in the period would seem to be borne out by the comments of contemporary playwright Thomas Heywood who wrote that some actors 'thinke it against their peculiar profit to haue' their plays 'come in Print'.[77] On the other hand, plays were published and while some may have been pirated, others were implicitly sold to publishers by the acting companies that owned them. While financial duress appears to have driven some companies to sell their plays to publishers, in other cases it seems that acting companies used selective play publication as a way of generating publicity for their work.[78]

Playwrights were not usually consulted about the sale of their plays to publishers, although resident playwrights such as Shakespeare may have had more influence over what happened to their works; and there are examples of writers involving themselves in the publication of their plays. Perhaps most famously, Jonson is reported to have overseen the printing of the 1616 Folio edition of his *Works*. A. W. Pollard used to believe that you could distinguish between those plays which were published with the authority of the acting company and those which were illicit by studying the registers of the Stationers' Company. According to Pollard, those plays published without an entry in the Stationers' Register or by someone other than the person who registered them were probably illicit. He therefore deemed them 'bad' in contrast with those he regarded as being published legally which he deemed 'good'.[79] However, more recent research has shown that there was not necessarily anything irregular about plays published without an entry in the Stationers' Register.[80]

Printed plays were not necessarily the same as the performed versions, not least because material cut from performances was sometimes reinstated in the printed text. That Shakespeare routinely wrote plays which were longer than could have been comfortably performed during the two- to three-hour slots generally allowed for performances has led scholars such as Lukas Erne to argue that he, at least, was writing with a potential audience of readers (as well as performance) in mind.[81] That Shakespeare and many of his contemporaries were interested in creating texts that were of literary as well as dramatic quality seems clear; that they were writing in the expectation of publication and an audience of readers is less so. Shakespeare, for instance, appears to have made little effort to ensure the publication of his plays: only 20 of the 36 plays included in the First Folio edition of his works (1623) had been printed before.

Just as the performance versions of plays were not necessarily exactly the same as those which were published so there are sometimes variations between early printed editions of a play, as has been noted. Some of these differences are accidental (including misreadings and typographical errors), others seem to be deliberate (as in the case of corrections), and some probably reflect the differing nature of the copy (or source) text used. This might be an authorial or scribal copy of the play, a copy of the theatrical 'book', the theatrical 'book' itself or an annotated early edition of the play. In each case there was a chance that the copy text would have been modified by people besides the author(s), just as further changes might be introduced deliberately or accidentally in the printing house. The fact that many people might have been involved in shaping the manuscript and printed plays we read today often makes it hard to distinguish the work of playwrights from the interventions of those they worked with, as will be explored more fully in the case studies below, but it also emphasizes the collaborative culture in which plays were produced, whether or not they were initially authored by one person or a team of playwrights.

Case studies

The Second Maiden's Tragedy

The Second Maiden's Tragedy (BL, Lansdowne MS 807) is thought to have belonged to Shakespeare's company, the King's Men. The playwright's name is not given on the manuscript, but modern research suggests that its author was Thomas Middleton.[82] As one of only five surviving manuscript plays to carry the official licence of the Master of the Revels (in this case of Sir George Buc, dated 31 October 1611) it affords rare evidence of Renaissance playwriting and censorship practices. The tragedy tells the story of the deposition of rightful ruler Govianus by a Tyrant, who is himself deposed at the end of the play. As well as taking Govianus's throne the Tyrant woos Govianus's beloved, named only as the 'Lady'; but she will not succumb to his desires, even when her father, a noble courtier (Helvetius) tries to coerce her into complying with the Tyrant's wishes. Instead the Lady chooses to be imprisoned alongside Govianus and, later, commits suicide rather than be taken prisoner and raped by the Tyrant. A sub-plot tells the story of Govianus's brother (Anselmus), whose excessive jealousy leads him to ask his best friend, Votarius, to test the fidelity of his wife. Unlike the virtuous Lady, Anselmus's Wife succumbs to Votarius's seductions. The Wife manages to persuade Anselmus of her fidelity but a series of cross-plots laid by the Lady, her maid (Leonella) and the maid's lover (Bellarius) back-fire and lead to the deaths of all three, along with Anselmus and Votarius.

The play, which is the second piece in Lansdowne MS 807, appears on folios 26 to 56. Five of these folios are inserted slips of paper including textual additions or alterations (f.31, f.36, f.46, f.47, f.53). The manuscript appears to be a scribal copy (Hand S) of the author's draft of the play but W. W. Greg identified at least three other contemporary hands at work in the manuscript: that of the censor, Buc

(Hand B), a book-holder (Hand P) and another theatrical corrector (Hand C). It would seem that the scribe copied out the play; this copy was then possibly revised by the corrector before being submitted to Buc who appears to have gone through the play first with a pencil and then again with ink; further revisions were made post-censorship by the scribe and corrector, including the insertion of additional material on the five slips already mentioned. These additional slips appear to be in the scribe's hand. This could mean that they are scribal compositions, although Greg thought that they were likely to be authorial in origin.[83] If Greg is correct, the playwright and scribe were both involved in the post-censorship revision of the play, something which would point to the close collaboration of playwrights and their theatrical associates. After these revisions were completed the play appears to have been passed to the book-holder for marking up for performance. That the book-holder's annotations were added at a late stage would seem to be confirmed by the fact that one of his added stage directions ('Enter Soldiers', f.48, l.1696) derived from the need to make visible an existing entry direction obscured by one of the additional slips (f.46), while a second added entry direction ('Enter Mr Goughe', f.48, ll.1723–4) precedes and provides the entry for an added speech on an inserted slip (f.47).

Buc is responsible for marking text for deletion or revision at several points in the manuscript; he also supplies one insertion (see p. 84). The book-holder's hand (Hand P) appears to be confined to a series of annotations designed to prepare the play for the stage, including a series of additional stage directions for sound effects and music and the adding of a number of entries. He also includes the names of two actors: Richard Robinson and Mr Gough (f.48, ll.1723–4; f.50, ll.1928–9). Richard Robinson is thought to have been Richard Burbage's apprentice and a member of the King's Men, as is Gough (probably Robert Gough, fl.1590–1625).[84] The two other hands (that of the scribe and the unidentified corrector) appear to be responsible for the revisions made to the original scribal copy of the manuscript. These revisions include deletions, alterations and additions to the text. Some of the revisions are minor (such as small linguistic changes); others are more substantial. These more significant changes include the shortening of several of the hero Govianus's longer reflective speeches and several cuts to the final scene, some of which seem designed to streamline the action, others of which may show the scribe removing potentially provocative allusions to Catholic practices such as the deletion of Soldier 1's refusal to bow to the corpse of the Lady (f.54, ll.2237–40). They also include a series of additions (on inserted slips) which alter aspects of the plot. Thus, the Tyrant originally allowed that Govianus and the Lady should be imprisoned together at one of Govianus's houses. During the revision of the play this scene and the Tyrant's orders are altered by the insertion of additional lines (f.31) which have the Tyrant change his mind about imprisoning the pair together. Instead he decides that they will be kept in the same house but apart: where Govianus 'may only haue a sight of her / to his myndes torment' (f.31, ll.3–4). This perhaps makes his order more plausible, adds to the growing picture of the Tyrant's perversity and renders the suffering of the lovers potentially more acute. The other significant plot change resulting from the revisions relates to the sub-plot featuring Govianus's brother. Originally, Anselmus died believing in his wife's constancy. An inserted piece of text (f.53) changes this so that Anselmus wakes to hear his friend Votarius's confession that he had seduced the wife; consequently, Anselmus dies lamenting the deceitfulness and lustiness of women (f.53, ll.6–16). This is another change seemingly intended to rack up the tragic suffering experienced by the play's characters and that emphasizes the contrast between the idealized picture of womanhood offered in the play's main plot and the fallible picture of women offered through the sub-plot.

The play's first modern editor, W. W. Greg argued that the hand of the censor, Buc, can only be clearly identified at four points in the manuscript. The first clear example that Greg identifies is in line 1354 (f.43) spoken by the Lady, when the word 'great' is deleted (possibly by Hand C) and the word 'some' is interlined in the black ink used by Buc so that the Lady states that she 'scornes / death as much as some men feare it' instead of 'as great men feare it'. He also suggests that Buc was responsible for the crosses that appear in the left margin at lines 1425 (f.43v) and 1841 (f.49v). The first cross occurs next to an unflattering comment on court women by Govianus deleted in lines 1424–6 (f.43v): 'twas a straunge trick of her, few of yor ladies / in ordinary will beleiue it, they abhor it / theile sooner kill them selues wth lust, then for it'. The second cross appears next to another line in which a critical comment on women is modified (f.49v, ll.1840–1). Finally, Greg attributes the interlineation 'I am poisoned' which replaces the deleted phrase 'yor kings poisoned' in line 2403 (f.55v) to Buc, along with the ink cross which appears next to the line in the left margin. While the change to line 1354 points to a censor keen to avoid satire of great men, and the revision of lines 1424–6 and 1841 suggest that he was averse to satire of court women, too, Buc's alternative formulation in line 2403 seems to be designed to avoid the potentially provocative identification of the Tyrant as a king at the moment of his overthrow. Such instances of censorship tend to confirm that the Master of the Revels was usually most sensitive to potentially provocative political satire, in this case of the court and its members, although Anne Lancashire has speculated that there may have been a more specific cause for Buc's removal of some of the satire of court women in the emerging scandal surrounding Lady Frances Howard who was to become infamous after she petitioned for the annulment of her marriage to Robert Devereux, third Earl of Essex, on the grounds of impotence (May 1613) and later married her alleged lover, Robert Carr, Earl of Somerset.[85]

These are not, however, the only instances where Buc may have intervened in the manuscript or the only evidence of the text being shaped by his concerns. Oaths are consistently deleted, in keeping with the requirements of the 1606 Act of

Abuses. At least some of these deletions are likely to be the work of Buc, but others may have been deleted by the scribe or corrector. There are other deletions in the text that seem to derive from the censor's concerns, too. This includes the removal of several other potentially unflattering allusions to courts and courtiers. On f.33v, for example (l.442) Votarius originally spoke of having to 'put on / a Courtiers face'; but 'Courtiers' is deleted and replaced by the interlined word 'Brazen' (possibly in the hand of Buc). If this is not Buc's change, it seems to be a response to his distaste for courtly satire. The marking of other critical allusions to women for deletion (as at f.30v, ll.196–9 and f.40, ll.1080–3) could, likewise, be the work of Buc or of the corrector in response to Buc's revisions elsewhere in the manuscript. Such readiness to self-censor plays – along with the appearance of the corrector and Buc revising the text – would seem to confirm the extent to which the relationship between players, playwrights and censor was collaborative.

That Buc trusted the players to make the requested revisions would seem to be confirmed by the phrasing of the licence which says that the play 'may wth the reformations bee acted publikely' (f.56). There is no suggestion here that he expected to see the play again before issuing its official licence. In this case, Buc might have been wise to see the play again because Anne Lancashire suggests that some of the revisions (apparently made post-censorship) add a new topical dimension to the play. In particular, she sees the additions regarding the imprisonment of Govianus and the Lady as possibly alluding to Arabella Stuart and her secret marriage with William Seymour (June 1610). After its discovery the lovers were imprisoned separately, like Govianus and the Lady, but they 'managed to correspond and even according to popular rumour, to meet occasionally by bribing their jailors' as do the play's lovers.[86] Although we cannot rule out the possibility that Buc did see these lines and simply missed the topical parallel, the absence of any alterations suggests that the additional slips with this material were added post-censorship.

In some ways what is most striking about *The Second Maiden's Tragedy* is the fact that it was licensed at all, but the presence in the manuscript of several hands associated with the playhouse also confirms the extent to which the readying of plays for performance was a collaborative affair in which playwrights, scribes and book-holders might work alongside each other metaphorically if not literally. The example of *The Second Maiden's Tragedy* also confirms that the production of the theatrical book from which a play might be performed was not necessarily a straightforwardly linear process. Plays might not only be revised on their initial submission to the playhouse and then by the censor, but they might be revised again on their return to the theatre and by more than one hand. Finally, if the evidence of *The Second Maiden's Tragedy* is represent-ative, the collective work done upon plays in the playhouse and by the censor could be as attentive to detail as that which went in to a play's creation and is arguably a testimony to the value placed upon plays by those working with them within the theatrical business as well as by their authors.

King Lear

Unlike *The Second Maiden's Tragedy* no contemporary manuscript of Shakespeare's *King Lear* survives today. Instead we rely for our knowledge of the play on the early printed editions. The first printed edition was registered for publi-cation on 26 November 1607 as 'A booke called Mr William Shakespeare his historye of King Lear'.[87] Recent research on the play's printing shows that the edition was subsequently printed between mid-December 1607 and mid-January 1608.[88] There are a number of obvious mistakes in the first Quarto (hereafter Q1). These errors led some early scholars to speculate that the edition was based on a pirated copy of the text. More recently, Adele Davidson has suggested that the text was prepared from a manuscript in which short-hand was used;[89] and other scholars have argued that the edition was based on an authorial manuscript of the play that was at various points difficult to decipher.[90] These difficulties, combined with the fact that the two compositors (or type-setters) who worked on setting the text appear to have been relatively inexperienced, are thought to explain some of the implicit errors in the quarto edition (such as the setting of verse as prose and vice versa).[91] A second quarto edition of *King Lear* was published in 1619 (Q2), but it appears to have been printed from Q1 and does not have any independent textual authority. The play was printed for a third time in 1623 in the First Folio, the first collected edition of Shakespeare's plays, compiled by two of Shakespeare's fellow King's Men, John Heminges and Henry Condell. In the Folio text (hereafter F1) *King Lear* appears as one of the tragedies. The extent and significance of the differences between the Q1 and F1 editions suggests that they were based upon differing textual versions of the play. Scholars continue to debate the nature of that used as the basis for F1, although it is generally thought to have been a later version than that on which Q1 was based.[92]

The Folio text of *Lear* varies from that found in Q1 not only in its title (being described as a tragedy rather than a history) but in numerous details. Some of the differences are minor (such as variations between, or the omission or inclusion of, individual words and phrases). Other differences are more significant. Perhaps most strikingly, the Folio text lacks 285 lines found in Q1 and contains more than a hundred lines not found in Q1. The two largest absences from F1 are the 'mock-trial' (3.6.17–55) and 4.3 (in which a Gentleman reports on Cordelia's response to her father's sufferings). The additional lines in F1 are all found in existing scenes and vary in length from a couple to several lines, while the most common variations between the two editions are between individual words or phrases, as when Q1's 'ear-bussing' appears in F1 as 'ear-kissing' (2.1.9).

Some of the small differences between the two texts are likely to be compositorial or editorial in origin (that is, derived from those working in the printing house): this includes some probable misreadings and errors, some correct readings where Q1 is clearly wrong, and some consistent linguistic variations between the two texts. Richard Knowles, for example, argues that there is a 'consistent attempt throughout' the F1 edition 'to polish its verse' through the omission, addition or substitution of 'individual words or phrases' in at least '130 places', and suggests that this regularization of the text probably derives from a scribe or editor, rather than Shakespeare. The same hand may be responsible for modernizing the text grammatically consistently changing 'older forms' such as '*hath* and *hast* to *has* or *haue*, as well as *a* to *he* and *and* to *if*'.[93]

Similarly, the censor's hand may account for some of the absences of Q1 material from F1 (including the Fool's allusion to monopolies in 1.4.145–6). Other variations – including some of the possible cuts and additions of text – are less likely to have originated from or in the printing house, and might instead be evidence of a 'deliberate reworking' of the play.[94] That Shakespeare and his contemporaries revised their plays is a possibility that has gained increasing acceptance in recent years, not least because of the pioneering work of scholars such as Michael Warren and Gary Taylor on the two texts of *King Lear*,[95] but the question of whether the F1 text of *Lear* preserves a later, revised version of the play remains contentious, with some scholars questioning whether the differences between the two editions reflect a 'deliberate revision of the earlier text'.[96] Whether Shakespeare was responsible either wholly or in part for the apparent reworking of *Lear* evidenced in F1 is similarly controversial. Some scholars have argued that he was responsible;[97] but others such as Richard Knowles are less convinced by the theory of authorial revision, noting that at least some of the additional material in F1 seems 'suspiciously un-Shakespearean' and that 'there is copious evidence that a great many people other than or in addition to Shakespeare affected the text'.[98] Whoever was responsible for them, the systematic nature of some of the differences between the two texts is intriguing. For the sake of discussion, I am going to refer hereafter to words present in F1 but not Q1 as additions and vice versa as cuts, although scholars do not all agree that the relationship between Q1 and F1 can be simply described in terms of conscious revision.

The part that differs most substantially in F1 is that of the Fool. His is not an especially long role (roughly 225 lines in Q1) but it is symbolically important because of his close relationship with Lear. The role does not change much in length (F1 omits roughly 30 lines found in Q1 and adds 22 new ones), but it differs subtly in tone in F1. There are two important changes to the Fool's part in his first scene, for example: the omission of the mock-serious dialogue about the difference between a bitter and a sweet fool during which the Fool implicitly identifies himself as the 'sweet' fool and Lear as the 'bitter' (1.4.137–48) and the reassignment of Lear's answer to the poignant question 'Who is it that can tell me who I am?' (1.4.221) to the Fool rather than Lear: 'Lear's shadow' (1.4.222). The cutting of the Fool's dialogue with Lear about folly could point to a desire to streamline the scene but it also diminishes the playfulness of the Fool, while the reassignment of Lear's answer to the Fool and Lear's apparent failure to acknowledge this answer is suggestive of a more distanced relationship. The Fool is also more enigmatic in F1, as is reflected in the rhyming jingle added to his part in 2.2 which closes: 'Fathers that wear rags / Do make their children blind, / But fathers that bear bags / Shall see their children kind: / Fortune, that arrant whore, / Ne'er turns the key to the poor' (2.2.41–6). Here the Fool implicitly comments on the plight of Lear but indirectly, in a manner more akin to a chorus. A similar choric quality characterizes the gnomic prophecy added to his part at the end of 3.2 (ll.78–95) about the 'great confusion' that will come to 'Albion' (3.2.91, 90), while the fact that he must remain on stage to deliver this speech solo instead of leading Lear into the hovel and away from the storm (as in Q1) emphasizes the pair's 'growing separation'.[99] The Fool's marginalization in F1 is intensified by the changes to his final scene, including the omission of the mock trial (3.6.17–55) and of Kent's request that the Fool help him to carry Lear in (3.6.95–9). As scholars such as John Kerrigan have observed, the collective effect of the differences is to render the Fool's character 'a wise and worldly jester, more urbane and more oblique than his predecessor', a change perhaps influenced, as Bart van Es argues, by Shakespeare's 'engagement' with the comic philosophy and writings of the role's probable performer, Robert Armin.[100]

Lear's role differs in some similarly subtle but significant ways between Q1 and F1. Unlike the Lear of Q1, the F1 Lear gives an explicit rationale for his division of the kingdom (1.1.39–44), thus making it (and him) seem more reasonable as the action opens, while a pair of additional lines in the play's final scene raises the possibility that F1's Lear dies in the deluded belief that Cordelia revives: 'Do you see this? Look on her: look, her lips. / Look there, look there! (5.3.309–10). The roles of Cordelia and her sisters also differ slightly between the two texts, in length and in characterization. Cordelia's role in F1 is shorter but it is also (arguably) stronger than in Q1. In 1.1 the Folio adds to her exchange with Lear so that she repeats her answer of 'Nothing' (1.1.88) in a way that emphasizes her shared stubbornness with Lear, while the cutting of the Gentlemen's idealized report of her tears for Lear (in 4.3) and the alteration of the stage directions for her return so that she enters in F1 'with drum and colours' (4.4) arguably change her from 'a saintly figure, emblematic of pity, to a warrior determined to put her father back on the throne'.[101] Just as the F1 Cordelia is less idealized, so, too, Goneril and Regan seem to be less unequivocally demonized. F1 cuts the lines from Q1 in which Goneril explicitly plans to overrule Lear (1.3.17–22) and the claim that she wishes to 'breed from hence occasions …, / That I may speak' (1.3.25–6). At the same time F1 gives Regan additional lines in which she appears to corroborate Goneril's claims that Lear and his knights are ill-behaved (2.2.332–7), thus, potentially, making Goneril's actions seem more reasonable. Perhaps equally significant is the fact that F1 trims Albany's speeches castigating Goneril and does not include his denunciation of her (4.2.32–51) or his accusation that she is a 'fiend' in the guise of a woman (4.2.63–9). While these could be cuts designed to shorten the final act they also serve to downplay the demonization of Goneril and are in keeping, more generally, with the F1 changes which 'make it less clear who is right and who is wrong in the relations between Lear and his daughters'.[102]

The roles of Kent, Albany and Edgar are also altered. Each role is shorter in F1, but their significance within the action is also changed. In Kent's case, the differences to his role are most evident in the second half of the play. Not only is one whole scene in which he features cut (4.3) but so is Kent's conversation with a Gentleman about himself and Edgar (4.7.85–97) and Edgar's account of meeting with Kent over the dead body of Gloucester (5.1.203–20). Cumulatively, the effect of these cuts is to diminish Kent's part in the second half of the play, as Michael Warren observes, and to reduce his role as a commentator on events. The cutting of Kent's role in the latter stages of the play also appears to be part of a wider pattern of reducing 'the number of passages of static speech or dialogue about moral issues'.[103]

The changes to Edgar's and Albany's roles are, in some respects, similar. Both lose lines in which they moralize about the play's sad events (as at 3.6.100–13 and 4.2.47–51). But the alterations to their roles are also interlinked, some of Albany's speeches being reassigned to Edgar. In F1 it is Edgar rather than Albany who commands the messenger sent to rescue Cordelia to 'Haste thee for thy life' (5.3.249). Even more significantly, perhaps, the play's closing lines about the future of the realm (5.3.324–5) are reassigned from Albany (in Q1) to Edgar (in F1). Taken together, these changes serve to make F1's Edgar more decisive and commanding, while the changes to Albany's part serve, by contrast, to diminish his prominence in the action.

Interesting in their own right, cumulatively, the series of substantive differences described above suggest that the 1623 edition does, indeed, represent a revised version of *Lear* (whether prepared by Shakespeare and/or others), a *Lear* which is less emblematic and overtly moralistic. Whether this *Lear* represents an improved version of the play prepared as a result of authorial or company second thoughts, as some scholars have suggested, is another question. Arguably, what is more significant is the fact that the two texts of *Lear* seem to confirm what other sources suggest: that Renaissance plays continued to be seen – by playing companies as well as playwrights – as living works of art, and thus potentially available for reworking, even after their licensing and first performance.

3

Stages and staging

Quince.　　　... *here's a marvelous convenient*
place for our rehearsal. This green plot shall be our
stage, this hawthorn-brake our tiring-house.

A MIDSUMMER NIGHT'S DREAM, 3.1.2–4

Today when we think of the 'theatre' we are as likely to think
of the buildings used by actors as we are to think of the plays
that they perform or the industry of which they form a part.
The same would not have been true in early Elizabethan
England with the first playhouse only being built in 1567
and the theatre only gradually becoming a recognized trade
from which one might make a living. Before the founding
of the first playhouses in Elizabethan London, players were
accustomed to performing in a variety of spaces and this
tradition did not end with the opening of the metropolitan
theatres: acting companies continued to perform periodically
at the royal court and customarily went on annual tours,
performing in diverse spaces. Like Bottom and his fellow
artisans-turned-players, Shakespearean acting companies had
to be versatile, ready to adapt their performances and their
plays for whatever audience and whatever 'theatre' or 'green
plot' might be available to them. This helps to explain why
the staging demands of many of the period's plays are minimal

by modern standards, setting and atmosphere often evoked through the language of the play rather than through scenery, and many plays of the period requiring little more than a platform backed by a pair of doorways for their performance. As Andrew Gurr and Mariko Ichikawa note, 'staging had to be minimal to cope with the radical variations in the resources the companies encountered'.[1]

How Shakespeare and his contemporaries staged their plays in the period's playhouses and temporary playing venues is one of the most intriguing but least documented aspects of the English Renaissance theatre world. None of the playhouses of Shakespeare's day survives intact to the present and detailed accounts of performances are rare (see p. 153), but a variety of sources exists which shed some light on the history, make-up and functioning of the theatres and which can tell us something about how plays were usually staged within them. These include legal records relating to the playhouses (such as the building contracts for the Fortune and Hope Theatres); the diary and theatrical papers of theatre manager Philip Henslowe and his son-in-law, actor Edward Alleyn; contemporary descriptions of, and allusions, to the London theatres; contemporary illustrations of the playhouses and their stages; the evidence afforded by the texts and stage directions of extant plays associated with the London theatres; and, more recently, the results of archaeological investigations at the sites of the Theatre, Rose, Globe and Hope Playhouses.

Stages

Between 1567 and 1642 when the civil war led to their temporary closure, 23 playhouses had been created in London. The playhouses were divided into two main types: open-air and indoor playhouses. The first open-air theatre was the short-lived Red Lion, established by John Brayne in Stepney (1567). His example as would-be theatrical entrepreneur was followed more famously and successfully by his brother-in-law and joiner-turned-player, James Burbage with his building of the Theatre in Shoreditch (1576). Together these two playhouses set a precedent for the creation of dedicated open-air playing venues that limited entrance to play performances to those willing to pay a fee in advance. Their example was to be followed by a variety of other businessmen and impresarios keen to turn a profit from Londoners' appetite for plays. By 1621 London had seen the erection of at least eight further purpose-built, open-air playhouses: the Curtain (1577), the Rose (1587), the Swan (1595), the Globe (1599), the Fortune (1600), the Hope (1614), the second Globe (1614) and the Second Fortune (1621). Other open-air playhouses were converted in or from existing buildings, including at Newington Butts (c. 1576), the Boar's Head (1598) and the Red Bull (1607).[2]

The first indoor playhouses were established around the same time as Burbage's Theatre. In 1575 Sebastian Westcott, master of the choristers at St Paul's Cathedral appears to have created a playhouse for use by his pupils in the cathedral almonry, which functioned periodically between 1575–89 and 1599–1606. The opening of the Paul's Playhouse was soon followed by the establishment of a rival boys' theatre. In 1576 Richard Farrant, deputy to the Master of the Children of the Chapel Royal, oversaw the creation of a playhouse for his choristers within the buttery of the former Blackfriars Monastery which was used by his pupils until 1584.[3] Theoretically, both playhouses were designed to be rehearsal spaces in which the pupils could practise for their regular performances at court, but the audiences for their 'rehearsals' grew and the custom of making a gift to the pupils for their efforts soon became a formal charge, thus setting the precedent for commercialized indoor theatres.

In 1596 James Burbage sought to emulate the choristers' example, buying the Upper Frater of the ex-Blackfriars Monastery and converting it into a second indoor playhouse in the precinct. Burbage implicitly intended to make the playhouse available to his son Richard's acting company, the

Lord Chamberlain's Men, knowing that the lease on the land on which his other playhouse (the Theatre) stood was soon to expire and that he might not be able to secure its renewal. In this aim he was frustrated, local residents in the Blackfriars precinct petitioning successfully to the Privy Council against the opening of a 'public' playhouse in their midst.[4] After Burbage's death, his sons temporarily sub-let the theatre to Henry Evans who used it as a new playhouse for the Children of the Chapel Royal, but on 9 August 1608 the Burbages signed six new leases on the property to William Shakespeare, Richard Burbage, Henry Condell, Thomas Evans, John Heminges and William Sly. Four of the new tenants were fellow players of Richard Burbage in the King's Men indicating that the royal troupe planned to take over the indoor venue, which they duly did, although plague in the city may have prevented them from opening the theatre until early 1610.[5] Thereafter the King's Men alternated between performing at the Globe Theatre (their open-air playhouse since 1599 when it was built from the timbers of the Theatre) and, in the winter, at the Second Blackfriars. They became the first adult company to perform regularly in an indoor playhouse. At least some scholars such as Andrew Gurr see this innovation as marking a 'radical' departure in terms of playing conditions with potential ramifications for the kinds of plays performed by troupes such as the King's Men post-1609.[6] Whether the popularization of indoor theatres had any impact on acting styles and playwriting will be considered more fully below, but it is perhaps worth noting here that indoor playhouses like the Second Blackfriars probably afforded more familiar playing conditions than Gurr allows. As Alan Somerset notes, most acting companies, including Shakespeare's, were used to using halls as temporary theatres from their experience of performing on tour and at court.[7]

The two main varieties of London playhouse differed most conspicuously in terms of the shelter that they did and did not offer from inclement English weather. They also differed in location. Most of the open-air theatres were located in

London's suburbs, where land was more readily available for new buildings and where players were not subject to the authority of the city council who had increasingly sought to restrict theatre within the city walls since the mid-sixteenth century. Other forms of illicit and controversial entertainment, such as brothels and bear-baiting arenas, tended to be found in the suburbs for similarly pragmatic reasons. Such associations led some contemporaries to look down upon the open-air theatres and their theatrical fare, equating their location with a propensity to offer vulgar, licentious entertainment. By contrast, the indoor playhouses of London were generally created in buildings within the city walls and close to the city's wealthiest districts. The fact that the indoor playhouses charged far higher entrance fees than the open-air playhouses made them potentially much more lucrative and is a sign that they catered primarily for London's wealthier playgoers, although the latter still seem to have attended the open-air playhouses on occasion, too (see p. 139).

What evidence we have about the physical design and facilities available at the period's many playhouses suggests that although there were variations in size, and sometimes in the shape of the auditoria and the stage, most of the period's playhouses offered players essentially similar staging facilities. The majority of the purpose-built, open-air playhouses were polygonal timber-framed buildings, with three sets of galleries around an open yard. Spectators with money could sit under cover in the galleries; those with less money or who wished to be closer to the action could stand around the stage in the yard. Into this yard jutted a large, raised wooden stage: at the Red Lion the stage measured 30 by 40 feet; and at the Fortune the stage measured 27 feet 6 inches by 43 feet. As these examples indicate, the stage platform was often large and usually rectangular, although there were exceptions to this, as at the Rose Theatre, modern archaeological investigations suggesting that the stage tapered at the front, measuring 'about 37 feet wide at the back', 'about 27 feet at the front' and being 'about 16 feet 6 inches deep'.[8] At the rear of the stage there was usually a tiring house (in which actors got dressed), fitted with at least two side doors and possibly a central door too, with a balcony above, part of which may have been used for Lords' rooms and part of which was available for action 'above'. These are, in essence, the stage conditions shown in the only surviving interior illustration of an Elizabethan open-air playhouse, a copy of Johannes De Witt's sketch of the Swan Theatre (c. 1596).[9] The stage itself was sometimes fitted with a trap door to allow characters to ascend to, or descend from, the stage. Above the stage it became customary for there to be a stage cover or 'heavens', usually carried on two stage pillars and decorated underneath to resemble a night sky. At the later open-air playhouses there is reason to believe that the stage cover was sometimes fitted with a trap door as well through which characters could be lowered on to stage, as perhaps occurred in Shakespeare's *Cymbeline* when the stage directions state that '*JUPITER descends in thunder and lightning, sitting upon an eagle*' (5.4). While the outside of the buildings appears to have been plain, playhouse builders went to great lengths to make the interiors visually splendid. At the Swan the stage pillars were cunningly painted so that they resembled marble and contemporaries frequently commented on the beauty of the London playhouses, even their critics describing them as 'gorgeous'.[10] Performing in the open-air, actors were reliant on sunshine to light their performances and therefore traditionally performed in the afternoon, while it is thought that the use of wood and the rounded shape of most of the auditoria probably helped actors with voice projection, wooden stages at theatres like the Globe acting 'as a gigantic sounding board'.[11]

London's indoor playhouses were generally much smaller than their open-air counterparts – the Second Blackfriars, for example, measured only 66 by 46 feet, whereas the Globe's outside diameter may have been as much as 100 feet.[12] Consequently, the indoor playhouses generally had smaller stages and could accommodate fewer spectators. While the acoustics indoors were probably superior than when playing in the open air, poorer light conditions meant that it was common for acting companies performing indoors to make use of candlelight in the winter at least, although the natural light afforded by windows appears to have been used, too, and may have been relied on wholly in the summer.[13] In other respects, the surviving evidence suggests that the playing facilities at the indoor theatres did not differ significantly from those found at the open-air playhouses. Again, it appears to have been usual for the indoor playhouses to be fitted with galleries for spectators and a raised wooden stage, backed by a tiring house with two or more doors. Some of the indoor stages appear to have been fitted with one or more trap doors and there is evidence to suggest that there was a trap door above the stage in some of the indoor theatres, too. Where the arrangements at the two types of playhouses differed significantly was in relation to the disposition of the audience. Unlike at the open-air theatres, there were no standing spectators indoors. Spectators in the 'pit' (the equivalent of the 'yard') sat on benches and the most expensive seats were those closest to the stage, whereas at the open-air playhouses places in the yard were cheapest and those in the galleries the most expensive. It was also possible to sit upon the stage at the indoor theatres, a practice which appears to have been uncommon outdoors.

Staging

It became customary for performances to be staged daily at most of the open-air playhouses, with the theatres usually only closing on Sundays, for Lent and during serious outbreaks of plague, when public playing was prohibited. Performances at the early indoor theatres were less frequent at first (limited to once or twice a week), but once the adult companies started using indoor playhouses it seems to have been usual for performances to be staged regularly indoors, too, again, usually, in the afternoon. Performances at the playhouses were advertised in advance with playbills posted about the city. On days when plays were to be given it was usual for the open-air playhouses to fly their flag and for the commencement of performances to be signalled by the sounding of trumpets, while at the indoor playhouses it appears to have become usual for performances to be preceded by, and for the acts to be interspersed with, musical entertainment.[14]

The repertory system

The day-to-day routine of the playhouses was an intensive one, with Philip Henslowe's records of performances at the Rose Theatre suggesting that it was customary for a different play to be staged each day. From June 1594 to June 1595 the Lord Admiral's players staged 'as many as thirty-seven different plays' at the Rose 'twenty-one of them new' to the repertory, with new plays 'added at more or less fortnightly intervals'.[15] Only on rare occasions, mostly in the seventeenth century, was the same play performed on successive days. More usually there was a delay before a play was reperformed, some plays enjoying more revivals and staying longer in the repertory than others. Henslowe's records also reveal the incredible speed with which plays could be prepared for performance after their purchase. While it usually took about two weeks to prepare a new play for performance at the Rose, on occasion plays were prepared in a matter of days.[16] Confirmation of the alacrity with which players could prepare for performance and of their adaptability occurs later too. On the morning of 18 October 1633 the King's Men learned that the Master of the Revels had forbidden them from staging their planned revival of John Fletcher's *The Tamer Tamed* that afternoon; rather than cancelling the show they instead performed Francis Beaumont and Fletcher's *The Scornful Lady*.[17]

Casting and rehearsal

The intensive nature of the repertory system and the little time allowed for the readying of new plays, especially in the Elizabethan era, has raised questions about how players prepared for productions, the nature and extent of rehearsals and casting and acting practices. Having obtained a new play, it was necessary to gain official permission for its performance, so a copy would be sent to the Master of the Revels. At least one other copy was probably retained so that the company could arrange for the casting of the play and the preparation of actors' parts. In theory actors were not supposed to learn their parts until the play had received the Master's approval. Whether they always waited for the Master's authorization before commencing their play preparations is less certain. It must have been tempting not to wait, especially if the company foresaw no problems with a play's text. That this temptation may have been too strong on occasion could find some confirmation in a comment made by Sir Henry Herbert when he forbade the King's Men from performing Fletcher's *The Tamer Tamed* (1633) until it had been revised. Herbert instructed the troupe's book-holder to 'Purge' the actors' 'parts, as I have the booke'. Elsewhere in relation to his suppression of the same play he noted that the 'players ought not to study their parts till I have allowed of the booke', a statement which hints that the players might have already begun learning their parts. This could have been a default of Fletcher's play being an old work that already existed in parts but the practice might not have been unique to this revival. That the actors did sometimes begin learning their parts in advance of receiving the Master's approval could help to explain the occasionally short period between the licensing and performance of a play, as when Herbert licensed James Shirley's *The Ball* on 16 November 1632 and apparently saw it performed on 18 November 1632.[18]

The evidence of casting preserved in the few surviving theatrical 'plots' (see p. 67) suggests that it was usual for the longest parts to be assigned to the company's sharers, while female roles were assigned to boy apprentices and minor parts were assigned to hired men. Some scholars such as Andrew Gurr and Tiffany Stern have suggested that type-casting was the norm, at least for sharer actors.[19] There is certainly evidence of playwrights thinking of dramatic characters in terms of types, as is reflected in *Hamlet* when the Prince welcomes the travelling players who visit Elsinore in terms of the stock roles he expects them to play (2.2.321–7); and some actors did specialize in familiar roles, such as clown parts, including William Kemp and Robert Armin. On the other hand, famous actors such as Edward Alleyn and Richard Burbage were praised by contemporaries for their versatility as performers and it is clear that they and other leading actors played a variety of character types during their careers. This continued to be true in the seventeenth century, as is suggested by the career of King's Man, John Lowin, who played roles as diverse as the sensualist Sir Epicure Mammon (*The Alchemist*), the malcontent Bosola (*Duchess of Malfi*) and the tyrannical Caesar Domitian (*The Roman Actor*).[20] This leads scholars such as T. J. King to argue that while there may have been some type-casting what determined the roles assigned to players was more often their length, more senior actors usually being assigned the biggest roles.[21]

As it was usual for plays to include more characters than there were actors in the company, doubling was customary though not for those playing the largest roles.[22] The doubling schemes employed could be complex and other members of the playhouse staff were sometimes drafted in to serve as non-speaking supernumeraries. The annotated manuscript of *The Two Noble Ladies* (1622) calls for the stagekeeper to appear twice in non-speaking roles and the plot of the lost play *Frederick and Basilea* calls for the use of 'gatherers' (who collected the theatre entrance fees) as extras three times, including in the final scene.[23]

Having been assigned their roles it was usual for actors to be given their 'parts'. Only one such part survives from the English Renaissance professional stage, that of Orlando in Robert Greene's *Orlando Furioso* (see p. 68). It suggests that it was usual for the actor's part to be copied out on a long manuscript roll. This would include the text that the actor was expected to learn along with short cues, usually only two or three words long, from the preceding character's speech.[24] Having been given their parts the first job of the actors was to memorize the text, although in the case of clown parts it seems that some impromptu improvisation was also expected.[25] According to Tiffany Stern, actors would study their parts alone, although pairs or small groups of actors may have later rehearsed shared scenes together. This may have been especially likely in cases where more experienced actors were sharing scenes with their own or company boy apprentices. There is certainly evidence of older actors training younger players in the period.[26] Whether playwrights were often involved in the rehearsal process is less clear, although there is some evidence to suggest that Shakespeare might have been consulted on aspects of the staging of his plays by his company, the Lord Chamberlain's/King's Men. Andrew Gurr discusses how some of the early printed versions of Shakespeare's history plays, which are thought to have been based on performance texts, include stage directions which show detailed knowledge of Shakespeare's sources suggesting that the playwright was on hand to advise on their staging, as when Clifford is directed to enter '*wounded, with an arrow in his neck*' in *The True Tragedy of Richard, Duke of York* (an earlier version of *3 Henry VI*), a detail not given in the text of the play but 'the correct place for the wound', according to Shakespeare's sources.[27]

How many (if any) company rehearsals took place before productions has been the subject of much debate, but there is little direct evidence of company rehearsal practices. Peter Thomson suggests that 'special attention was given to certain scenes and exchanges, but that the rest was left unrehearsed'.[28] Other scholars, such as Tiffany Stern, suggest that full company rehearsals were 'a luxury and not a necessity', probably occurring at least once but possibly not more than that in most cases.[29] Rehearsals certainly took place before many amateur play performances in the period (as is suggested in *A Midsummer Night's Dream*) and professional company rehearsals evidently did occur on at least some occasions, as is indicated by the articles of agreement signed between Philip Henslowe, Jacob Meade and actor Robert Dawes (7 April 1614). Dawes bound himself to play for the pair for three years and agreed that he would 'duly attend all such rehearsall which shall the night before the rehearsall be given publickly out' or face a fine of 12 pence if he arrived late and a fine of 'twoe shillings' should he fail to attend at all.[30] Given that performances usually took place in the afternoon, most playhouses would have been free in the morning and this is, perhaps, the most likely time for such rehearsals, although experience at the reconstructed Globe Theatre in London suggests that it may have been possible to rehearse at the open-air theatres in the evenings, too, at least in the summer.[31]

How performances themselves were managed is, likewise, little documented, although the evidence suggests that there was no equivalent of the modern director. The business of controlling the entry and exit of actors, the preparation of properties and the timing of special effects appears to have been overseen instead by the book-holder, who was usually based in the tiring-house with a marked up copy of the play. The surviving theatrical 'plots' may also have been designed to help with the traffic of people on and off the stage, perhaps being hung up on a peg in the tiring house as a guide to the characters required in each scene.[32] It seems to have been usual for actors to be readied 'roughly nine lines in advance' of their textual entrance, while characters were usually allowed between two to four lines to make their exit once on stage.[33] Whether the book-holder also functioned as a prompter, as became common in the eighteenth century, is less certain, although experiments at the reconstructed Globe Theatre in London suggest that it might have been difficult for the book-holder to hear the on-stage dialogue.[34] Other evidence suggests that playwrights were occasionally back stage before or during performances, too. In the induction to Jonson's *Bartholomew Fair*, for example, the stage-keeper claims that the playwright has 'kicked' him 'three or four times / about the tiring-house' for making suggestions for the play's improvement.[35]

Acting styles

There were no handbooks to acting in English in this era and the first English acting school did not open until the Restoration era.[36] Most actors therefore learned their profession either through imitation or informal training, for example as boy apprentices (see pp. 19–20). Precisely what they learned and how they acted has been the subject of much scholarly interest, but little agreement. Following the lead of early scholars such as B. L. Joseph, some critics argue that Shakespearean acting was usually formal and rhetorical, involving an emphasis on individual brilliance in the 'delivery of speeches', rather than ensemble work, and the use of stock gestures and conventional ways of blocking group scenes.[37] It has also been suggested that 'the rapid turnover of plays and the familiarity between players and audience inhibited truly individualistic characterizations'.[38] But other scholars such as Marvin Rosenberg have challenged such assumptions and point out that the period's leading actors were specifically praised not just for their versatility but for their convincing impersonation of the characters played.[39] In 1664 Richard Flecknoe praised Richard Burbage, for example, as 'a delightful *Proteus*, so wholly transforming himself into his Part, and putting off himself with his Cloathes, as he never (not so much as in the Tyring-house) assum'd himself again until the Play was done'.[40] One finds contemporary writers, such as Shakespeare, implicitly advocating naturalistic acting, too (even if Elizabethan and Jacobean ideas of what was 'naturalistic' may differ from ours). Perhaps most famously Hamlet calls upon the players who visit Elsinore to: 'Suit the action to the word, / the word to the action, with this special observance, / that you o'erstep not the modesty of nature' (3.2.18–20). That acting on the Shakespearean stage was not as formalized in its delivery and gestures as scholars such as Joseph have suggested might also find some confirmation in a contemporary academic play, *The Second Part of the Return from Parnassus* (written around 1602). The academic playwright invents a conversation between contemporary actors Richard Burbage and Will Kemp in which Kemp implicitly mocks university acting as non-naturalistic and implicitly different in this respect from professional acting:

> 'tis good sporte in a part, to see them neuer speake in their walke, but at the end of the stage, iust as though in walking with a fellow we should neuer speake but at a stile, a gate, or a ditch, where a man can go no further.[41]

Other scholars have argued for changing acting styles across the period with an early fashion for rhetorical, declamatory acting, especially at the open-air playhouses, gradually giving way at the indoor playhouses to a more naturalistic style of impersonation. This gradual shift has been linked to a growing divide between the open-air and indoor playhouses and the allegedly differing tastes of their audiences, with the older style of acting becoming associated with the open-air playhouses and the subtler acting with the indoor playhouses. In similar vein, it has been suggested that playwrights started to write different types of play once they had regular access to the indoor playhouses. Perhaps most famously Gerald Eades Bentley argued for a change in Shakespeare's writing style after his company's acquisition of the Second Blackfriars Theatre.[42] Although Bentley's theory has been much criticized, not least because Shakespeare's 'late' plays were performed at the Globe as well as the Blackfriars, it continues to have its supporters.[43]

In part, critics who argue for a divide between the plays and playing styles associated with the open-air and indoor playhouses are mirroring the comments of Jacobean and Caroline critics of the stage. By the 1620s 'disparagement of the large outdoor theatres' and the plays associated with them 'had become a cultural fashion', as John Astington notes.[44] This was particularly true of the Red Bull and the Fortune Theatres which had become popularly associated with old plays and jigs, both of which were equated, as Andrew Gurr notes, with supposedly 'debased standards of literary sophistication'.[45] It is no coincidence that when Thomas Goffe's citizen playgoer, Thrift, decides to leave the Salisbury Court Theatre in the Prealudium to *The Careless Shepherdess* he talks of going instead 'to th' Bull, or Fortune' where he may 'see / A Play for two pense, with a Jig to boot'.[46] If popular stereotype is to be believed, the amphitheatres' specialization in such plays was accompanied by their favouring of an older, showier form of acting, which their critics condemned as 'noisy over-acting'.[47] Edmund Gayton dismissed the players of the Fortune and Red Bull as 'terrible teare-throats'.[48] Individual actors such as Richard Fowler, famous for his performance of 'Conquering parts' at the Red Bull and, later, the Fortune, were mocked too, with playwright Thomas Rawlins alluding to him as 'the widest / Mouth'd Fowler of them all'.[49]

While there is evidence of the indoor playhouses commissioning new plays on courtly themes and of old, heroic plays being revived regularly at the open-air playhouses, in other respects the evidence of the period points to continuity between the repertories at the open-air and indoor theatres, not least because of the regular traffic in actors and plays between indoor and outdoor venues (see p. 142). For instance, although there may have been some plays that the King's Men only performed at the Globe Theatre and some that they only performed at the Blackfriars Theatre, generally, they appear to have used the same repertory of plays for their indoor and outdoor theatres, at least up until the Caroline era, just as they drew on the same repertory of plays for court performances. The main exception appears to have related to plays featuring battles which were more difficult to stage on the much smaller indoor platform and which consequently do not seem to have been performed often at the Blackfriars.[50]

Staging practices and customs

When Richard Flecknoe looked back upon the English Renaissance stage (1664) he characterized its staging as 'plain and simple, with no other Scenes, nor Decorations of the Stage, but onely old Tapestry'.[51] The general absence of scenery on the Renaissance stage is probably one of the most conspicuous differences between the playhouses of Shakespearean London and those of the modern day. On the English Renaissance stage, setting and place were more usually evoked through the text, the 'bare island' (*The Tempest*, Epilogue.8) of the stage generally becoming whatever or wherever the characters said it was. This meant that the setting could change between scenes, too, as English playwrights and actors increasingly favoured a 'successive' staging style (whereby the stage became different places in succession) over the 'simultaneous' staging style that had predominated in medieval drama (whereby different settings were represented simultaneously).

Most English Renaissance plays are comparatively simple in their staging demands, too: although some implicitly require a 'discovery' space at the rear of the stage for moments of revelation, tableaux or the thrusting on of large properties such as beds, and some call for an acting area above and/or trapdoors in the stage and/or heavens for ascents and descents, many English Renaissance plays require only a wooden platform and two entrances. Indeed, T. J. King's research suggests that the latter was all that was needed for as many as 86 of the 276 extant plays that he looked at written between 1599 and 1642.[52] These minimalist demands derive from the need for plays to be portable, originally between court and touring venues and later between playhouses, too. But the comparatively modest staging demands posed by the period's plays should not lead us to conclude that English Renaissance staging was crude. On the contrary, Shakespearean acting companies went to great efforts to present productions that were visually as well as aurally striking.

The players' rich, colourful costumes were especially memorable for many contemporaries. Acting companies traditionally owned a stock of playing clothes but the establishment of permanent playhouses with their provision of secure storage space allowed actors to expand their wardrobes, troupes generally spending far more on playing apparel than on any other aspect of their productions. The payments relating to George Chapman's now lost play for the Lord Admiral's players, *The Fountain of New Fashions* (1598), preserved in Henslowe's *Diary*, are indicative in this respect. While Chapman was paid 4 pounds for the play, Henslowe lent members of the company at least 17 pounds for 'dyvers thinges' for its production including 7 pounds 'to bye wemenes gownd & other thinges'.[53] Such was the importance of the costume wardrobe that players could be fined for leaving Henslowe's playhouse with them.[54]

Many of the costumes owned by playing companies were implicitly adaptable for various productions, as is suggested by an inventory of playing apparel in Edward Alleyn's hand (c. 1590–1600), thought to list playing clothes owned by his company, the Lord Admiral's Men. It divides the costume wardrobe into different types of garment and styles of outfit such as 'Clokes', 'Gownes' and 'Antik sutes'.[55] Other costumes were specifically prepared for individual actors or productions, as appears to have occurred with *The Fountain of New Fashions*. Hence we find Alleyn also listing 'will somers cote' and 'faustus Jerkin his clok', while another 1598 inventory of the troupe's playing clothes includes items such as 'Tamberlynes cote with coper lace' and 'Tamberlanes breches of crimson vellvet', implicitly for the company's productions of Marlowe's *Tamburlaine the Great* plays.[56] The players seem to have made some effort to represent characters from other times and countries in appropriate costumes, too; and, having acquired such costumes, sometimes commissioned multiple plays that could make use of them. The fact that the King's Men 'put on no fewer than eight plays calling for Spanish dress' between 1620 and 1625 might be explained not only by the fact that Anglo-Spanish relations were topical in this era, as Jean MacIntyre and Garrett P. J. Epp note, but by a pragmatic desire to make good use of specially made Spanish costumes.[57] Thomas Platter claimed that players bought at least some of their costumes second-hand from servants who had inherited them from their masters or mistresses. Henslowe's records at the Rose suggest that players also bought costumes 'from secondhand clothing dealers, pawnbrokers' and 'original owners', including fellow actors.[58]

In a culture in which what you wore was partly dictated by your class or social role and in which people were accustomed to reading colours symbolically, costumes provided actors with a powerful way of conveying information about the social station and qualities of the characters that they played.[59] In *Hamlet* the Danish Prince's 'inky cloak' (1.2.77) would have been an immediate indicator of his character's melancholy disposition as well as his persistence in mourning, unlike his fellow Danish courtiers who have implicitly stopped wearing black for their dead king, while in *Tamburlaine the Great, Part I* the protagonist's casting off of his shepherd's weeds to reveal his 'armour' and his 'curtle-axe' would have made clear to audiences at the Rose Theatre Tamburlaine's belief that he is a soldier and conqueror by nature.[60] Equally, actors could expect audiences to be sensitive to breaches of dress codes, as when an ambitious character is revealed by his/her wearing of finer clothes than his/her class merits, or when an elite figure conceals his/her true class by donning a lowly disguise, as does Edgar in *King Lear*, or when the declining fortunes of a character are reflected by the diminishing quality of his/her clothing, as is true of Lear himself. As the latter examples suggest, costume changes could be written into the plot and/or used for symbolic effect, as well as to conceal actors playing multiple roles.

The importance of visual spectacle on the English Renaissance stage was reinforced by the use of stage furniture, most playing companies owning a stock of playing gear, ranging from smaller items such as targets, foils, fake heads and animal skins to larger properties such as the 'j rocke, j cage, j tombe, j Hell mought' listed in a (lost) 1598 inventory '*of all the properties for my* Lord Admeralles *men*'.[61] If the 1598 inventory is indicative, property stocks were smaller than costume stocks (perhaps because they were harder to transport and store) and it was more common for properties to be specially prepared for specific productions. Hence we find a number of items in the Admiral's Men's list identified by the play they are for, including 'j tome of Dido' (implicitly for *Dido and Aeneas*, in production at the Rose in January 1597–8), 'Tamberlyne brydell' (for *Tamburlaine the Great*, first listed in production in Henslowe's *Diary* on 28 August 1594) and 'j dragon in fostes' (for *Doctor Faustus*, first listed in production on 30 September 1594).[62] Up until the early seventeenth century, most acting companies' properties included a selection of musical instruments, too, although players sometimes owned their own instruments as well. In 1598 the Lord Admiral's owned 'iij trumpettes and a drum, a trebel viall, a basse viall, a bandore' and 'a sytteren'.[63] Such instruments could be used to advertise performances when on tour, to mark the start of performances and to provide the musical accompaniment and sound effects called for in plays of the period. Players are likely to have used other items of playing gear not included in the known inventories, too, such as wigs, fake beards and make-up, the latter possibly supplied by the 'grocers and apothecaries' who also 'sometimes provided the chemicals necessary for pyrotechnic effects'.[64]

Renaissance plays often draw attention to their own theatricality, but this did not prevent acting companies from seeking a degree of realism in their performances. This included using live weapons such as guns and cannons to mimic the sounds and smells of the battles staged in the period's many history plays, and the use of fireworks to mimic lightning during storm scenes of the kind with which Shakespeare's *The Tempest* opens. Careful attention seems to have been paid to the creation of realistic depictions of violence and gore as well, acting companies using wine, vinegar and animal blood and organs to create the bloody effects called for in some of the period's plays.[65]

Playwrights and players also seem to have been interested in the creation of striking visual spectacles. Marlowe's *Tamburlaine the Great* plays, for example, incorporate a series of memorable shows of Tamburlaine's power, drawing upon the symbolic staging traditions of the medieval theatre, including his use of Turkish emperor Bajazeth as a footstool to rise into his throne in Part I (4.2), and his use of the conquered kings of Soria and Trebizon to pull his chariot in Part II (4.2). Later plays make use of the special stage facilities available in the London playhouses, incorporating scenes in which characters miraculously ascend or descend from below the stage through trap doors (as probably occurred with the ghost in *Hamlet*) and/ or scenes in which heavenly figures appear dramatically from above. Just as Marlowe's spectacles invite symbolic interpretation so, too, moments calling for the use of trap doors in the stage or the stage canopy were potentially invested with added meaning and theatrical power by the traditional association of the areas above and below the stage with 'heaven' and 'hell', respectively. Indeed, while Renaissance playwrights and actors may have been interested in incorporating elements of realism in their plays they also continued to exploit the older traditions of symbolic theatre inherited from the medieval stage. Like the acting of the day, staging in the playhouses of Shakespeare's London is probably best described as stylistically eclectic.

Case studies

The Alchemist

Ben Jonson's *The Alchemist* was written for the King's Men and first performed by them in 1610. The earliest recorded performance occurred in Oxford but it has long been suspected that the play was written with performance at the troupe's new indoor playhouse, the Second Blackfriars, in mind, and that it was premiered there in early 1610 shortly after the theatre's delayed opening, following a prolonged plague epidemic in the city. Jonson had previously written for the King's Men but also had experience of writing for the boy companies, including the Children of the Chapel Royal when they used the Second Blackfriars Playhouse, a fact which may have influenced his offering of the play to the King's Men or their commissioning of the play from Jonson. *The Alchemist* tells the story of a trio of con-artists (Subtle, Doll and Face) who take over the house of Face's master (Lovewit) while he is out of London during an outbreak of plague and who proceed to extort money, gold and gifts from a cross-section of gullible Londoners in return for 'magical' advice and/or the promise of riches to be gained from assisting Subtle who poses as a learned alchemist on the verge of discovering how to transform base metals into gold.

The theory that Jonson's play was written, and perhaps even specifically commissioned, for performance at the King's Men's new indoor playhouse rests in large part on the play's setting. With the exception of one scene, all the action takes place in Lovewit's house in the Blackfriars district of London and thus within a building analogous to the theatre in which the King's Men hoped to be playing at this time. The location of Lovewit's home within the former monastic precinct is alluded to several times, including in the opening scene when Subtle mentions that the house is 'here in the Friars'.[66] Jonson appears to render the play even more apposite for performance at the newly opened theatre by setting its action on a day in 1610, so that the play's 'earliest audiences' would have been encouraged to see the action as 'occurring in the immediate present: right now' and to see its world as an extension and reflection of their own world and its vices.[67]

By confining most of the action of the play to a single room inside Lovewit's house and to a single day Jonson also appears to have been exploiting the staging conditions presented by the King's Men's new playhouse, itself created in a room in an ex-Blackfriars building. Indoor playhouses and their stages were generally much smaller than their open-air counterparts. This meant that their acoustics were superior and that actors could speak more quietly, if they wished; but, with their smaller, covered auditoria the indoor playhouses were also potentially more claustrophobic than the amphitheatre playhouses. The Second Blackfriars, for example, had a stage perhaps half the size of that at the Globe. In *The Alchemist*, Jonson exploits these differences and the 'structural power of claustrophobia' creatively, writing limited privacy and confinement into the plot, and using them to generate growing dramatic tension and suspense.[68] The trio is always listening for the next knock on the door and wary of being overheard by their Blackfriars neighbours. The danger of being overheard is written into their role-playing with their victims, too: Subtle and Face pretend not to want to be overheard when they discuss the Queen of Fairy's interest in Dapper (1.2.107) and Face warns Mammon not to let Subtle 'hear, or see' (4.1.12) him when he comes to woo Doll disguised as a Lady driven mad by 'studying Broughton's works' (2.3.238). Managing the entry and exits of their customers from Lovewit's house, while avoiding inadvertent meetings and the possible exposure of their scams, is another challenge heightened by the confined space within which Jonson has his trio of tricksters working, especially in the second half of the play when customers arrive in increasingly rapid succession.

Jonson's play appears to be tailored for performance at the Second Blackfriars Theatre thematically, too, Jonson setting up a series of suggestive parallels between alchemy, the deceptive activities of Subtle, Face and Doll and the professional playing of the King's Men. Perhaps most obviously Subtle and his conspirators liken alchemy and, by implication, their deceptive practices, to an art (see, for example, 1.1.46, 77), involving skill and an ability to improvise akin to that called for in the acting profession. The potential theatrical analogies are reinforced by the trio's description of their alliance as a 'venture tripartite' (1.1.135) – a legalistic phrase which recalls theatrical contracts, as well as contemporary joint-stock companies – and by their allusion to their 'parts' and their 'shares' in the venture, terms which again have theatrical as well as commercial connotations, as when Doll angrily asks Subtle 'Do not we / Sustain our parts?' (1.1.144–5), meaning their roles and their 'shares' in the business. Elsewhere, we find Face directing the performance of the others telling them to 'take but the cues I give you' (3.3.80), in another borrowing from theatrical terminology. As these examples suggest, the manner in which the con-artists perpetrate their deceptions invites comparison with the stage, too, as they (like the King's Men who portrayed them) conjure their illusions and deceive their patrons through convincing role-play; and they encounter some of the same practical challenges as professional players, such as having to change apparel quickly on occasion as they shift between the roles that they double, as when Face longs 'for a suit, / To fall now, like a curtain: flap' (4.2.6–7) when he has to change costumes quickly.

Just as the con-artists have something in common with the King's Men as professional deceivers, so Lovewit's house as a temporary house of illusions invites comparison with the Blackfriars Playhouse. Indeed, as Ian Donaldson notes:

> These two houses of illusion are in fact *the same house*, and the charlatans who arouse and exploit the fantasies of their victims are (when all is said and done) members of the company of the King's Men, who use similar arts to somewhat similar ends.[69]

Playwrights and players were sometimes criticized by their opponents as deceivers and condemned because they 'made' nothing real.[70] Jonson's awareness of this perspective on the profession of playing and his own ambivalence about the professional stage is arguably reflected in the play's epistle 'To the Reader' in which he warns him/her to 'beware at what hands / thou receivest thy commodity; for thou wert never more fair in the way / to be cozened (than in this age) in poetry, especially in plays' (2–4), implying that they, like the Londoners in the play, may not get what they have bargained for and that players and playwrights do sometimes cheat audiences. On the other hand, Jonson was a playwright who clearly believed that drama could and should have an important social role, not just entertaining but educating its audiences, as he implicitly aims to do in *The Alchemist* when he promises his audience 'fair correctives' (Prologue.18) and punishes the folly of his characters. Interestingly, the punishment of Jonson's erring Londoners is effected by his 'con-artists'. This, like Jonson's own implication in the professional theatre world, perhaps helps to explain why Subtle, Doll and Face escape serious punishment at the end of the play.

Jonson's implicit tailoring of *The Alchemist* for the Blackfriars and the King's Men may not be limited to aspects of the play's content. The play's casting demands might also be designed for the troupe as it was in 1610. The play includes 21 parts, 2 of which are female and which would therefore have been played by boys (Doll and Dame Pliant). This is a comparatively small cast for a Renaissance play and might easily have been performed by as few as 12 players. In fact, up until the fifth act the play features only 12 characters so that a cast of 12 would not need to engage in any doubling until this point when, as Richard Fotheringham notes, 6 of the actors would have needed to appear briefly as the 'six neighbours' who descend on the returning Lovewit with news of the goings on at his house (5.1). In designing a comparatively small-cast play Jonson may have been considering the smaller stage available at the Second Blackfriars, but Fotheringham suggests that he could also have been catering for a reduction in the size of the King's company during the plague closures.[71] If Fotheringham is right, this tailoring of the play's casting demands would be fresh evidence of how familiar playwrights like Jonson implicitly were with the acting companies for whom they wrote.

We do not have a full cast list for the play but the 1616 Folio edition of Jonson's works does list some of the King's Men who were involved in its performance in 1610 (Richard Burbage, John Heminges, John Lowin, William Ostler, Henry Condell, John Underwood, Alexander Cook, Nicholas Tooley, Robert Armin, William Egleston).[72] And a contemporary annotated copy of the 1616 text preserves evidence about which roles were played by which actor. According to the latter, the company's leading player, Richard Burbage took the role of Subtle, while his apprentice Nicholas Tooley played the fiery young puritan, Ananias; Henry Condell played the play's sceptic, Surly; John Underwood played the hapless lawyer's clerk, Dapper; William Egleston (or Eccleston) played the feisty young gentleman Kastril; and John Lowin played Mammon, Lowin's famously wide girth perhaps making him seem especially well suited to the portrayal of a character who epitomizes the indulgence of one's appetites.[73] The roles of the other King's Men said to have performed in the play in 1610 – Robert Armin, John Heminges, William Ostler and Alexander Cooke – are not given.

That Burbage should take the role of one of the play's chief characters and con-artists is no surprise, but it is perhaps interesting that he apparently took the role of the older con-artist not the role of Face, who is arguably the play's main character. Later, Face was to be played by Nathan Field, a talented boy-turned-adult player and playwright. This could suggest that the role was first played, likewise, by one of the company's younger stars. Such a casting might make sense in a play in which Face is the younger, wilier of the two male criminals, while Burbage's age (roughly 41) in 1610 might have suited him to the role of the older trickster. The actors unassigned to any part were all adults in 1610 and therefore are likely to have taken adult roles in the play, rather than either of the female roles. R. L. Smallwood suggests that Robert Armin may have played Drugger.[74] If this was the case then John Heminges (the other older unassigned actor, aged around 44) might have played Lovewit, with the younger men, Cook (26 or 27) and Ostler (22) perhaps taking the roles of the up-start butler, Jeremy/Face and the hypocritical puritan, Tribulation Wholesome. That one of the company's younger promising players should play Face would have made particular sense, given the fact that, as 'Lungs', he plays the servant or apprentice to Subtle's doctor (Burbage). Neither Cook nor Ostler was actually an 'apprentice' at this date but Cook, at least, had started in the company as an apprentice to John Heminges, claiming his freedom (as a grocer) in 1609; as a comparatively newly freed man Cook might have seemed an especially appropriate choice for the part of Face, the apprentice-soon-to-turn master con-artist, while the death of Cook in 1614 might explain why the role was then recast with Nathan Field taking it on after 1615 when he joined the troupe.[75]

In other respects *The Alchemist* is less obviously company- and venue-specific. This is particularly true of the play's staging demands. These are comparatively simple, as was customary in the period, requiring only a playing space backed by a couple of doors through which the play's multiple visitors can enter and exit (one possibly fitted with a keyhole through which Face is able to speak to Mammon in 3.5), and a window through which Doll is able to look to inspect arriving visitors (1.1.180). What we know about the Blackfriars Playhouse suggests that the tiring house would have afforded two and possibly three doors, while four of the contemporary illustrations of playhouse stages on 'the titlepages of play quartos' show 'windows in the rear wall', thus suggesting that such windows were a common feature and might have been found at the Second Blackfriars, too, although the latter need not have been depicted realistically.[76] However, although *The Alchemist* might easily have been staged at the Blackfriars almost the same facilities would have been available at most of the outdoor playhouses and might have been contrived at other venues visited by the troupe.

The Alchemist requires no elaborate stage furnishings either. Few props are called for: those that are mentioned in the text are generally small, including coins, tobacco, a ring, trunks and keys. Similarly, the play poses no great demands in terms of costuming. Most of the outfits required for the play are items of everyday, contemporary English dress and might therefore be supplied by the actors or from the company's general playing stock, including Subtle's doctor's robes, Face's captain's and butler's outfits (the latter probably a blue servant's coat), Doll's 'velvet gown' (5.2.24), Sir Epicure Mammon's implicitly fine clothes and Dame Pliant's dress and 'French hood' (5.2.22). The play's most exotic costume is arguably that worn by Surly when he disguises himself as a Spanish Don, the text suggesting that he should wear a 'deep ruff' (4.3.24), Spanish trousers and a 'lewd' Spanish hat (4.7.55), and that he should have a 'dyed' beard (4.7.97) and his face darkened with umber (5.5.52). However, plays featuring Spanish characters were not without precedent and it is possible that the King's Men owned some Spanish costumes already, perhaps including a 'Hieronimo' costume of the kind Face tells Drugger to borrow from the players (4.7.68), complete with 'old cloak, ruff, and hat' (4.7.71) and which Lovewit later uses as part of Face's plot to marry him to Dame Pliant. That the King's Men had performed a play featuring Hieronimo, and therefore might have owned a Hieronimo costume, could find some confirmation in John Webster's induction to John Marston's *The Malcontent*, written for its performance at the Globe in 1604, in which the adult players joke about having obtained the play from the boy players in return for their claiming of an adult play about 'Jeronimo'.[77] Other costumes might have been specially made, such as Subtle's and Doll's outfits as the priest and queen of Fairy, respectively, and Face's costume as Subtle's assistant 'Lungs', the latter perhaps wearing a 'Ficrdrackes' suit like that listed as belonging to the Lord Admiral's Men in 1598.[78]

The play's demands in terms of special effects are similarly modest. The most common demand is for off-stage knocking or bell-ringing, to signal the arrival of each new visitor to Lovewit's house. The play's most challenging requirement is its call for an off-stage explosion. The stage direction describes a '*great crack and noise within*' (4.5) as Subtle's laboratory supposedly explodes and his alchemical experiments are ruined. As noted above, players were no strangers to creating loud sound effects using musical instruments and/ or to using materials such as gunpowder and fireworks. In this case we do not know how they achieved the requisite noise but it is possible that they used gunpowder, perhaps supplied by the same grocer or apothecary from whom they might have bought the make-up for darkening Surly's face when in disguise.

In conclusion, while it would seem that *The Alchemist* was designed with performance by the King's Men at the newly opened Second Blackfriars Theatre in mind, and would have been invested with additional meaning and topicality when performed there in 1610, its staging requirements are not specific to the troupe's new venue, the royal company or the original occasion of performance in the same way. On the contrary, the play seems to have been written by Jonson so that it could be staged fairly easily in any venue in London and/or on tour at any time, as appears to have been customary until well in to the seventeenth century when the leading companies came to concentrate on metropolitan playhouse playing. Hence, the troupe had no difficulty in taking the play on tour (as they did to Oxford in 1610), to court or in reviving it on later occasions at the Second Blackfriars.[79] Although the play may have been at its most topical in 1610 and its most suggestive in its exploration of the links between deceivers and actors when performed at the Second Blackfriars Theatre, the play was portable (between venues and audiences) as was traditional of the plays written for the professional theatre companies.

Bartholomew Fair

Ben Jonson's *Bartholomew Fair* was first performed by Lady Elizabeth's Men in 1614. The first recorded performance took place before the king at court on 'the firste of November' (All Saints' Day), but Jonson's induction to the play suggests that it was premiered the day before at the Hope Theatre (Induction.62).[80] In 1614 the Hope Theatre was London's newest open-air playhouse, having been built for Philip Henslowe and Jacob Meade on the site of the old Beargarden. It was unique amongst its fellow theatres in being designed 'bothe for players to plaie In, And for the game of Beares and Bulles to be baited in'. The surviving contract for the theatre (29 August 1613), between carpenter Gilbert Katherens and Henslowe and Meade describes how the playhouse was to be 'of suche large compasse, fforme, widenes, and height as the Plaie house called the Swan'. To facilitate its use for baiting as well as playing, it was to include a stage that could be 'carryed or taken awaie', while the 'Heavens all over the saide stage' was 'to be borne or carryed without any postes or supporters to be fixed or sett uppon the saide stage'.[81] Just as the Hope was a distinctive playing venue, so the playing company who occupied it in 1614 was unusual. The first company of Lady Elizabeth's Men was officially formed by a royal patent of 27 April 1611. Its patron was King James I's daughter Elizabeth, later wife of Frederick, Elector Palatine and Queen of Bohemia. At this point the troupe appears to have consisted of 13 core players.[82] The troupe was to enjoy a comparatively long but unstable life, possibly splitting at an early date into a touring and a metropolitan branch, the latter of which underwent a series of reorganizations. One of the earliest shake-ups in the troupe's make-up occurred in 1613 when Philip Henslowe oversaw an apparent merger between the troupe and the Children of the Queen's Revels, led by Philip Rosseter (see p. 36). The result appears to have been a troupe which was both larger than average at first and that contained more youth players than was usual in the other adult companies. It was for this newly amalgamated company that Henslowe and Meade reportedly built the Hope Theatre and for which Jonson wrote *Bartholomew Fair*.

Keith Sturgess suggests that the play was written 'expressly for the court performance' at Whitehall, with the preceding performance at the Hope being 'in the nature of a public dress rehearsal'.[83] That the play was commissioned by the court might explain why it speaks to some of James I's concerns, including the dangers of tobacco and puritanism, the power of Justices of the Peace, and royal and divine authority. Leah Marcus, for example, reads the play – and its final delegation of the 'power to judge' to James alone (Epilogue.10) – as a topical and 'elegant defence of royal prerogative' and 'particularly the king's power to "licence" plays and pastimes' in a year in which James had faced open criticism in the so-called Addled Parliament (1614), in part for his support of traditional pastimes which some regarded as 'popish'.[84] Whether or not the play was commissioned by the court Jonson seems to have borne the play's performance at the Hope Theatre as much (if not more) in mind. Thus, in its 'highly ambivalent adaptation of "popular" forms', such as the puppet play and its satirical treatment of classical learning, contemporary debates about the theatre and popular audiences, the play can be seen as a caustic response to the theatrical failure of Jonson's preceding play for the public stage, his classical tragedy *Catiline*, while the text of the play alludes specifically to its performance at the new dual-purpose Hope and its use by bears as well as players.[85] Not only does the book-holder joke about the stage-keeper 'gathering up the broken apples for the bears within' (Induction.47) and about the author having 'observed a special decorum' the playhouse 'being as dirty as Smithfield, and as stinking every whit' as the real fair (Induction.142, 143), but the teasing of Ursula (or the play's 'she-bear', 2.3.1) during the game of 'vapours' at her pig booth in 2.5 is seemingly designed to recall the sport of bear baiting.

Jonson's choice of setting and some of his characters may also have been inspired by where and when the play was to be performed. As a place which brought together a cross-section of English society, one can see why the annual St Bartholomew's Fair at Smithfield, along with its temporary booths, might have seemed a useful setting for Jonson's exploration of human vanity and folly, but it perhaps also seemed well suited to the venue in which *Bartholomew Fair* was to be performed, the Hope's demountable wooden stage being suggestive of the temporary fair booths and playhouses being associated – like the fair – with 'licence and excess'.[86] Similarly, the play's intended performance for James I on All Saints' Day (along with the Fair's association with St Bartholomew) may have suggested to Jonson the idea of making the play partly one about judgement (a known interest of the king's and a concept with which St Bartholomew was traditionally associated) and for making one of his main characters a 'satirical analogue for Saint Bartholomew', the infamous flaying of the saint echoed in the fleecing of Cokes by the fair people.[87]

Other internal evidence suggests that Jonson wrote the play with the unusual nature of the newly amalgamated Lady Elizabeth's Men in mind, too. As well as being one of the longest surviving English Renaissance plays, *Bartholomew Fair* is noteworthy for the size of its cast, including 36 roles as well as extras, and several large-cast scenes, the play's final scene implicitly calling for nearly 20 players to be on-stage at once. At the same time there is no obvious lead role. Plays of the period would not usually call for so many characters or for scenes with so many people on-stage together. Given his experience, the fact that Jonson does so is unlikely to be an accident and may be a sign that he knew he was writing for a larger than average troupe. Internal allusions to size also suggest that Jonson sought to exploit the company's larger than average number of youth players to creative effect, deliberately inviting the casting of young players in the role of some of the older characters and the casting of adults in younger roles, as well as the casting of larger and smaller performers alongside each other.

Textual allusions suggest that Jonson imagined the infantile Bartholomew Cokes being played by an adult or a taller player, while he imagined his irascible tutor Wasp being played by a boy or a smaller player: so there are jokes about Cokes and his long, thin 'Sir Cranion legs' (1.5.87), while Wasp is referred to as the 'little man' (4.4.27). Similar allusions suggest that Jonson wanted Mrs Overdo to be played by a tall boy actor and Win by a smaller boy player, Whit referring to the former as the 'tall lady' and the latter as the 'shmall lady' (5.4.22, 21). As well as the 'boys o' the Fair' who follow Cokes (5.3), other possible youth roles include the parts of Mooncalf (described as a 'boy', 2.2.116), Ezekiel Edgworth (said to be 'a fine boy of his / inches', 2.3.49–50), and Troubleall (referred to as the 'mad child o' the Pie-powders', 4.6.2). Besides the obvious visual comedy to be gained from the spectacle of taller actors alongside smaller actors, Jonson seems to have seen the casting of youthful players in adult roles and the preponderance of younger players in the new company as a way of drawing attention to 'the childishness of adults'.[88] In this respect, the effect appears to have been rather similar to that implicitly achieved in the satires Jonson had previously written for the boy companies, such as *Cynthia's Revels* for the Blackfriars Boys in 1601. Jonson's satire and his technique of parody through 'belittlement', as Jonas Barish puts it, arguably reach their apogee with the puppet play (5.4).[89] Puppet plays were sometimes performed at fairs and 'often followed the bear-baitings in Paris Garden (where the Hope Theatre stood)', but it is clear that in *Bartholomew Fair* the puppet play, and its parodic, anglicized version of the stories of Hero and Leander and Damon and Pythias, is not there just to recall the traditions of the fair or the site of the playhouse in which Lady Elizabeth's Men performed, it also represents a parodic version of the players and the debased theatre Jonson thinks popular audiences favour.[90] Its world mirrors and parodies the world of the fair, in the same way that Jonson uses the fair to mirror and parody his own world and to satirize what he perceives to be its debasement of classical learning and values such as love and friendship. The potential connections between the puppet play and Jonson's play, and further evidence of his familiarity with the troupe and its unusually youthful make-up, would seem to be found in the meta-theatrical jokes made about the puppets. This includes likening the puppets to child players, Littlewit describing them as 'Pretty youths, sir, all children' (5.3.45) and alluding to leading members of the company such as Nathan Field (5.3.73) and Joseph Taylor (5.3.67).

The staging demands of the play are, like its casting needs, greater than usual in some respects. Although the play requires no challenging special effects it does implicitly call for a large number of contemporary costumes, including multiple women's gowns and accessories such as Mrs Overdo's velvet gown (4.5.16) and French hood (1.5.13), Win's velvet cap (1.1.19) and high shoes (1.1.21), the masks worn by the two women (5.6.43) and Dame Purecraft's straight stomacher (3.2.118–19) and small ruff (3.2.95). Some of the play's characters change costumes, too, as when Justice Overdo dons a guarded coat (2.6.14) to disguise himself as mad Arthur of Bradley and later disguises himself as a porter (5.2) or when Quarlous adopts Trouble-all's madman's 'habit' (a ragged cap and gown) (5.2), so that the company would have needed in the region of 40 different outfits. Although the troupe may have invested in some new costumes for the production, Philip Henslowe and Jacob Meade having agreed in 1613 that they would disburse the money needed for 'the furnishing of the said company with playing apparel towards the setting out of their new plays', we can assume that the company also made use of their own clothes and the old stock of playing clothes Henslowe reportedly held on its behalf.[91]

The play implicitly calls for a similarly large array of small properties. Indeed, Keith Sturgess may be right when he says that *Bartholomew Fair* 'probably requires more props than any other contemporary play', including a lockable box, a book, baskets, gingerbread men, pears, ballads, a scalding pan and firebrand for Ursula, toys and Leatherhead's puppets.[92] The play also implicitly requires several larger items of stage furniture including at least two booth structures (for Ursula's pig booth and the puppet theatre), stocks (capable of holding three people – Wasp, Overdo and Busy), Lantern Leatherhead's shop and Joan Trash's stall. The booths, at least, may have been represented with actual wooden canvas-covered booth structures, the court records relating to the play's performance including expenditure on 'Canvas for the Boothes and other neccies' [necessaries] 'for a play called Bartholomewe ffaire'.[93] Whether Lady Elizabeth's Men used similar specially made structures for their performances at the Hope is not known though not unlikely, as it would not have been especially difficult or costly to build such temporary structures. Similarly, it would not have been difficult to buy or build the 'shops' for Leatherhead and Trash and a set of stocks. If Lady Elizabeth's Men did use actual booths, like those one might have seen at the actual Bartholomew Fair, it would have been another way of emphasizing the realism of the setting and the parallels between the play's fictional setting and the Hope, with its temporary, removable stage. Gabriel Egan also suspects a theatrical joke: 'Rather than employ the convention whereby the booth might be understood to represent a house, a shop, or a palace, Jonson used the booth to represent a booth.' He may have been deliberately provoking an expectation of 'simultaneous' staging only to 'frustrate' this, too.[94] In terms of setting and time the play largely (if loosely) conforms to the classical unities: after the first act (which is set in Littlewit's house) the action takes place in one location (the fair) and during the course of a single day (as in *The Alchemist*). It does not, however, have a single plot. Rather, like most English Renaissance city comedies, it depicts a series of interconnected plots and thus seems to conflate classical and popular English dramatic traditions.

This melding of classical and native dramatic traditions arguably extends to other aspects of the play, too. As many scholars have noted, Jonson's play incorporates a number of tableaux which appear to invite emblematic or symbolic interpretation, as was common of medieval English drama, but which at the same time allude to classical myth. When Ursula emerges from her booth in 2.5 'with a firebrand' and an injured leg, her appearance seems designed to recall that of the goddess of discord, who was 'usually represented in the emblem books' of the period 'as an untidy woman, lame in one leg, with a fire-brand in one hand and her feet obscured by clouds – a metaphor like the "vapours" of quarrelling'.[95] While the likening of Ursula to a goddess is partly ironic, the association of the mistress of the pig booth with discord is in keeping with Ursula's verbally and morally disruptive role in the play and thus symbolically apt. Similarly, Wasp's brief carrying of Cokes on his back in 2.6 appears designed to recall and to parody both the story of Anchises, carried from the burning city of Troy on the back of his loyal son (Aeneas) – an episode 'commonly adduced in Renaissance emblem books to illustrate the virtue of filial piety' – and the stock scene in medieval morality plays in which the devil carried the vice off on his back.[96] In this case, the symbolic point of the echo seems to be to suggest the extent to which Wasp and Cokes are comically afflicted by vice and fail to live up to their social and moral duties as a paternalistic tutor and a gentleman, respectively. A similar symbolic point appears to be made when the play's representatives of reason, justice, and truth – Wasp, Overdo, and Busy – end up in the stocks (4.6), in an episode that parodically recalls contemporary emblems showing virtues in the stocks.[97] While such emblems were usually used to indicate 'the trials that this world imposes on the virtuous', the point of Jonson's scene seems to be that these authority figures have brought about their own suffering and fallen short of their ethical and social responsibilities.[98] The play's incorporation of such emblematic scenes may have encouraged Lady Elizabeth's Men to adopt the symbolic staging traditions of the medieval stage for other aspects of their performance of the play, too. R. B. Parker, for example, argues that Ursula's pig booth 'is pretty clearly associated with hell' and might therefore have been located stage left, the traditional location of 'hell' on the medieval stage, while the puppet booth as the place where the people of the fair come together and perhaps learn some lessons, might have been located stage right, the 'usual site of heaven or paradise', and the stocks might have been 'down-centre at the front of the stage' in keeping with the emblematic association of the stocks with worldly trial.[99]

If the play's requirements in terms of casting and stage furnishings are comparatively demanding, in other respects the play's staging requirements are fairly simple, the action requiring no more than a playing place on to and from which players can enter and exit, facilities that de Witt's illustration of the Swan Theatre (upon which the Hope was modelled) suggest that the Hope would have afforded. There is no call for use of a below-stage area, no action above, no requirement for multiple doors and no ascents or descents. In this regard the play is not venue-specific and could have been performed elsewhere in London and on tour, although the large size of some of the scenes would have made staging it in smaller venues, such as indoor playhouses like the Cockpit, more challenging. The fact that the play could be taken to court the day after its performance at the Hope Theatre is its own evidence that the play was portable and could be staged elsewhere. Similarly, although the play would have been at its most topical and its theatrical jokes most meaningful when it was performed at the Hope by Lady Elizabeth's Men, *Bartholomew Fair* is not wholly company-specific either. It could be acted, and much of the same comedy could be achieved, by another company if it was of sufficient size and included actors of varying heights. There are, however, no records of the play being performed again in the seventeenth century. Although subsequent performances may have escaped record, this could also be a sign that the play did not stay long in the repertory, perhaps in part because of the staging challenges it poses and because of the ways in which it was tailored to its original company and occasion of performance.

4

Audiences

Every Writer must gouerne his Penne according to the Capacitie of the Stage he writes too, both in the Actor and the Auditor.

THE TWO MERRY MILKMAIDS, 1620[1]

The printer of *The Two Merry Milkmaids* argues above that Renaissance playwrights accepted the need to tailor their plays for their audiences as well as their performers. This chapter looks at the complex relationship between English Renaissance playwrights and the main audience for which they 'governed their pens': London playgoers.[2] Public theatre was big business in the late Elizabethan metropolis: by 1595 it is estimated that around 15,000 people were attending the theatres every week; by 1620 the 'weekly total was probably nearer 25,000 people'.[3] Who were these spectators? Why did they attend? How did they respond and how were they affected by the experience of theatre going? These are thorny questions, not least because of the comparative paucity of evidence about individual playgoers and the inherent bias in the surviving evidence towards those who were literate. But, they are questions which have received growing attention in the last half century as theatre critics have become more interested in audience response; and scholars of the Renaissance stage ave increasingly acknowledged, with Andrew Gurr, that the 'history of the writing of plays in Shakespeare's time is not really complete without an account of the audiences'.[4]

One of the first scholars to pay serious attention to theatre audiences in Shakespearean London was Alfred Harbage. In *Shakespeare's Audience* (1941) he surveyed the known evidence about Renaissance theatre audiences, identifying three main types of audience in the period – the 'genteel', the 'plebeian' and the socially mixed – with the working classes being the predominant group generally, he argued. For him the fact that public theatre audiences were characteristically 'socially, economically, [and] educationally heterogeneous' helped to explain what he regarded as the 'universality' of Shakespeare's plays.[5] Plays written for such an audience needed wide-ranging appeal. Later Harbage refined his views arguing that the development of the indoor theatres charging higher prices and implicitly catering for a more elite clientele in the early seventeenth century contributed to the evolution of two rival 'dramatic' traditions: the 'popular' and the 'coterie', the 'popular' tradition thriving at the open-air playhouses where audiences continued to be socially mixed and the 'coterie' tradition flourishing at the new, more elite indoor playhouses.[6]

Harbage's valorization of the working classes as the chief spectators at the Elizabethan theatres and his picture of a heterogeneous audience inviting the composition of plays of universal appeal have proved seductive to many scholars; but they faced a serious challenge by Ann Jennalie Cook in 1981. Cook questioned Harbage's thesis that there were two rival dramatic traditions and his argument that working-class spectators made up the bulk of the London audiences. Her research led her to conclude that the dominant spectator at the open-air and indoor playhouses of Shakespearean London was what she termed 'the privileged playgoer'. Although she did not dispute that there were 'plebeian' playgoers she argued that they were always likely to have been in the minority, apprentices and other working men and women usually being required to work on weekday afternoons (when the plays took place) and generally having less money available for such recreations. For her it seemed clear that 'London's large and lively privileged set ruled the playgoing world quite as firmly as they ruled the political world, the mercantile world, and the rest of the cultural world'.[7]

However, Cook's own thesis has in turn been critiqued, most notably by Martin Butler and Andrew Gurr. Butler takes issue with various aspects of Cook's thesis, disputing her contention that the 'privileged' were 'virtually, if not absolutely, the only spectators who counted' and arguing that it is 'patently obvious ... that the unprivileged did go to plays, in quantities, and that at least some of the time or in some theatres they constituted the principal audience'. Equally, Butler does not accept Harbage's thesis that the working classes were the dominant audience across the Elizabethan and early Stuart theatre worlds or the idea that there were two dramatic traditions. Instead, he suggests that scholars think of the Renaissance stage in terms of three main dramatic traditions: the courtly, the elite and the popular, the boundary between the latter two often being blurred at the indoor playhouses.[8]

Andrew Gurr is not wholly convinced by Butler's theory of three overlapping dramatic traditions in the period, but he echoes Butler in questioning Cook's privileging of the 'privileged' playgoer, pointing out in the preface to his own study of *Playgoing in Shakespeare's London*, that Cook's definition of the privileged is so broad as to be of questionable usefulness as a social category and that this group cannot fully account for the more than 50 million theatre visits thought to have been made in the era.[9] In Gurr's opinion, the evidence up to the turn of the sixteenth century points to socially mixed audiences at the open-air theatres, being catered for by companies with similar repertories. Only after the King's Men's acquisition of the Second Blackfriars Theatre popularized indoor theatres for adult players from 1609, and the establishment of other indoor venues does Gurr believe that there was a gradual differentiation between the social composition of theatre audiences, the higher prices charged at the indoor theatres making them inaccessible to some plebeian spectators and the number of elite spectators possibly declining at the more remote northern amphitheatres.[10] Whether this divergence in audience make-up was matched by a divergence in theatrical tastes and the fare that was offered at the indoor and open-air theatres, as has sometimes been assumed, is a point about which Gurr is more cautious, arguing that the 'fact that the hall playhouses could perform plays taken from the amphi-theatres, not only Globe plays at the Blackfriars but Red Bull plays at the Cockpit, suggests the division was more of social class than audience taste'.[11] On the other hand, he does seem to accept that there was some differentiation between the northern amphitheatre playhouses and the indoor theatres by the 1630s, the northern playhouses favouring an older repertory of 'predominantly masculine and heroic' plays 'more and more designed for citizens' and the hall playhouses recruiting most of 'the new plays' and catering for more elite audiences and interest in the court.[12]

The make-up and tastes of Renaissance audiences are not the only points about which modern scholars have disagreed. Perhaps most contentious of all has been the question of whether, and to what extent, the period's extant plays can be used as evidence regarding the audiences that watched them. Both Alfred Harbage and Ann Jennalie Cook are cautious about reading the plays for evidence about early theatre audiences. Harbage argues that 'any approach to the audience through the plays must be highly subjective', while Cook argues against using the playgoers 'as an expla-nation for the plays'.[13] By contrast, more recent critics have looked to the plays as an important source when reflecting on audiences of the time, including Martin Butler who argues that 'it is surely clear that the nature of the plays is profoundly implicated in the kind of audiences which were going to see them'.[14] Jeremy Lopez goes even further and suggests that 'one can better understand the audiences of the

English Renaissance if one better understands the plays they watched'.[15]

Audiences: An overview

The surviving evidence about Shakespearean playgoers takes a variety of forms, including: records specifically documenting play attendance (such as playhouse receipts; private household payments for playhouse attendance; allusions to and descriptions of specific play performances in sources such as letters, diaries and memoirs); general allusions to and comments on audiences and playgoers; addresses to and representations of playgoers in play dedications, prefaces, prologues, epilogues, inductions, plays-within-plays; the physical evidence of the spaces in which audiences saw performances; the indirect evidence of playgoers' tastes preserved in the period's extant plays and lists of lost works; and, finally (and more contentiously), the indirect evidence of what Andrew Gurr describes as the 'mental composition' of audiences of the time.[16] As a whole, the evidence is comparatively slim and, relying mostly on written records, is generally fuller in what it tells us about literate and privileged playgoers than about those who were not literate. Indeed, more than half of the 250 'real' people identified as having 'attended plays on some occasion through the period' in Gurr's latest edition of *Playgoing in Shakespeare's London* are members of the elite, including 114 gentry and 19 nobles.[17]

The make-up of audiences

The combined evidence of building contracts for theatres such as the Fortune and the Hope, modern archaeological investigations at the sites of the Theatre, Rose, Globe and Hope Playhouses, contemporary illustrations and descriptions of playhouses and their audiences, and the playhouse receipts for the Rose Theatre preserved in the *Diary* of Philip Henslowe have taught us much about the possible, the actual and the perceived size of Renaissance theatre audiences. The open-air playhouses appear to have been able to accommodate large audiences of between 2,000 and 3,000 spectators. Indoor playhouses are thought to have been much smaller, the Paul's Playhouse perhaps accommodating as few as 200 people and the larger hall playhouses such as the Second Blackfriars and the Cockpit thought to accommodate a maximum of 700 spectators.[18] On some occasions, it seems that the theatres did play to capacity (or near capacity) crowds. New plays, holiday performances and performances of plays which dealt with scandalous or topical events all seem to have drawn large audiences.[19] When the King's Men staged Thomas Middleton's topical anti-Spanish drama *A Game at Chess* at the Globe in August 1624 in the aftermath of failed negotiations for a Spanish marriage for Prince Charles, the play ran for nine consecutive days during which the Spanish ambassador claimed that there were 'more than 3000 persons there on the day that the audience was smallest'.[20] On the other hand, if the evidence of the takings at Henslowe's Rose Theatre is typical it was more usual to play to audiences of around 'half to 60 per cent capacity'.[21]

Anyone who had the money and the time could go to performances in the capital's public theatres and the starting price at the open-air playhouses was comparatively low: 1 penny. At a time when the 'average weekly wage for artisans in England … was about 5s. 3 ½d' this was a cost potentially within the reach of many London workers and it compared favourably with the costs of other recreations, being the same, for instance, as the cost of attending puppet shows and the bear-baiting arenas.[22] Inside the playhouses there were other opportunities to spend one's money, including on refreshments and superior seating as Thomas Platter, a Swiss visitor who attended the Globe Theatre (1599) reveals, describing how spectators could pay an extra penny to sit in the galleries, while anyone desiring 'to sit in the most comfortable seats which are cushioned, where he not only sees everything well, but can also be seen, ... pays yet another English penny at another door'.[23] As Platter's description suggests, the configuration of the audience within the open-air playhouses was hierarchical with the seats in the galleries and the 'cushioned' lords' rooms more likely to be occupied by those with more money, and thus higher up the social ladder, and the poorer spectators or 'groundlings' (as they became known) standing in the yard, although there are stories of more humble spectators sitting in privileged positions and of elite spectators choosing to stand in the yard, including Venetian ambassador, Antonio Foscarini. In 1613 fellow Venetian Antimo Galli reported that the ambassador went to the Curtain Playhouse, where

> in order not to pay a royal, or a scudo, to go in one of the little rooms, nor even to sit in the degrees that are there, he insisted on standing in the middle down below among the gang of porters and carters.[24]

Those particularly keen to show off may have been able to sit on the stage itself (for a further payment), as became customary at the indoor playhouses.[25] This custom may explain how feltmakers' apprentice Richard (or John) Gill came to be hurt on-stage by a player at the Red Bull (1623).[26]

Visiting the indoor playhouses was a more costly business. Prices at the Second Blackfriars are thought to have started at 6 pence for a seat in the galleries going up to 2 shillings for a stool on the stage and half a crown for a box by the stage.[27] As the price gradations hint, there was a seating hierarchy, as at the open-air theatres, although in the indoor playhouses it reversed that which operated at the open-air theatres, the seating closest to the stage being the most costly and the seats in the galleries the cheapest. The considerably higher entry costs are likely to have made a difference to the clientele that frequented the indoor playhouses. Based in the wealthier western part of the city, and close to the Inns of Court and

Westminster, the indoor playhouses implicitly targeted a more elite audience than the open-air playhouses.

Alfred Harbage described Shakespeare's audience at the Globe as socially heterogeneous. What evidence there is about specific playgoers tends to confirm that audiences at the open-air playhouses were socially mixed, particularly in the Elizabethan period. Up until the early seventeenth century and the establishment of regular indoor playing by the King's Men, this is perhaps unsurprising. Before this the main option for anyone who wanted to see plays regularly would have been visiting the open-air playhouses which staged performances daily. The early indoor theatres at St Paul's and the Blackfriars operated periodically during this period, too, but staged performances only once or twice a week.

Whether the working classes dominated audiences, especially at the open-air playhouses, as Harbage thought, is less clear, but they certainly attended in numbers. There are records of a variety of spectators at the mainly open-air Elizabethan playhouses, ranging from apprentices, servants and craftsmen, to law students, nobles and foreign ambassadors. The one apprentice London playgoer known by name is John or Richard Gill, the feltmakers' apprentice injured at the Red Bull (see p. 135), but it is clear that other apprentices attended the theatres, too, despite the fact that (theoretically) they were expected to be at work on weekday afternoons and were not supposed to receive any wages.[28] As Charles Whitney's research has shown, a number of the London craft guilds issued ordinances which complained about apprentices' 'haunting' of 'plaies', while the company of bakers issued an order in 1589 which sought to 'curb "divers servauntes" who "usually in the werking Daies resort to play howses and other such like places"'. Those 'out of service' or 'in between jobs or indentures' are known to have attended plays, too.[29]

Evidence about qualified craftsmen attending the open-air playhouses is even more plentiful, named playgoers from these groups including: Gilbert Borne, butcher (1611), Thomas Collins, glover (1611), William Frend, ale-brewer (1614),

William Hawkins, barber (1600) and Thomas Pinnocke, silkweaver (1638). There are also several records of named servants attending – including Elizabeth Hatrell, serving-woman (1611) and Joseph Mulis, servant to Dudley Norton (1612) – and sailors, such as the group of seamen led by Thomas Alderson involved in an affray at the Fortune Theatre (1626).[30]

At the more privileged end of the spectrum, named spectators at the open-air theatres include gentlemen and nobles such as Sir Edward Dering (1623–4), Sir Humphrey Mildmay (1633), Henry Rich, Earl of Holland (1628), Sir Ambrose Vaux (1612) and George Villiers, first Duke of Buckingham (1628). A number of foreign ambassadors went to the open-air theatres, too, including at least two Venetian ambassadors, Antonio Foscarini (1613) and Giorgio Giustinian (1607–8), Spanish ambassador, Sarmiento de Acuna, Count Gondomar (1621) and French ambassador, Antoine Le Fevre (1607–8). There are also known to have been other continental visitors at the open-air playhouses including Johannes De Witt (1596), Samuel Kiechel (1584) and Prince Frederick Lewis of Württemberg (1610).[31]

Although it seems that young men were predominant we know that open-air audiences included older members of society, children and women. Luke Bryan, a member of the king's guard, was 60 years old when he got into a dispute with Joan Hewes, one of the gatherers at the Red Bull in 1607, and Simon Forman, the well-known physician-cum-astrologer was nearly 60 when he went to the Globe to see *Macbeth* and *The Winter's Tale* in 1611, while Dr John Lambe, a later infamous quack-doctor and associate of the Duke of Buckingham, was over 80 when he was set upon by a mob after visiting the Fortune Theatre in June 1628.[32]

The names of the children who attended the open-air theatres are generally not known (the attendance of Lady Anne Cecil at the Globe when she was 15 is a rare exception) but we know that minors were sometimes present. Another payment in the Cecil family records in 1633–4 may preserve evidence of such visits, being 'For the children going to see plays at several times this year'.[33] That younger children were present at least occasionally at the open-air theatres is, likewise, suggested by Philip Gawdy's account of a tragic event in 1587 when the Lord Admiral's Men used a gun during a performance and accidentally 'killed a child, and a woman great with chyld'.[34]

Women playgoers appear to have represented an even more significant presence at the open-air theatres, as at the later indoor theatres. In the Elizabethan period women playgoers faced being stigmatized and could only attend the theatres acceptably if escorted by men; but female playgoing became increasingly respectable in the Jacobean and Caroline periods, a shift reflected in playwrights' increasing acknowledgement of the presence of women spectators in prologues and epilogues, and in the growing fashion for plays focused on women (see pp. 142–3). Most of the individual women known to have attended playhouses in the period belong to Cook's 'privileged' classes, such as Lady Anne Cecil, Elizabeth Williams, gentlewoman and sister-in-law of Sir Dudley Carleton (1614) and Elizabeth Wybarn, widow of William Wybarn and later wife of Ambrose Lord Vaux (1612). But this is in large part a result of there being more evidence about such spectators generally. Other evidence makes it clear that they were not the only women to be found at the theatres. While contemporary allusions suggest that the open-air theatres were infamous for the presence of prostitutes, extant records provide specific evidence of working women and women of humbler social status attending the open-air playhouses. These include women such as Marion Frith the transvestite and reputed cut-purse who provided the inspiration for *The Roaring Girl* and who reportedly attended a performance of this play at the Fortune Theatre (1611) and a number of women gatherers at the open-air theatres, such as Joan Hewes, Mary Phillipps and Elizabeth Wheaten.[35]

The apparent diversity of the known spectators at the open-air playhouses would seem to challenge Cook's argument that the privileged classes dominated all the period's playhouses in the Elizabethan period. Whether audiences at the open-air playhouses continued to be as socially mixed after the popularization of indoor playing in the early seventeenth century is harder to know, as direct evidence of the individuals attending both kinds of playhouse in the period is slim. It has been argued that there was a gradual distinction between theatre audiences. Such a view finds support in James Wright's later history of the early English stage in which he describes the theatres in operation on the eve of the civil war and observes that the Fortune and Red Bull Theatres 'were mostly frequented by Citizens, and the meaner sort of People', in contrast with the more elite audiences at the indoor theatres.[36] Contemporary allusions also lend some weight to the theory that there was some differentiation in social make-up between the open-air and indoor playhouses, the open-air theatre audiences often being caricatured as lowly in class and character. In his verses attacking Jonson's *The Magnetic Lady*, which flopped when it premiered at the Blackfriars Theatre in 1632, Alexander Gill suggests that Jonson would have been better sending his play to the Fortune Theatre with its audience of 'Prentizes and Apellwyfes', while John Tatham caricatures the same audience as 'a noyse / Of *Rables*, *Apple-wives* and Chimney-boyes'.[37] On the other hand, there is plenty of evidence to show that members of society's elites continued to frequent the open-air playhouses throughout the early seventeenth century; and some were actively targeted by open-air playhouses, as when 'small handbills advertising' a revival of John Fletcher's *Wit Without Money* at the Red Bull 'were specifically "thrown into Gentlemens Coaches"'.[38]

The higher entry charges at the period's indoor theatres have led most scholars to assume that the audiences were more elite. What evidence there is tends to confirm this, showing that the indoor playhouses were popular venues with members of the gentry, students of the neighbouring law schools and the nobility. Named visitors to these playhouses include: James Butler, twelfth Earl, first Duke of Ormond (1632), Sir William Cavendish (1600, 1601, 1602), Sir Richard Cholmley (1603),

John Digby, gentleman (1634), Philip Herbert, fourth Earl of Pembroke (1636), Sir Arthur Ingram (1638), John Newdigate, student of the Inner Temple (1620–1) and James Stuart, second Duke of Lennox (1636).[39]

The Blackfriars Theatre was host to royalty, too: Prince Charles of the Palatine visited on 5 May 1636, and Charles's aunt, Queen Henrietta Maria visited four times.[40] In doing so, she helped to seal the respectability of female playgoing in the period. Other known women spectators at the indoor theatres in this era include elite women such as the Countess of Essex (1632) and Anne, Countess of Newport (1637), members of the minor gentry, such as Joan Drake, and at least one apparently lowlier figure, Katherine Greene who was arrested (possibly as a prostitute) but who was later released because it was discovered that she was pregnant (1631).[41]

Richer members of the merchant classes would have been able to attend the indoor playhouses, too, and there is some evidence that they did.[42] Jonson alludes to the presence of 'the shops Foreman' amongst those in the audience for Fletcher's *The Faithful Shepherdess* (c. 1609) at the Blackfriars; Thrift, a citizen, is included amongst the representative playgoers in the Praeludium to Thomas Goffe's *The Careless Shepherdess* (Salisbury Court Theatre, c. 1629); and, as late as 1640, Richard Brome included the 'City friend' amongst those he addressed in the epilogue to his topical drama *The Court Beggar*, performed at the Cockpit.[43]

Perhaps more surprisingly, there is also some evidence of humbler figures attending such theatres. Sir William Cavendish's servant Hallam accompanied his master to the Paul's Playhouse in 1601; and Jonson alludes to 'the faeces or grounds of your people, that sit in the / oblique caves and wedges of your house, your sinful six-penny mechanics' as late as 1632 in his induction to *The Magnetic Lady* (performed at the Blackfriars).[44] One might think that writers such as Jonson were exaggerating the lowliness of some of the spectators at the indoor theatres but the evidence of apprentices and other modestly paid craftsmen attending plays regularly and, in

some cases, choosing to sit in more expensive seats at the
open-air playhouses suggests that such figures did sometimes
choose to occupy privileged positions at the theatre, despite
the high costs involved, especially in proportion to their likely
income. It is possible, therefore, that audiences at the indoor
playhouses were not without some social diversity, even into
the Caroline era; a point which would tend to reinforce the
arguments of scholars such as Jeremy Lopez that the differences between the audiences of the various early London
theatres were 'differences of degree rather than kind'.[45]

Audience tastes

Just as there have been disputes about the social make-up
of the audiences at the diverse theatres in Shakespeare's
London, so there has been debate about the extent to which
the different playhouses catered for different audience tastes.
In the Elizabethan period the evidence for any great differentiation between the playing repertories at the main playhouses
is slim. On the contrary, most of the evidence points towards
the development of similar company repertories, perhaps
because the acting troupes were competing for the same,
socially diverse audiences. Consequently, in the 1590s, we
find the Lord Chamberlain's Men and the Lord Admiral's
company competing with each other with very similar repertories, including a wave of history plays in the early 1590s
and a taste for humorous comedies in the late 1590s. In the
Jacobean period there is similar evidence of a fashion for
tragicomedies across the companies and their theatres. This is
not to say that there were no differences in the theatrical fare
that the leading companies offered but they do not seem to
have been great or to have been connected to any conspicuous
differences between their audiences.

   That there were not huge differences between the fare offered
at outdoor and indoor playhouses is perhaps not surprising
given that acting companies and their plays frequently moved

backwards and forwards between the indoor and open-air playhouses in the Caroline era. Indeed, most of the early seventeenth-century acting companies changed theatrical venues periodically. Sometimes this involved moving between theatres of the same kind, as when the Red Bull players moved from the Fortune Theatre back to the Red Bull Playhouse during 1640; on other occasions it involved a company moving from an indoor to an outdoor venue or vice versa. Prince Charles's players started life, for example, at the new Salisbury Court Theatre (1631) but moved to the Red Bull in 1633 and the Fortune Theatre in 1640, while the King's Men alternated between playing at the Second Blackfriars and the Globe from around 1609–10.[46] At the heart of many of these relocations was Christopher Beeston, owner of the Red Bull and Cockpit Theatres and of a stock of plays that he appears to have transferred between the two venues and the companies he presided over. Although there seem to have been some plays that Beeston chose not to move between the theatres he oversaw, there were many others that he did transfer from the Red Bull to the Cockpit, suggesting that 'the playhouses became distinct in the social identity of their audiences more through their prices and their locality than their repertoire'.[47]

Further evidence of continuing overlaps between the theatrical traditions and repertories of the Caroline indoor and outdoor theatres is found if we look more closely at the plays being performed. While more of the new plays written in the era appear to have been commissioned for the indoor playhouses, the open-air theatres were not wholly reliant on old or 'drum and trumpet' plays; they performed new plays, too, although most have been lost. Equally, it is clear that the nostalgic taste for Elizabethan and Elizabethan-style plays was not confined to the open-air theatres. The companies based in the indoor theatres also relied increasingly on revivals of old plays in the Caroline era, including for their visits to court.[48]

There is some evidence of shared fashions across the Stuart playhouse world, too, as in the Elizabethan era. The vogue for plays focused on women from the 1610s onwards, with which John Fletcher is often identified, was not one confined to the indoor playhouses, for example. Although there is more evidence of playwrights specifically addressing women in plays written for the indoor theatres, plays that appealed to the 'gender concern or even gender loyalty of women spectators' were performed at the open-air theatres, too, including Shakespeare and Fletcher's *King Henry VIII*, with its sympathetic portrayal of Katherine of Aragon (at the Globe, 1613), Middleton and Dekker's *The Roaring Girl* (at the Fortune, 1611) and Massinger's *The Maid of Honour* (at the Red Bull, 1621–2).[49] The fashion for romance with which Beaumont and Fletcher, and the King's Men, are particularly associated in the Stuart era, and which is often seen as influenced by court tastes, was not confined to the indoor theatres either. At the Fortune Theatre, the Red Bull players also performed romance, staging John Kirke's *Seven Champions of Christendom* sometime before 1638 (when it was printed), a play based on Richard Johnson's 'very popular chivalric romance of the same name'.[50]

There is evidence of a shared interest in topical and political drama across the indoor and open-air playhouses, too, especially in the late 1630s and early 1640s. Thanks to the pioneering work of scholars such as Martin Butler and Julie Sanders, it is now well recognized that the Caroline dramas performed at the indoor playhouses by playwrights such as Massinger, Brome and Shirley were politically engaged. Scholars have been slower to recognize the similar fashion for topical, political drama at the open-air theatres, and yet there is plenty of evidence that the players at the Red Bull and the Fortune were just as interested in such fare. Just as Brome and Beeston's Boys found themselves in trouble in May 1640 for performing a play which seemed to allude to the recent, ill-fated war with the Scots in 1639, so the players at the Red Bull and the Fortune courted scandal and arrest by staging topical works in the late 1630s. In 1639 Prince Charles's players at the Red Bull got into trouble with the Privy Council for staging a lost play called *The Whore New Vamped* which allegedly satirized 'monopolies and ecclesiastical officials'. The Red Bull players at the Fortune Theatre reputedly faced punishment twice for staging topical plays in the same year: first, a lost play called *The Cardinal's Conspiracy* which implicitly satirized Archbishop William Laud; and secondly, for reviving *The Valiant Scot*, an old play which in its sympathetic treatment of Scottish rebellion had become newly topical in the wake of the conflict between England and Scotland (see pp. 157–64).[51] Indeed, if anything, these cases suggest that the theatrical fare offered at the open-air theatres in the Caroline era may have been even more politically engaged and radical than that being staged at the indoor theatres.

Finally, it is worth noting that spectator tastes were not necessarily uniform at any of the period's theatres, any more than they are at individual theatres today. That different audience members had differing preferences is something which one finds playwrights alluding to throughout the Renaissance era, in texts ranging from John Lyly's *Midas* (1592) in which the prologue describes how 'at our exercises soldiers call for tragedies, their object is blood; courtiers for comedies, their subject is love; country-men for pastorals, shepherds are their saints', to the epilogue to Fletcher and Shakespeare's *King Henry VIII* in which it is acknowledged that 'ten to one this play can never please / All that are here' (1–2).[52]

Audience behaviour and response

The flourishing of the professional theatre industry and the swelling of audience numbers did not go uncontested. As well as having to weather periodic civic attempts to curb their activities, the theatres faced fierce attacks from a small but vocal minority, especially during the 1570s and 1580s when a spate of anti-theatrical tracts was published. While the city authorities worried about the disorder, disease and crime potentially attendant upon the crowds drawn to the playhouses, the anti-theatricalists were most concerned with the effect plays had on spectators, arguing that plays corrupted people by teaching them immoral lessons. Young people and women were deemed especially susceptible to theatre's 'ill' lessons. Hence, one finds the anonymous author of *A Second and Third Blast of Retrait from Plaies and Theaters* (1580) accusing plays of corrupting 'the good disposition & manners of youth', while the special danger posed to women spectators is suggested by his account of 'some citizens wiues' who,

> have euen on their death beds with teares confessed, that they haue receiued at those spectacles such filthie infections, as haue turned their minds from chaste cogitations, and made them of honest women light huswiues.[53]

Whereas concerns about the influence of theatre appear to have had little direct impact on the functioning of the playhouses, the danger of spreading disease, and plague specifically, provided one of the few reasons for their periodic closure, the theatres generally being required to shut their doors once the level of weekly deaths from the plague in the city exceeded an agreed maximum.[54] Civic concerns about the possibility of crime and disorder at the theatres were not without foundation either, although examples of crimes being committed inside playhouses and/or of serious disorder are comparatively few. There were 'only two major disturbances' inside theatres in the period, one at an indoor theatre and one at an open-air theatre, as Ann Jennalie Cook notes.[55] There are other examples of smaller-scale disputes and violence, as when Lord Thurles and Captain Charles Essex became involved in a fray at the Blackfriars (1632) after the former blocked the view of the latter and his companion, the Countess of Essex, or the incident which led to George Wilson being 'kild at ye play house in salesburie court' in March 1634; and there is some evidence of petty crimes such as pick-pocketing being committed at the theatres; but the theatres do not appear to have been the sinks of crime and disorder which they were sometimes described as by their opponents.[56]

Defenders of the stage challenged the association of playhouses with the perpetration and encouragement of crime, immorality and disorder by stressing the positive educative function of the stage. Thomas Heywood specifically inverted the claims of the anti-theatricalists to argue that plays taught people to be moral by rewarding virtue and heroism and by punishing sin and showing men the 'vglinesse' of their vices to make them 'the more to abhorre them'.[57] In some ways, what is most fascinating about these debates is that, while they disagreed about the nature of drama's effect on audiences, critics and defenders of the stage alike agreed that plays had the capacity to influence their audiences powerfully.

Going to the theatre in Renaissance London was a communal experience for many spectators, not just because audiences were large and usually visible to each other, but because people often appear to have attended plays in groups. Most often people went to plays with family members and/or friends as is illustrated by the accounts of the Dering family of Surrenden Dering in Kent, which reveal that Sir Edward Dering (a famous lover of drama) usually attended the theatre with others in the 1620s. Sometimes Dering went with male family and friends, sometimes with female companions, and occasionally with a mixture of both, as when he went to see a play in 1623–4 with 'my lady *william* Tuffton, and my sisters ffranc*es* and Mary Tuffton' (the 'lady' was probably Dering's mother-in-law Frances, Lady Tufton; William Tufton was his brother-in-law; and Frances and Mary are likely to have been his sister, Lady Frances Wotton, and his sister-in-law, Mary Tufton).[58] But there is evidence of groups of workers and young men, such as apprentices, attending together, too, including the butchers and glovers involved in an affray at the Fortune Theatre (1611) and the group of sailors bound over after a fracas at the same theatre in 1626.[59] There is some evidence of women attending in groups, too. In her memoirs, Anne Murray Halkett tells of how she 'loved well to see plays' in her youth, encouraging groups of her female friends to attend the theatres together.[60] In each case, the responses of individual playgoers were potentially informed as much by the views and reactions of their immediate companions as by the responses of the wider audience.

With this possibility in mind, Mary Blackstone and Cameron Louis offer a fascinating account of the ways in which the party of largely 'privileged' playgoers led by Elizabeth Wybarn to the Globe in 1612 might have responded to the performance of a play such as John Webster's *The Duchess of Malfi*. This includes paying special attention to the group's connections with each other (such as the shared recusancy of several of them) and how these connections might have informed their responses to, and distinguished their reactions from, those of other 'privileged' spectators. In doing so, they highlight a potential problem with the past habit of categorizing audiences primarily in terms of social class, showing how other loyalties and aspects of individual identity (such as religious allegiance and gender) might be as important in shaping audience reactions.[61]

What evidence we have about audience responses tends to emphasize the communal nature of the theatrical experience, contemporaries often describing collective responses. These were often more vocal than is customary in modern western theatres. There are, for instance, numerous allusions to audiences expressing their distaste with performances by hissing, calling out and even throwing missiles at the stage![62] By contrast, audience pleasure might be marked with laughing and clapping, sometimes of a hearty variety, not to the tastes of all contemporary playwrights, Beaumont consequently calling for 'soft smiling, not loud / laughing' in the Prologue to *The Knight of the Burning Pestle*.[63] There are also accounts of mass excitement, Stephen Gosson describing how 'in publike Theaters, when any notable shew passeth ouer the stage, the people arise vp out of their seates, & stand upright with delight and eagernesse to view it well'.[64] There are similar accounts of spectators being moved to tears, men and women alike, although women were thought to be especially susceptible to the emotion of pity.[65] Representations of 'strong passions' were thought to be especially powerful, Edmund Gayton writing of how some spectators were 'so transported, that they have gone weeping, some from Tragedies, some from Comedies; so merry, lightsome and free, that they have not been sober … a week after'. If contemporary anecdotes are to be believed, there were also occasions when spectators were so moved by performances that they attempted to intervene in the action, as in the story recalled by Gayton about a 'passionate Butcher of our Nation', who 'being at the Play, called *the Greeks and Trojans*, and seeing *Hector* overpowered by *Mirmydons*, got upon the Stage, and with his good Battoone tooke the true *Trojans* part so stoutly, that he routed the *Greeks*'.[66] The anecdote is very possibly fictitious and is, in part, an example of class-based satire, but it again points to theatre's perceived ability to influence spectators in powerful fashion.

Hamlet's conduct as an on-stage spectator of 'The Mousetrap' (3.2) illustrates another way in which spectators might intervene in performances, that is as interrupters of, and commentators on, the play being performed. On-stage spectators in the plays of Shakespeare and his contemporaries are frequently disruptive in this way. Sometimes this is because they are theatrically naïve (often this is linked to their being of middling or humbler class, as in Gayton's story of the butcher). This is true, for instance, of Beaumont's Citizen and his wife (Nell) in *The Knight of the Burning Pestle*, who are supposed to be making their first visit to the Blackfriars Theatre when they interrupt the action to demand a play of their own choice, opting for a play about a grocer who 'shall do / admirable things' (Induction.34–5) and volunteering their apprentice Rafe for the lead role. Bartholomew Cokes proves a similarly naïve on-stage spectator of Lantern Leatherhead's puppet play in Jonson's *Bartholomew Fair*. Cokes disrupts the performance, as do Beaumont's Citizen and his wife, asking a series of foolish questions and repeating the dialogue in ways that illustrate his limited understanding of the workings of theatre and of illusion.

Arguably even more common than representations of supposedly naïve spectators are dramatic depictions of on-stage spectators who comment mockingly on performances because they are, or consider themselves to be, theatrically sophisticated. This is partly the case with Shakespeare's theatre-loving Danish prince who cannot resist offering a satirical commentary on the visiting players' performance of 'The Mousetrap' at Elsinore, prompting Ophelia to note that he is as 'good as a chorus' (3.2.247). Similar instances of elite spectators wittily mocking performances occur in several of Shakespeare's plays. In *Love's Labour's Lost* the royal and noble spectators at the amateur show of the Nine Worthies interrupt each of the performers to ask mocking questions, prompting Holofernes (who plays Judas Maccabeus) to observe that their behaviour 'is not generous, not gentle, not humble' (5.2.624); and in *A Midsummer Night's Dream*, Theseus, Hippolyta and their courtiers make a series of satirical remarks during the Mechanicals' performance of their play of Pyramus and Thisbe, despite Theseus' initial observation that 'what poor duty cannot do, noble respect / Takes it in might, not merit' (5.1.91–2).

The stereotype of the disruptive and/or critical spectator is, in fact, a very common one especially in the early seventeenth century. Jonson was especially critical of such spectators, consistently mocking them in his plays. In *Every Man Out of His Humour* (1600) Asper alludes mockingly to the type of gallant who, 'to be thought one of the judicious, / Sits with his arms thus wreathed, his hat pulled here, / Cries "mew" and nods, then shakes his empty head'.[67] Jonson is even more scathing about such exhibitionist critics and their self-advertising disruption of plays in the dedication to his late play, *The New Inn* (1631), claiming that the audience that first saw the play came: 'To see and to be seen. To make a general muster of / themselves in their clothes of credit, and possess the stage against the play'.[68] Satire of ill-behaved and critical spectators occurs in non-dramatic texts, too. Thomas Dekker's comic advice-book for foolish gallants, *The Guls Horne-booke* (1609) implicitly confirms that the kind of disruptive attention-seeking behaviour that Jonson describes in *The New Inn* had long been a problem at the playhouses, satirically recommending that gallants behave in precisely such ways at playhouses. Hence, he advises paying to sit on a stool on the stage, observing that by 'sitting on the stage you haue a signd patent to engrosse the whole commodity of Censure' and 'may lawfully presume to be a Girder' (or critic).[69] As such advice and stories of disruptive spectators indicate, 'the action in the audiences competed with the entertainment on the stage'.[70]

Some scholars have linked the popularization of the stereotype of the 'critical' spectator to the growing interest in theatrical criticism and the emergence of what Michael Neill calls 'theatrical connoisseurship' in the early seventeenth century, as the establishment of the professional playhouses made it possible for at least some members of society's elites to become regular playgoers.[71] The perceived right to judge plays was not confined, however, to experienced playgoers. As Beaumont's portrait of the Citizen and his Wife in *The Knight of the Burning Pestle* suggests, less experienced and humbler playgoers were not necessarily slow to make their wishes or opinions felt. Edmund Gayton claims that, like Beaumont's Citizens, audiences at the open-air theatres sometimes interrupted performances to demand that they play 'what the major part of the company had a mind to; sometimes *Tamerlane*, sometimes *Jugurth*, sometimes the Jew of *Malta*, and sometimes parts of all these'.[72] True or not, this account is testimony to the agency associated with audiences in English Renaissance theatrical culture.

Evidence that real audiences did sometimes influence what was performed on the London stages has, likewise, emerged from the research of Tiffany Stern. She describes how it became customary at the end of performances for 'an announcement' to be 'made asking the audience to sanction a particular choice of play for the following afternoon'. Although this was intended to be a 'courtesy', audiences did sometimes demand a different play, as at the end of a performance at the Curtain Theatre (22 August 1613) attended by the Venetian Ambassador. Perhaps even more significantly, Stern's research suggests that audiences may have been invited to judge 'whether or not' new plays 'would "survive" to be performed again' at the end of their first performance (as was customary in Restoration theatres). She thinks audience judgement may have had a part in what was 'altered or cut' from texts following their initial performance, too, plays being 'written in long form first and potentially shortened in the light of performance'.[73] If Stern's supposition about post-performance revision of play-texts is correct, it would be further evidence of the collaborative nature of play production in the period and testimony to the important role of audiences in shaping the period's plays.

The implicit importance of audience judgement, especially for a commercialized industry, in which acting companies and theatres were competing for playgoers' pennies, helps to explain why playwrights sought to shape audience responses in increasingly explicit ways over the course of the Renaissance. Evidence of author anxiety about audience responses and an overt concern with engaging spectators is most often displayed in theatrical framing devices such as prologues, inductions and epilogues, devices which appear to have become increasingly common in the Jacobean and Caroline eras. We find playwrights such as Shakespeare courting kindly responses to plays through their characterization of their audiences as 'gentle' in character (whatever their birth), and through invitations to clap; while we might see Prospero's call for Ferdinand and Miranda to 'be mute / Or else our spell is marred' (4.1.126–7) during the performance of his masque in *The Tempest* as Shakespeare's indirect plea for audience silence and attention during performances. Other playwrights tried to control audience responses by describing what they hoped to prompt more directly, as when Beaumont wrote of his wish 'to move inward delight, not outward light- / ness' (ll.8–9) in the Prologue to *The Knight of the Burning Pestle*. Other writers condemned in advance undesirable responses, as in the prologue to Lyly's *Midas* where he asks the 'gentlemen' of the audience that the players be not 'hiss'd' (27) or in the prologue to Jonson's *The Staple of News* where he 'prays you'll not prejudge his play for ill, / Because you marked it not and sit not still'.[74]

The extent to which dramatists were conscious of negotiating a relationship with their audiences and of the commercial imperative which led almost all spectators to feel entitled to judge plays is perhaps made most explicit in the induction to Jonson's *Bartholomew Fair*, with the Book-Holder presenting the audience with a contract relating to the forthcoming play. This contract outlines what the audience can expect and is entitled to, and what Jonson believes the playwright can expect in return, although, as Jonson was painfully aware, the rights of authors were not generally acknowledged and were hard to assert when working in a commercial industry in which the customer was almost inevitably the boss.[75]

The other aspect of audience response that at least some playwrights hoped to shape was the interpretation of their plays, but here, too, the power of the dramatist had its limits. We know from playwrights' own testimony that audiences did not always respond to their plays in the ways that playwrights desired, and it was not simply a case of audiences disliking or being unimpressed by plays. While playwrights like Jonson complained about contemporaries' preoccupation with application, or the habit of looking for topical allusions in their plays, other evidence suggests that audiences sometimes misunderstood or did not care about authors' intentions.[76] The publisher of *The Knight of the Burning Pestle* in 1613 alludes to the play's failure in the theatre, arguing that when it was first performed the audience misinterpreted its satirical style (Epistle, 4–6). While it might be convenient for authors and their supporters to blame audience miscomprehension and deficiencies for the commercial failure of plays, such comments illustrate that dramatists were not able to control audience interpretations fully, just as they were not able to control the uses to which audiences put their plays, whether that was noting down the jokes for personal recycling or noting down whole speeches and perhaps even plays with a view to their private study or their piracy, as occurred with sermons of the day. Tiffany Stern discusses the evidence for the transcribing of plays in shorthand during performances and the possibility that at least some printed plays, including those previously characterized as 'bad quartos', could find their origin in such texts in a recent, fascinating paper on the 'bad' quarto of *Hamlet*.[77] At the same time, it is important to recognize that not all playwrights sought to control the audience's interpretation of their plays in the same way or to the same degree. On the contrary, at least some appear to have been keen to accommodate the 'appropriation' of their plays in differing ways and to differing ends by their audiences.[78] How audiences responded to plays could be informed or changed by the contexts in which they were performed, too. There are, for instance, examples of plays taking on new significance or becoming topical in ways not originally foreseen or intended by their playwrights, as we shall see in the case of *The Valiant Scot* (p. 159).

The quotations from, and allusions to, plays and theatres preserved in contemporary memoirs, commonplace books and letters afford valuable evidence about the 'diversity and creativity' of the 'early reception' of English Renaissance plays, as Charles Whitney's pioneering research has shown.[79] Evidence about how individual spectators responded to specific performances is less plentiful. There are, for instance, only a handful of detailed eye-witness accounts of public theatre performances in the period: physician-cum-astrologer Dr Simon Forman's accounts of seeing plays at the Rose and the Globe (in 1600 and 1611); John Holles's account of the performance of Middleton's controversial anti-Spanish allegory, *A Game at Chess* (Globe, 1624); and Nathaniel Tomkyns's report of seeing Heywood's and Brome's play about a group of alleged witches brought to London for trial,

The Late Lancashire Witches (Globe, 1634).[80] Like other accounts of Renaissance play performances, these examples are comparatively brief and mainly consist of plot summary. Simon Forman writes, for example, of the opening of *The Winter's Tale*, which he saw in 1611, 'Obserue ther howe Lyontes the kinge of Cicillia was overcom with Jelosy of his wife with the kinge of Bohemia his frind that came to see him';[81] John Holles describes the main events and the conceit behind the use of chess symbolism in Middleton's play as being about recent events between England and Spain:

> The whole play is a chess board, England y[e] whyt hows, Spayn y[e] black: one of y[e] white pawns, wth an vnder black dubblett, signifying a Spanish hart, betrays his party to their aduantage, aduanceth Gundomars propositions, works vnder hand y[e] Princes cumming into Spayn: w[ch] pawn so discouered, y[e] whyt Kyng reuyles him.[82]

And Nathaniel Tomkyns opens his account of *The Late Lancashire Witches* with a brief outline of its subject: 'The subiect was of the slights and passages done or supposed to be done' by the 'witches sent from thence'.[83] But each of these eye-witness reports also affords an insight into the diverse, sometimes idiosyncratic, ways in which contemporaries might respond to the plays that they saw.

The accounts of Holles and Tomkyns demonstrate that playgoers might be very alert to dramatists' use of topical, controversial material, for example, and that they might be able to decode symbolic references to current affairs (as when Holles identifies some of Middleton's chess piece-characters with real individuals). In Holles's case, we also have an example of the way in which plays might divide audiences, the popular success of *A Game at Chess* seemingly at odds with Holles's disapproval of the play and its satire of the Spanish (see p. 190). Tomkyns gives us a similar insight into the potential diversity of spectator responses and of the differing criteria playgoers might bring to bear on the plays that they watched when he notes that *The Late Lancashire Witches* proved very popular

> though there be not in it (to my vnderstanding) any poeticall Genius, or art, or language, or iudgement to state oʳ tenet of witches (wᶜʰ I expected,) ₐ or application to vertue but full of ribaldrie and of things improbable and impossible.

Tomkyns is implicitly a little surprised by the play's success, finding it wanting when measured by some of his implicit criteria of quality, which include 'genius', poetic skill, linguistic eloquence and political or moral instruction. At the same time, he shows his awareness that others have enjoyed the play and that there are reasons for this – by his assessment, 'the newnesse of yᵉ subiect' and its combination of comic 'fopperies' with 'diuers songs and dances'.[84] Tomkyns's account thus offers not only an individualized reaction to the play but evidence of differing responses amongst audience members and of spectators' recognition that they might respond in different ways from each other.

Four of Simon Forman's play accounts are preserved in his 'Booke of plaies and Notes hereof per formans for Common policie' and relate to performances that he saw in 1611 at the Globe: *Macbeth* (20 April 1611), *Richard II* (30 April 1611), *The Winter's Tale* (15 May 1611) and *Cymbeline*.[85] But these were not the first plays that Forman had been to see or his first accounts of play performance. His papers suggest that he may have been a regular playgoer, as S. E. Cerasano observes, and they include an additional play summary of a now lost play (*Cox of Collumpton*) which Forman saw at the Rose Theatre (9 March 1600).[86] For Forman playgoing was not simply a recreation 'but part of his social world', Forman using theatre visits 'for courtship and accompanying negotiations'.[87] His play accounts can be seen as similarly self-interested in that they are implicitly shaped by his own concerns and are clearly designed to be of specific use to him. Thus, Forman seems to have been drawn, as Whitney observes, to 'plays featuring specialities of his own, prognostication, magic, and medicine'.[88] This may be why in his account of *Macbeth* Forman pays particular attention to the witches' prophecy and the supernatural encounter with Banquo's ghost, and why Leontes's sending to the oracle of Apollo and the hanging of the wise man who prophesies that John of Gaunt's son will be king feature prominently in his accounts of *The Winter's Tale* and *Richard II*, respectively. Forman's reports suggest a similar interest in feigning, hypocrisy and trickery (reflected in the attention he pays 'the Italian' Iachimo in his account of *Cymbeline* and his listing of several instances of betrayal and perfidy in his summary of *Richard II*). Forman's account of *Macbeth* also points to a special interest in the handling of guilt: as well as an extended description of Macbeth and Lady Macbeth being unable to wash the blood of Duncan from their hands, and an account of Banquo's visitation, Forman concludes his summary by recalling the scene (5.1) in which Lady Macbeth sleepwalks and reveals her guilt before her doctor.[89]

As the full title for Forman's 'Booke of plaies' suggests, he sought to draw lessons in 'Common policie' from the plays that he watched, too, and he does so explicitly in the case of two of the productions: *Richard II* and *The Winter's Tale*. In the case of the now lost play on *Richard II*, he reflects on the downfall of Jack Straw, who is outwitted as a result of what Forman describes as his 'overmoch boldnes', and he draws a pragmatic political lesson: 'in such a case or the like, never admit any party, without a bar betwen, for A man cannot be to wise, nor kepe him self to safe'.[90] Forman reflects rather more bitterly on the case of the 'wise man' hung by John of Gaunt, observing that this 'was a pollicie in the common wealthes opinion. But I sai yt was a villaines parte, and a Judas kisse to hange the man for telling him the truth'. From this example he draws the following distinctly 'anti-aristocratic' lesson:[91] 'Beware by this Example of noble men, and of their fair words, & sai lyttell to them, lest they doe the like by thee for thy good will'.[92] In this instance Forman suggests (like Tomkyns) an awareness that his perspective on the play will not be shared by all, his sympathy for the wise man perhaps heightened by his own experience of being hounded for his pursuit of his magical and oracular arts.[93] Forman concludes his account of *Cymbeline*'s action with a discussion of the play's 'Rog' (presumably Autolycus), this time drawing the moral, 'Beware of trusting feined beggars or fawning fellouss'.[94] In his implicitly pragmatic, utilitarian interest in drama and how it might serve him in his life, Forman is not wholly unusual. The research of scholars such as Charles Whitney has shown that many (especially literate) playgoers of the period were similarly interested in the use(s) to which they might put the plays that they watched and read, suggesting that audience members could be highly active and independent agents when it came to shaping the meaning of contemporary plays.[95]

Case studies

The Valiant Scot

The Valiant Scot is a play that is comparatively little known today and yet its history on the Renaissance stage affords a fascinating example of the way in which the meaning and topicality of plays could change over time. It also affords implicit evidence of audience interests at the open-air Fortune Theatre where it is recorded as being performed in 1639. The play, which borrows from Blind Harry's *Wallace* (a 12-book narrative poem, written c. 1476–8), tells the story of William Wallace, the Scots hero who fought for Scottish independence from the rule of King Edward I (1239–1307) before being captured and executed (1305).[96] In the play, Wallace's resistance of English rule is initially prompted by his father's enforced surrender of his place as Sheriff of Ayre to one of the English-appointed Scottish commissioners and by the seizure of his wife-to-be Peggy by the son of one of the commissioners, Young Selby, both acts which infringe the traditional rights and liberty of the individual in a fashion that would come to seem increasingly topical during the rule of Charles I, the king being accused of a similar disregard for the rights of subjects. Wallace is spurred on in his rebellion by the subsequent murder of Peggy and his father, Old Wallace.[97]

Like the history plays of the Elizabethan stage, *The Valiant Scot* demands a comparatively large cast and incorporates various scenes of on-stage violence, including a sword fight between Wallace and Young Selby (Act 1), a series of running battles between the English and the Scots (Acts 3 and 4), complete with '*Drums and Colours*' (Act 4), and the killing of the two Scots men who betray Wallace, Mentith being killed by Wallace's '*fists*' (Act 5, sig.K2v) and Comin being stabbed in the final moments of the play by Robert the Bruce, the newly appointed ruler of Scotland (Act 5, sig.K3v). Like Blind Harry's treatment of the story, *The Valiant Scot* is implicitly sympathetic to Wallace, presenting his rebellion and quest for revenge as understandable, and characterizing him as charismatic and brave. By contrast, while the play avoids critiquing Edward I directly its representation of the English-appointed commissioners in Scotland and its portrayal of the English is generally unflattering. The notable exception to this ambivalent representation of the English is Clifford, who is shown to be noble and fair, as exemplified by his readiness to acknowledge Wallace's bravery and his sympathy for Wallace's cause (Act 2).

The author of this surprisingly positive treatment of Scottish rebellion in the face of misused English power is not known, the only clue to the author's identity being the initials J. W. and his identification on the play's title-page as a gentleman. The original date of composition of *The Valiant Scot* is also unrecorded, although the play's modern editor argues that internal allusions to war with France, and parallels between Grimsby and infamous Stuart court favourite George Villiers, first Duke of Buckingham, point to a date of composition in the early part of King Charles I's reign (c. 1626–9).[98] Where and for whom the play was written and whether it was performed following its initial composition are other questions for which we have no answers. What we do know is that on 26 April 1637 the play was entered in the Stationers' Register, being printed for the first time later that year by John Waterson. It appeared with a dedication to one of the leading Scottish nobles, James Hamilton, first Duke of Hamilton (sig. A2v). The occasion for printing the play would seem to lie in unfolding events north of the English border. As John Kerrigan has recently pointed out, the publication of J. W.'s celebration of Scottish rebellion in the face of 'tyrannous' English rule was both 'timely' and prescient in 1637: 'This was the year in which the union of 1603 began to fragment. On top of decades of distant, sometimes uncongenial government from London, the Scots were now required to accept a crypto-Anglican prayerbook', an imposition that led to mass protest and the founding of the so-called Covenanting movement after the national Covenant they signed in 1638 signalling their opposition to interference by the Stuart kings in the Church of Scotland.[99]

With the outbreak of open conflict between Scotland and England in mid-1639 and England's failure against the Scottish forces in the so-called First Bishops War the play became even more topical. The war with Scotland was one for which there was little appetite in England, many contemporaries reportedly feeling 'considerable support for the Covenanters'.[100] This appears to have been especially true amongst English puritans, many of whom felt similar reservations to those expressed by the Covenanters about the religious policies of Charles I and his Archbishop, William Laud. It is against this complex political and religious backdrop that we learn that *The Valiant Scot* was reputedly staged at the Fortune Theatre in May 1639.

Our only record of the play's revival is preserved in a contemporary pamphlet, *Vox Borealis, or The Northern Discoverie* (1641), presented as a dialogue about recent events in Scotland between two Scotsmen, Jamie and Willie. The pamphlet is prefaced by a satirical poem that mocks prelates. It is signed by its printer, 'Margery Mar-Prelat' (sig.A2v), the choice of name an obvious homage to 'Martin Marprelate', the pen-name adopted by the author(s) of a series of scurrilous attacks on bishops and the prelacy in the Elizabethan period. It is in the context of the pamphlet's sustained attack on the prelacy that we learn of *The Valiant Scot*'s alleged performance, Jamie telling the story as one of two cases of the prelacy acting 'against the poore Players of the *Fortune* Play-house'. According to Jamie, the company got 'a new old Play', called *The Cardinal's Conspiracy* which

> they brought upon the *Stage* in as great *state* as they could, with *Altars*, *Images*, *Crosses*, *Crucifixes*, and the like, to set forth his pomp and pride. But wofull was the sight to see, how in the middest of all their *mirth*, the Pursevants came and seazed upou the poore Cardinall, and all his Consorts, and carried them away. And when they were questioned for it, in the High Commission Court, they pleaded *Ignoranse*, and told the Archbishop, *that they tooke those examples of their Altars, Images*, and the like, *from Heathen Authors*. This did somewhat asswage his anger, that they did not bring him on the Stage: But yet they were fined for it, and after a *little Imprisonment* gat their *liberty*. And having nothing left them but a few old Swords and Bucklers, they fell to Act the *Valiant Scot*, which they Played five dayes with great applause, which vext the Bishops worse then the other, insomuch, as they were forbidden Playing it any more; and some of them prohibited ever Playing againe.[101]

Although the polemical use to which the tale is put and the fact that there is no other reference to *The Valiant Scot* being performed at the Fortune Theatre could suggest that this is a politic fabrication, the specificity of the story and the fact that another contemporary source confirms the performance of *The Cardinal's Conspiracy* at the Fortune in May 1639 tends to reinforce its veracity.[102] Jamie's account of the two play performances provides a context for understanding why and how *The Valiant Scot* was revived and the ways in which it might have been tailored for audiences at the Fortune in 1639 by its players, if not its original author.

In 1639 the acting company performing at the Fortune Theatre and implicitly responsible for the performances of both *The Cardinal's Conspiracy* and *The Valiant Scot* was a troupe known as the Red Bull players. Not much is known about this 'shadowy group of players', although the company appears to have been formed around 1626, starting life at the Red Bull Theatre before moving to the neighbouring Fortune Theatre (1634) and then back to the Red Bull around Easter 1640.[103] Comparatively little is known about the troupe's repertory. Andrew Gurr lists only four plays as definitely belonging to the troupe: J. W.'s *The Valiant Scot*, the anonymous *The Cardinal's Conspiracy* (lost), J. D.'s *The Knave in Grain* and *The Seven Champions of Christendom*, a tragicomic romance written by company member John Kirke which glances at contemporary religious tensions between Catholics, Protestants and Puritans.[104] Although their known plays are few, collectively they point to a generically diverse repertory including history, tragedy, tragicomedy and comedy, while the obvious contemporary relevance of the plays performed in 1639 suggests an interest in topical political and religious drama.

Like Prince Charles's players who performed at the Red Bull in the 1630s, the Red Bull company at the Fortune had a reputation for loud, grandiose acting and for the performance of old-fashioned heroic and comic drama, while their audiences were often stereotyped by contemporaries as predominantly plebeian and vulgar in their tastes; but there are reasons to question both stereotypes, as noted above (p. 107), and closer consideration of the troupe's performance of *The Valiant Scot* arguably provides further grounds for doing so. On the face of it, the decision to perform *The Valiant Scot* might seem to confirm conventional prejudices about the taste of players and audiences at the Fortune for old 'drum and trumpet' dramas. The play was not new in 1639 and it does include drums, trumpets and a series of on-stage battles; it also features clowning of the kind often associated with vulgar tastes in the Caroline era. However, when the Red Bull players chose to revive the play they implicitly did so not because it was old-fashioned or full of battles (although these may have been part of its appeal); they revived it because it was politically topical. It invited the drawing of parallels with contemporary events in Scotland, parallels that would have been even more obvious and provocative in performance, as the company brought on stage actors dressed as English and Scottish soldiers, the latter complete with their traditional 'blew Caps' (Act 3, sig.G3) and the former carrying the same 'old Swords and Bucklers' reputedly employed by the English troops sent to Scotland.[105]

Given the play's sympathetic treatment of the Scots and the unflattering representation of most of the English characters, *The Valiant Scot* was a provocative and politically engaged choice of play in mid-1639, offering an implicit critique of Charles I's 'contemporaneous attempt to impose ecclesiastical conformity on the Scots by military force'.[106] In this context, the troupe's production of *The Valiant Scot* can be seen as complementing its preceding performance of *The Cardinal's Conspiracy*. Although the players claimed that the latter was an 'old' play, too, and denied that they made any reference to current affairs or individuals, it is clear that *The Cardinal's Conspiracy* was understood to offer a critique of the Church reforms promulgated by Archbishop Laud within the Church of England, with the support of Charles I. In choosing to follow up its suppressed performance with a production of *The Valiant Scot* the Red Bull players were implicitly continuing their critique of royal religious and political policy, J. W.'s Scottish play open to symbolic interpretation in 1639 as an attack on royal policy in Scotland and upon Charles I's perceived infringement of the rights of subjects on both sides of the border during the 1630s. That the two performances were seen as connected in this way is suggested in Jamie's account, in which he claims that those most angered by the production of *The Valiant Scot* were the bishops.

Whatever the players' agenda, the production was a commercial success, reputedly running for 'five dayes with great applause'.[107] If the Fortune Theatre could accommodate up to 3,000 people like the Globe (as is thought likely), this could mean that the play was seen by as many as 15,000 people. While many of these spectators may have been 'plebeian' playgoers there is no reason to assume that these were the only kinds of people drawn to this production. We know that at least some members of society's elites continued to visit the open-air theatres up until the 1640s and it is entirely possible that a politically controversial production of the kind represented by the revival of *The Valiant Scot* owed its five-day run to its success in drawing large, socially diverse audiences, rather like the King's Men's production of Middleton's topical *A Game at Chess* (Globe, 1624).

The Red Bull players were not alone in their performance of topical, politicized drama in the late 1630s. There is evidence of Prince Charles's players at the Red Bull also performing satirical dramas about current affairs in this era and finding themselves in similar trouble with the authorities as a result, as when they staged *The Whore New Vamped* in 1639 (see pp. 143–4). In their implicit challenging of royal policies *The Valiant Scot* and *The Cardinal's Conspiracy* can also be seen as anticipating plays such as Brome's *The Court Beggar* and its satire of Charles's campaign against the Scots and Shirley's *The Cardinal* (written for the Blackfriars) which dramatizes the downfall of a scheming prelate who was probably seen as a figure for Laud, then in the Tower of London.[108]

Contemporaries may have caricatured the open-air theatres and their audiences as vulgar and conservative in their theatrical tastes but the example of the Red Bull players' performances in the late 1630s suggests that it is a mistake to equate the performance of old plays with being entirely old-fashioned or crude in one's tastes, for the Red Bull players appear to have used such texts in highly topical, politically challenging ways. This is in keeping with Martin Butler's observation that 'such traces as we have tend to suggest that it was the popular rather than the elite theatres which staged plays directly commenting on or dealing with recent affairs' in the Caroline era.[109] If the playing companies performing at the open-air theatres were suiting their repertories to the 'capacity' and tastes of their audiences, this suggests that spectators at the Fortune and Red Bull Theatres were not straightforwardly conservative or lowly in their interests, whatever their social background. They may have enjoyed theatrically old-fashioned genres, but their taste for plays such as *The Valiant Scot* suggests that they had as keen an interest in current affairs as those who attended the indoor theatres, and that the differences between repertories and audience tastes may not have been as great as contemporaries and critics have sometimes suggested. Indeed, the more overt political and religious satire associated with the open-air theatres in the 1630s could be evidence that these theatres played an earlier part in the emerging oppositional political culture in London than the era's indoor playhouses. As such they, their repertories and their audiences arguably merit more serious scholarly attention than they have generally received.

A Jovial Crew

Richard Brome's comedy *A Jovial Crew* belongs to the same theatrical era as *The Valiant Scot*, first being acted some time in 1641. The play tells the story of Master Oldrents, a rich and generous land-owner who is plunged into depression after a gypsy, Patrico, tells him that his two daughters, Rachel and Meriel, will be made beggars. Unable to cheer their father and unaware of the gypsy's prophecy, Rachel and Meriel decide to leave home and dress up as beggars, accompanied by their suitors, Vincent and Hilliard. They are helped in their adventure by Master Oldrents's steward, and a one-time vagabond, Springlove, whose enduring love of the wandering beggars' life leads him to request leave to return to that life temporarily every spring. The daughters and their lovers soon discover that the beggars' life is not as idyllic as they have imagined and that its freedoms come at the cost of hardship. Back home, the departure of his daughters and his steward leads Oldrents to give up his grieving and resolve to devote himself entirely to merriment in a way that is shown to be as 'over-done' as his previous grief over the prophecy.[110] The play culminates with the pretend beggars being arrested and having to earn their freedom by performing a play before Master Clack, the justice and his guests, including Oldrents. The play they choose to stage alludes to Oldrents's own story, dramatizing his meeting with the gypsy and featuring his disguised daughters, Springlove and Patrico. Oldrents interrupts the play to grant his forgiveness to his steward and daughters, who each renounce the wandering life of the beggar; then, in a further twist it is revealed that Oldrents once had a child with Patrico's now dead sister, and that this child is Springlove, whom Oldrents promptly grants a thousand pounds a year.

Brome wrote the play for the King and Queen's Young Company (also known as Beeston's Boys), formed by Christopher Beeston in 1637. Despite being first named as 'Boys' it 'seems to have been neither a boy company of the old type, nor yet an adult company like the others', mostly including youths but also some adult players.[111] The large number of youth players may help to explain Brome's inclusion of 4 female roles amongst the play's 24 speaking parts, while the play's incorporation of music, songs and dancing in three of its five acts could be evidence that the troupe included youths especially talented in music and movement and that they sought to exploit this, as did the early boy companies that emerged from the London choral schools. Beeston's Boys were based at the Cockpit, the indoor theatre set up by Christopher Beeston in 1616 to rival the Second Blackfriars Theatre. Converted from an old cockpit on Drury Lane, the theatre was much smaller than the open-air playhouses with a capacity for about 700 spectators.[112] Like the other indoor theatres, the prices at the Cockpit were much higher than at the open-air theatres and the audience is thus likely to have been dominated by privileged members of society, although this does not mean that its audiences were without social diversity.

Scholars have long recognized the topical nature of works such as Brome's *The Court Beggar,* but they have been slower to see *A Jovial Crew* in these terms. In fact, scholars have often regarded the play as escapist. R. J. Kaufman argues that *A Jovial Crew* 'though superficially realistic and buoyant' is 'more profoundly escapist than' his 'far more fantastic and remote heroic plays'.[113] However, in its preoccupation with personal liberty, duty and patriarchal power and responsibilities, the play can be seen as deeply topical, for these were contentious issues in a society in which many were worried about Charles I's apparent infringements of the rights and liberties of subjects. Indeed, it is probably no coincidence that Oldrents is, in many ways, set up as an exemplary patriarch, being praised as a 'Landlord', a 'Master', a 'Patron' (1.1.126, 127) and a 'great House-keeper' (4.1. 2016), who is prayed for by his tenants 'as duly as / For King and Realme' (1.1.106–7). Juxtaposed with this celebration of Oldrents's generous, kindly exercise of his patriarchal power is the play's early preoccupation with the limits of his authority and the importance of respecting the personal liberty of those subject to him. This is made most explicit in his conversation with Springlove about the steward's request for leave to go wandering for a time. Oldrents tries to persuade Springlove to overcome what he calls his 'gadding humour', but the steward defends his wish to roam citing the power of nature: ''tis the season of the year that calls me. / What moves her Noats, provokes my disposition / By a more absolute power of *Nature*, then / Philosophy can render an accompt for' (1.1.216–19). Perhaps even more pointedly, Springlove talks of his 'inborn strong desire of liberty' (1.1.302), and defends his right to exercise it, arguing that where 'duty is exacted it is none' (1.1.311).

That the play is engaged with, rather than seeking to escape from, current social and political anxieties is perhaps made even clearer in Brome's handling of the beggars' commonwealth, with Springlove and Oldrents's daughters and their lovers all prompted to reflect on the nature of liberty and what makes a 'free state' by their experience of this other society (see, for example, 2.1.575–99, 742–95). That Brome is concerned with the 'sad and tragic daies' (Prologue.3) in which he writes becomes even more apparent when the beggar-poet Scribble talks of wishing to stage a play in which he would 'present a Common-wealth' (4.2.2535), including 'a *Gentleman*, a *Mer- / Chant*, a *Courtier*, and a *Souldier*' as representatives of 'The *Country*, the *City*, the *Court*, and the *Camp*' (4.2.2538–40). He goes on to describe how he

> would have the *Country*, the *City*, and the
> *Court*, be at great variance for *Superiority*. Then would
> I have *Divinity* and *Law* stretch their wide throats
> to appease and reconcile them: Then would I have
> the *Souldier* cudgell them all together, and overtop
> them all.

> (4.2.2564–9)

As Julie Sanders notes, Scribble's drama is 'chillingly prescient of events in the country following the performance of Brome's play'.[114]

Whether *A Jovial Crew* teaches any moral or has any answers to offer in the face of the incipient social problems in his own society is something about which there has been less agreement, even amongst those who share the view that the play is a commentary on Brome's troubled times. Ira Clark argues that Brome's plays generally offer 'an exhortation to face sociopolitical problems' without offering 'principles on which change might be based or goals to which it could conform'.[115] By contrast, Rosemary Gaby argues that the play makes its audience aware of the 'foolishness' of indulging in 'romantic fantasy' and thus implicitly teaches a topically pointed lesson, especially to the Caroline court, with its well-known taste for pastoral romance.[116] In its consistent praise of Oldrents's generosity as a host and patron the play seems to advocate a paternalistic model of society and traditional country values such as hospitality which were felt to be in decline in the Caroline era. Indeed, as Garrett A. Sullivan Jr notes, the play can be seen as using Oldrents to offer 'an idealized image of estate management' and by extension an ideal model of rule for the larger body politic of England.[117] Equally, the play seems to acknowledge the need for society's patriarchs to be measured in their 'rule' and the importance of respecting the liberty of the individual; while the experiences of Rachel, Meriel and Springlove emphasize the importance of balancing one's desire for freedom and personal liberty with one's duty and responsibility to others. Indeed, 'absolute' freedom (2.1.594), like absolute authority, is shown to be problematic. In this way it could be argued with Martin Butler that the play offers both 'a sharp rebuke to the court for its economic and political bankruptcy' and 'a morality of social and political responsibility'.[118] Whether its audiences saw it in this way is not documented, although the play's underlying royalism perhaps explains the later support Brome gained from well-known royalist patron of poets and translators, and dedicatee of the first printed edition of the play, Thomas Stanley.[119] At the very least, the play's covert political agenda implies that the people who attended the Cockpit on the eve of the civil war were deeply interested in current affairs and in dramas which engaged with them, in which respect their tastes appear to have differed little from those attending open-air theatres such as the Fortune, whatever their differences in class or social status.

5

Patrons and patronage

Belch.   *But whose men are wee all this while:*
Post-hast. *Whose but the merry Knight's, sir* Oliver Owlets,
There was neuer a better man to Players.[1]

Patronage and players

Like Sir Oliver Owlet's players, most English Renaissance
acting companies performed under the name of a royal or
noble patron. The tradition of elite patronage of acting
companies can be traced back to the medieval era when it
became customary for the monarch and his/her leading nobles
to retain servants who could provide entertainment during
holiday periods. In 1591 Elizabethan commentator Samuel
Cox recalled how 'in ancient former times' such actors only
performed 'in the time of Christmas, beginning to play in the
holidays and continuing until twelfth tide, or at the furthest
until Ashwednesday'. According to Cox, those who enter-
tained the monarch 'had other trades to live of, and seldom
or never played abroad at any other times of the whole year',
while those who 'pertained to noblemen' were 'ordinary
servants in their house, and only for Christmas times used
such plays, without making profession to be players to go
abroad for gain'.[2] This system appears to have continued into

early Tudor period, but by the late sixteenth century the nature of aristocratic patronage of players and the relationship between players and their patrons was rather different, players usually being entitled to use the name and to wear the livery of their patron but not generally being based in their patron's household or receiving board or regular wages from him/her.[3]

That patrons' financial commitment to playing companies was often negligible by the Elizabethan era would seem to be confirmed by instances of companies collapsing as a result of financial failure, sometimes in dramatic fashion, as in the case of the Earl of Pembroke's troupe in the summer of 1593. As Philip Henslowe reported to Edward Alleyn (28 September 1593), Pembroke's players were 'all at home ... for they cane not saue ther carges' [charges] and had been forced to pawn their apparel.[4] That players were expected to fend for themselves economically by the Elizabethan era probably explains why in 1572 James Burbage and his fellow players were careful to ask their patron Robert Dudley, Earl of Leicester, only for their 'liveries as we have had, and also your honors License to certifye that we are your houshold Servaunts when we shall have occasion to travayle amongst our frendes as we do usuallye once a yere'.[5] By the late sixteenth century most patronized companies, including Burbage and his peers, implicitly expected to earn their money not as household servants but by performing in London and/or on tour, in towns, cities and private houses for a variety of other patrons. It was not a change that all welcomed, as is suggested by the scathing complaint of the anonymous author of *A Second and Third Blast of Retrait from Plaies and Theaters* (1580) that noble players were now 'beggers' rather than the 'seruants' of the men and women whose names they used.[6]

Powerful men and women were expected to act as generous patrons of others, generosity and charity being regarded as duties and deemed markers of nobility, but lending one's name to an acting company, and especially one that toured or performed in the capital, was also a potentially powerful way of advertising one's name, wealth and status. This is

probably why 'it was not uncommon for membership on
the Privy Council to coincide with increased activity as a
patron of performers', as Mary Blackstone notes, nor is it
likely to be a coincidence that the royal company toured the
most regularly and widely in Elizabethan England.[7] Like the
country progresses of Elizabeth I, the touring of her players
served to carry her name and authority around the land, her
entertainers serving as her representatives and, some scholars
have argued, potential couriers and spies for her government.[8]
Such politic considerations may even have underpinned the
decision to form the new company of Queen's Men in 1583,
the 1580s being an era when 'good public relations between
crown and people were clearly of urgent importance', as
Elizabeth I faced growing threats at home and abroad,
especially from Catholics.[9]

For some at least, patronizing an acting company was a
way of indulging an interest in theatre, too. Indeed, Leeds
Barroll argues that 'a partiality to public drama' may have
been *the* 'incentive for aristocratic patronage' in many cases.[10]
Certainly, there is considerable evidence of contemporary
aristocratic interest in public plays. As well as attending the
London playhouses and sometimes hosting play performances
at their town and country residences, there is evidence of
aristocrats reading and sometimes even writing plays for the
public theatre. In June 1599 William Stanley, sixth Earl of
Derby, was rumoured to be 'busy penning comedies for the
common players', while his estranged wife apologetically
petitioned her powerful uncle, Sir Robert Cecil to ask that
her husband's players be allowed to perform in the capital
'for that my lord taking delite in them, it will kepe him from
mor prodigall courses'; and William Percy, the third son of
the twelfth Earl of Northumberland, wrote at least six extant
plays, including five composed between 1601 and 1603 which
he appears to have offered to the Children of St. Paul's.[11]

Theatrical interests were not confined to male patrons
either. We know that at least some noblewomen shared a taste
for drama, visiting playhouses, reading and writing plays

and occasionally patronizing acting companies.[12] Lady Mary Herbert (née Sidney) is one of the period's best-known women writers and the translator of Robert Garnier's Senecan drama *Marc Antoine*, but she was renowned for her patronage of individual writers and playwrights such as Samuel Daniel, too, and could have had some role in her husband's decision to patronize a London company in late 1591 or early 1592.[13] She certainly appears to have had connections with contemporary actors, being mentioned as a potential benefactor in the 1592 will of Simon Jewell, an actor thought to have been a member of the Queen's players.[14] Similarly, although Alice (née Spencer), Countess of Derby does not appear to have written plays she assumed the patronage of her husband's acting company briefly following his death in 1594, the troupe receiving a reward in Winchester in May under her name.[15] Leeds Barroll suspects that the Dowager Countess had some part to play in the transfer of several of the players later that same year to the newly formed Lord Chamberlain's troupe, too, her sister being married to the Lord Chamberlain's son, George Carey.[16]

Royal or noble patronage lent players status and potentially secured them lucrative invitations to perform at court and on tour, as is suggested by the career of the Earl of Leicester's players. Although Dudley did not pay his actors 'quarterly wages', his prestigious support as royal favourite is likely to have been responsible – at least in part – for his troupe's regular invitation to perform at court, the company playing at least once there at Christmas or Shrovetide every year from 1572 to 1581.[17] The name of a high-profile patron was likely to attract players more generous rewards, too, as is demonstrated by the fact that royal players generally enjoyed the most lavish payments when on tour.

That the way civic authorities treated patronized playing companies was often closely tied to the reputation of their patrons is occasionally made explicit, as in the records of Gloucester. In 1580–1 the city passed an ordinance regulating the number of performances visiting players were to be allowed to give in future, limiting them according to the social status of their patrons, 'the Queenes ma*iestes* Players' being allowed to perform three times during each visit, the players of barons being allowed to play twice and the players of lesser patrons only being allowed to play once.[18] As Peter Greenfield observes, such evidence strongly suggests that civic hosts saw players 'primarily as representatives of their patrons', and that when they treated them well it was out of respect for and, in some cases, a politic desire to curry favour with, the powerful patrons that the players represented, as much as a wish to display their own civic power and largesse.[19] The prestige of players' patrons appears to have informed the kind of welcome that they could expect at private houses, too. Indeed, some opponents of the stage accused players of using their patrons' names to extort generous rewards from those they visited on tour, as in *A Second and Third Blast of Retrait from Plaies and Theaters* where it is claimed that often 'the goodwill men beare to their Lordes, makes them drawe the stringes of their purses to extend their liberalitie to them'.[20]

Elite patronage became even more important for acting companies in 1572 with a proclamation calling for the execution of the statutes against unlawful retainers and a new Act for the Punishment of Vagabonds and for Relief of the Poor and Impotent that restricted touring performances to acting companies with royal or noble patrons or those with the permission of two Justices of the Peace.[21] These edicts appear to have prompted James Burbage and his fellow Lord Leicester's players to contact their patron to crave his written licence acknowledging them as his 'houshold Servaunts and daylie wayters'.[22] Mary Blackstone interprets the 1572 act, like the later formation of the new Queen's Men in 1583, as 'an indirect means of reminding ... civic officials of the prestige, privilege and power of the monarch and her noblemen'.[23] If this was indeed one of the motives for the 1572 act, its assertion of royal and aristocratic authority was made even clearer in 1598 when it was revised so that Justices of the Peace were no longer able to license players. Under the early

Stuarts the number of acting companies officially permitted to perform was curbed further with patronage of players officially limited to the royal family.[24]

Patrons and players

The nature of the connections between players and their patrons is more difficult to establish, not least because these relationships appear to have been little documented. There is, for instance, little information about the role patrons played (if any) in the formation and dissolution of companies. Thus, although there has been fascinating research upon the possible role of courtiers such as Sir Francis Walsingham in the formation of the Queen's Men in 1583 and about the part played by the Lord Chamberlain and Lord Admiral in the emergence of the so-called 'duopoly' of the Lord Chamberlain's and Lord Admiral's Men in 1594, there is no direct evidence for their involvement in these events.[25] Information about the relationships between patrons and players is similarly scarce. In some cases, there is little or no evidence of patrons engaging directly with their acting companies or their plays. Andrew Gurr argues that this is largely true of the successive patrons of the company which started life as the Lord Admiral's Men – Charles Howard (Lord Admiral), Prince Henry and Frederick V Lord Palsgrave (later Elector Palatine) – although Howard at least did act to assist his players on occasion and seems to have enjoyed a long-term connection with one of the troupe's leading actors, Edward Alleyn.[26]

Other patrons appear to have taken a more active interest in their actors, commissioning them to perform before them and on their behalf, and intervening to assist them on occasion. Although Robert Dudley, Earl of Leicester did not pay his players an annual wage and only seems to have hosted them at his residences occasionally, he made sure to take them on his military expedition to the Low Countries in 1585, as part of his politic display of his own power and the power of the English, and he is among those noble patrons known to have acted most directly to assist his players.[27] As early as June 1559 we find him supporting a group of players travelling under his name, writing a letter to the Earl of Shrewsbury, then Lord President of the North, asking that his 'plaiers of interludes' having the licence of 'diuerse of my lordis here vnder ther seales and handis, to plaie in diuerse shieres w[th]in the realme' might have the Earl's 'hand and seale to ther licence for the like libertye in yorke shiere'.[28] As William Ingram notes, Dudley's letter appears to have been written in response to the issuing on 16 May 1559 of a proclamation requiring that 'all ... interludes to be played either openly or privately' be licensed by two Justices of the Peace or 'such as shall be lieutenants for the Queen's majesty in the same shire'.[29] Dudley's readiness to act to protect his players' right to perform would also seem to be suggested by the fact that his players were the first to receive a royal patent to act (10 May 1574), implicitly following his lobbying at court on their behalf.[30]

Patrons sometimes intervened to defend their players, too, especially in the face of potential prosecution by civic authorities. In 1583 Sir Walter Waller of Groomsbridge in Kent, a man with a reputation for ambition and for being something of a bully, was quick to defend his players when they were arrested in Brasted by local puritan Justice, Thomas Potter, after allegedly proclaiming their intention to perform a play in the town without proper permission. Coming to the town Waller reportedly sent for the constable

> & seyinge his sayde warrant for y[e] caryinge of those .v. persons to y[e] gaole, he sayd, y[t] they were hys men all of them, & no rog*es* ..., & y[t] your supplyant was a knave & a villayne & y[e] soon of a vyllayne & of a knave.[31]

Waller later defended the men against the charge of being travelling rogues and vagabonds by claiming that they were not professional players but rather his 'howseholde s*ervauntes*' who had come to Brasted 'to meete wth me at my retorne from London'.[32] Waller's intervention was effective, in so far as the men were subsequently released into his custody, but his provocative language later got the self-proclaimed patron into trouble, Potter insisting that the case be brought to the attention of the Privy Council. While Waller may have been economical with the truth when he claimed that the players who visited Brasted were his paid household servants, it is clear that Waller's anger did not stem simply from a wish to protect the players, but rather from a perceived insult to himself and he later claimed in his pleading letter to Sir Francis Walsingham that Potter was motivated to arrest the players by the 'cankred mallice' the Justice bore himself.[33] There may have been some truth in the claim: as a suspected Catholic-sympathizer and vocal champion of players Waller was precisely the kind of man that a puritan-minded Justice such as Potter might be expected to oppose. At the same time, the case offers a fascinating insight into how fiercely some patrons were ready to defend their players and how seriously some officials took the 1572 act policing players and those allowed to be patrons.[34]

Patrons and players' repertories

One of the most intriguing questions posed by the system of elite patronage of playing companies in Elizabethan and Early Stuart England is whether patrons had any influence on the plays performed by the players carrying their names and thus might have used their players to advance their own ideological agendas. In some cases, especially in the early Elizabethan era, the question is all but impossible to resolve because of the loss of the plays performed by the royal and noble companies of the day. But the question remains difficult to answer even in the case of those companies whose history is better documented and whose plays are better preserved. In the case of many companies there appears to be no particular connection between the plays that they performed and the documented views and interests of their patrons; in others it seems that there is. Some acting companies appear to have commissioned plays which included strategic, flattering allusions to their patrons or their patrons' families. Andrew Gurr detects possible allusions of this sort to the Stanley family in Shakespeare's early history plays, thought to have been written for Lord Strange's Men, the company patronized by Ferdinando Stanley, Lord Strange.[35] More famously, Shakespeare's *Macbeth*, written for the King's Men, is often seen as a play written in response to King James I's well-documented fascination with magic; and *King Lear* appears to endorse the new king's wish to re-establish the ancient kingdom of Britain through the union of Scotland and England. As the latter example suggests, acting companies may have chosen to perform plays which promoted the views of their patrons, too, acting as potential 'apostles' for their patron within and beyond the patron's household.[36] Paul Whitfield White argues that there is strong reason to believe that at least some of the plays performed by the Earl of Leicester's players in the 1560s and 1570s advanced the militant Protestantism Leicester famously championed; and, in their pioneering study of the Queen's Men, Sally-Beth MacLean and Scott McMillin suggest that the royal troupe was formed from the cream of the Elizabethan acting world 'to spread Protestant and royalist propaganda through a divided realm' in similar fashion.[37] However, although there is evidence of 'state-sanctioned propaganda for the stage' of this kind in the early and mid-sixteenth century, there is no known evidence 'of any direct intervention by patrons with the players who wore their livery over what they might play in their repertory' in the Elizabethan and early Stuart eras, as Andrew Gurr observes.[38]

On the contrary, there is some evidence of acting companies performing plays either at odds with the reported views of their patrons or which engage with those views in more challenging ways, as when the King's Men performed a series of 'distinctly edgy' plays in the 1620s and 1630s. This included a series of dramas concerned with tyrannical rulers and the abuse of subjects' rights (such as Philip Massinger's *The Roman Actor*), which appear to reflect contemporary anxieties about the absolutist tendencies of the Stuart monarchs.[39] Indeed, the repertory of the King's Men is especially fascinating in what it reveals about the potentially varying, complex influence of a patron's interests upon a company's repertory, as will be illustrated in this chapter through a case study of two of their plays: Middleton's *A Game at Chess*, which infamously attacked the Spanish and an ex-Spanish ambassador shortly after King James had been seeking a Spanish match for his son and heir, Prince Charles (possibly with the support of the Lord Chamberlain, William Herbert, third Earl of Pembroke), and Brome's and Heywood's *The Late Lancashire Witches*, which dramatized the contemporary case of a group of women accused of witchcraft, and which appears to have made use of material presented privately to the Privy Council supporting the charges against them. The latter fact has led some scholars to speculate that the play was written at the instigation not of the company's official patron (Charles I), but of another powerful courtier with access to the case materials, Philip Herbert, fourth Earl of Pembroke, brother to William Herbert and leader of the puritan faction at court. Pembroke, it is argued, hoped to embarrass Archbishop Laud, the leader of the rival religious faction at court, and a well-known sceptic regarding witchcraft, by promoting the case against the Lancashire women. The possible involvement of the Herbert brothers in these plays' appearance on stage suggests that players and playwrights were not necessarily only answerable to their own named patrons but might have been persuaded to serve the interests of other informal patrons, too.

As the example of the Herberts and their relations with the King's Men suggests there is also evidence of individual royal and noble patrons taking an interest in, and sometimes helping, players and playwrights besides those who worked directly in their names, further complicating our understanding of elite patronage of drama in Renaissance England. Robert Dudley, Earl of Leicester, not only patronized his own company of players but reportedly 'befriended' the Elizabethan 'children's companies', intervening to protect Sebastian Westcote, the recusant manager of the Children of St. Paul's from prosecution and to assist William Hunnis, Master of the Children of the Chapel Royal, when he petitioned the company's landlord for permission to continue performing in the First Blackfriars Theatre.[40] Similarly, in 1599 the Earl of Derby was not only said to be writing plays for the common players but, according to contemporary Rowland Whyte, to have 'put up the playes of the children of Pawles to his great paines and charge'.[41] In the seventeenth century the Herberts were among the most famous champions of the players. In 1619 William Herbert intervened, in his capacity as Lord Chamberlain, to insist that the 'King's Men should continue to receive their accustomed allowances, even though Lionel Cranfield, the new Master of the Wardrobe, wished to cut them in his efforts to reduce court expenses'. He wrote to the Stationers' Company in the same year 'forbidding them to print any of their plays without the actors' consent'. It is possible that the family played host to players at their country residences, too. The Pembroke domestic accounts from this era do not survive but we know that the Lord Chamberlain's Men performed for King James during a visit to the Pembroke's house at Wilton (2 December 1603) and that players were frequent visitors to the neighbouring town of Marlborough between 1590 and 1622.[42] Given the town's small size, Peter Davison suggests that one of the main reasons for players' visits is likely to have been the proximity of Wilton, 'thirty miles to the south' and the possibility of visiting the drama-loving Herberts.[43] Confirmation of the Herberts' importance as patrons of drama is arguably found in the many play dedications that they received, including being joint dedicatees of the Shakespeare First Folio (1623). Evidence of more personal connections with the acting fraternity of the day survives, too. Setting aside the debates about whether William Herbert could be the mysterious 'Mr.

W. H.', dedicatee of Shakespeare's *Sonnets* (1609), we know that Herbert was well acquainted with the players, famously writing of his reluctance to attend a court performance in 1619 because he still mourned for the troupe's leading player, who had died earlier that year: as he explained he 'being tender harted, could not endure to see' the play 'so soone after the loss of my old acquaintance Burbadg'.[44]

There is evidence of aristocrats sometimes patronizing performances by players who were not their own, too. On more than one occasion the Earl of Leicester hosted performances by the Queen's players, a troupe that included several actors previously part of his own company, suggesting both his wish to honour his royal mistress but perhaps also an on-going connection with players that he had once sponsored.[45] More controversially the Lord Chamberlain's Men were paid by a group of supporters of the Earl of Essex to stage a special performance of *Richard II* at the Globe Theatre in 1601 on the eve of the Earl's ill-fated rebellion against the queen. As Leeds Barroll observes, it is striking that the Earl's followers 'seem to have had no qualms in actually hiring the Lord Chamberlain's Servants for their own subversive aims'. The Privy Council's subsequent intervention in the case, including the interviewing of a representative of the company (Augustine Phillips), is revealing in a different way, suggesting that 'the state did not require (or could not depend on) anticipatory policing of players even by those officers of the Crown whose names the companies bore', including the Lord Chamberlain.[46]

The decline of elite patronage of players

Suzanne R. Westfall, one of the leading scholars of Renaissance dramatic patronage, has argued that theatre in England up until 1583 and even 'well after that' was 'a patron's theatre', in that royal and aristocratic patronage was key to its existence and its growth.[47] By the eve of the civil war and the closure of the public theatres in London in 1642 this was no longer true in the same way: the traditional system of aristocratic dramatic patronage was in decline.[48] How and why elite patronage of acting companies declined in the early seventeenth century are complex questions. Part of the explanation probably lies in the changing nature of dramatic patronage and of attitudes towards patronage and patrons. Increasing legal restrictions on the patronage of players in the Elizabethan period, followed by the concentration of dramatic patronage in the hands of the royal family, left would-be aristocratic (and lesser) patrons of acting companies increasingly marginalized. Rather than patronizing his/her own company, aristocrats and gentry were obliged to show their support for the theatre and/or individual playwrights, players and playing companies in less formal ways, exercising influence 'through their positions at Court, or more informally as friends or acquaintances of the actors or playwrights'.[49]

The narrowing of opportunities for dramatic patronage, combined with the fact that there appears to have been growing antagonism to the centralization of power in the court and its officials and a decline in the prestige of patrons and in respect for the patronage system more generally, meant that patrons' names no longer exercised the same influence or afforded players the same protection, especially outside London.[50]

Just as the power of patrons and their names was in decline, so the thriving of the commercial theatres and the financial independence they offered meant that acting companies were increasingly autonomous economically and artistically. This 'may have led to' or encouraged what Mary Blackstone characterizes as 'a more distanced relationship between the player and the patron'.[51] At the same time, the London actors had a newly pressing patron to cater for: the paying public in the theatres. Players had long played publicly on tour and in the capital but the playhouses of late Elizabethan London promised regular access to large, controlled audiences and thus a steady income and a new stability, whereas players wholly reliant on individual patrons were always in some way vulnerable, as patrons could die or choose not to continue their patronage. Werner Gundersheimer wonders whether Shakespeare might have come to favour 'the support of the London crowds to that of a single *patronus*' and whether this might serve to demonstrate in microcosm a broader cultural shift from aristocratic patronage of the arts towards a commercialized – and more democratic – theatre world in which the paying 'customers' were 'the new patrons'.[52] This was certainly the way that some contemporaries saw it. In John Stephens's *Satyrical Essayes Characters and Others* (1615), a 'common Player' is defined as one who 'howsoever he pretends to haue a royall Master, or Mistresse, his wages and dependance proue him to bee the servant of the people'.[53]

There was, however, no simple displacement of one type of patronage (individual) by another (public), nor any straightforward transition from the system of individual dramatic patrons to the world of independent professional theatre. Like his contemporaries, Shakespeare arguably 'did not "prefer" either elite or public support, he enjoyed both simultaneously'.[54] As Suzanne R. Westfall notes, by 'the end of the sixteenth century ... companies such as Shakespeare's clearly had' at least 'two patrons – the King and the paying public. In some cases these two patrons worked at cross-purposes, but in most cases they appeared to be quite comfortable as bedfellows.'[55] While the theatres promised larger, more regular rewards than any individual patron could provide, players still 'needed aristocratic patrons to secure court performances and stand by them in their collisions with the censor, the Privy Council, or the civic authorities', as Margot Heinemann notes.[56] Nor was it an entirely new combination of patrons. As Kathleen McLuskie observes, 'a balance between patronage and commerce had funded players from the earliest times'.[57] The different benefits offered by public theatre audiences and elite patrons perhaps helps to explain why many troupes continued to seek out royal and aristocratic patrons long after the commercial theatres were well established and despite the fact that crown-led changes, especially in the Caroline era, meant that there were fewer opportunities for noblemen and women to act as patrons of playing companies.

Case studies

A Game at Chess

In August 1624 the King's players performed Thomas Middleton's *A Game at Chess* for nine consecutive days at the Globe Theatre.[58] In a theatre world in which it was customary for a different play to be performed daily such a run for an individual play was unprecedented. The play drew huge audiences with 'more than 3000 persons' said to be 'there on the day that the audience was smallest', according to the Spanish Ambassador, Don Carlos Coloma, and with many more spectators turned away, as Sir John Holles, our one eye-witness confirms: he reported how, having rowed 'to ye globe', he found the 'hows ... so thronged, y^t by scores y^ei came away for want of place'.[59] Although some of the open-air theatres had begun to acquire a reputation for serving citizen and apprentice audiences, contemporary reports make clear that Middleton's box-office smash was seen by 'all sorts of people old and younge, rich and poore, masters and seruants, papists and puritans, wise men ... churchmen and statesmen'.[60] The play's spectacular run only came to an end when the Privy Council intervened at the king's request to suppress the play and to order a (temporary) stop to all performances by the troupe.[61]

The play's incredible popularity derived from its controversial engagement with recent Anglo-Spanish relations and what contemporaries referred to as the 'Spanish business': King James I's attempt to marry his oldest surviving son and heir, Prince Charles, to the Spanish Infanta, which failed finally in March 1624. Controversially, Charles and royal favourite, George Villiers, Duke of Buckingham had left England for

Spain in 1623 with the aim of bringing the Spanish negotiations to a head. But, after a protracted stay, they returned
home without the Infanta and apparently disillusioned with,
and cynical about, the Spanish and their readiness to form a
match and to address England's other pressing concern – the
restoration of the County Palatine of the Rhine to James's
daughter Elizabeth and her husband Frederick, the Elector
Palatine, after the invasion of Archduke Ferdinand of Austria
in 1620 with Spanish aid. Encouraged by the Prince and
the Duke, the MPs and Lords involved in the parliament
subsequently called by James (19 February–29 May) advised
the king to break off all treaties with the Spanish. James
eventually acceded to the petition of the upper and lower
houses ordering the dissolving of the treaties and accepting
parliament's promise of money to assist with the preparations
for probable war against Spain (23 March).[62] As the country
looked forward to some kind of armed conflict with Spain,
anti-Spanish and anti-Catholic feeling was running high, as
was reflected in the publication of a series of anti-Spanish
sermons and tracts, including the Second Part of *Vox Populi*
by Thomas Scott in May 1624. Scott's work was to serve
as one of the main sources for Thomas Middleton's play,
not least in its impersonation of Diego Sarmiento de Acuna,
Count of Gondomar, Scott writing in the persona of the
one-time Spanish Ambassador to England.[63]

   A Game at Chess does not address the events described
above directly; rather it uses the conceit of a game of chess to
construct a political allegory which alludes to them symbolically. Superficially, the play is about the conflict between two
houses – the white, which is associated with 'noble candour,
uncorrupted justice / And truth of heart' and the black,
which is associated with 'serpent subtlety' and 'dissimulation
– with most of the action revolving around two plots: the
attempted rape and seduction of the White Queen's Pawn
by the Black Bishop's Pawn, and the attempted capture of
the White Knight by the Black Knight during a visit to the
Black House.[64] Allegorically, it is clear that audiences were

invited to view the White House as representing England and the Black House as Spain, and to draw parallels between the play's plots and recent events. Most obviously, the attempted capture of the White Knight by the Black House seemingly alluded to Charles's visit to Spain and the Spanish court's attempted seduction and corruption of the Prince. Similarly, the 'loud peal of joy' (5.3.219) with which the White King greets the safe and victorious return of the White Knight and White Duke has been seen as recalling the widespread celebrations witnessed when Charles and Buckingham returned from Spain.[65]

Contemporaries were only too aware of the controversial topicality of the play's allegory. Sir Francis Nethersole described the play's plot as 'a game of Chesse, vnder wch the whole Spanish busines is ripped vp'; while Sir John Holles saw the play as 'a representation of all our spannishe traffike' and decoded the allegory, explaining how the 'whole play is a chess board, England ye whyt hows, Spayn ye black' and that the 'moral' of the play was 'built vppon ye popular opinion, y^t ye Jesuits mark is to bring all ye christian world vnder Rome for ye spirituality, & vnder Spayn for ye temporalty'.[66] Such topical interpretations of the play appear to have been reinforced by the parallels apparently set up between various of the play's characters and real people from the Spanish and English courts, the Black King being seen as a figure for King Philip of Spain and the White King, Knight and Duke as figures respectively for King James, Prince Charles and the Duke of Buckingham.

In one case, the players are alleged to have gone even further with their 'application' of the allegory. Textual allusions – such as his description as 'the fistula of Europe' (2.2.46), the reference to his 'chair of ease' (4.2.30) and his appearance in a litter at the start of Act 5 – suggest that the Black Knight was to be interpreted as a figure for Gondomar. One-time Spanish Ambassador to England and reputed to be the original proponent of the Spanish match, Gondomar suffered from an anal fistula which meant that he required a special chair and sometimes used a litter to travel about the city during his time in London. In performance, the players are reported to have made the identification even more obvious by impersonating Gondomar in great personal detail, as John Chamberlain reported to Sir Dudley Carleton: 'they counterfeited his person to the life, wth all his graces and faces, and had gotten (they say) a cast sute of his apparel for the purpose, wth his Lytter'.[67] Many contemporaries would have been familiar with Gondomar's appearance and his chair and litter, either having seen him during his time in London or from the frontispiece of the second part of Thomas Scott's *Vox Populi*. Whether such specific impersonation was a feature of the performance of other characters is less clear, although the current Spanish Ambassador suggested that some attempt was made to suggest a physical resemblance between the Black King and King Philip of Spain, reporting to Spanish royal favourite, Olivares, that 'the king of the blacks has easily been taken for our lord the King because of his youth, dress and other details'.[68]

As a general rule, players were discouraged from representing living people and were not supposed to represent current kings. It is unsurprising therefore that it was the players' impersonation of contemporaries which received harshest official censure. The production was drawn to the attention of the authorities on 7 August when the Spanish Ambassador, Coloma wrote to the king to complain; James was on summer progress.[69] The king's secretary, Sir Edward Conway subsequently wrote to the Privy Council on 12 August to report that the king had received information

> of a very scandalous Comedie acted publickly by the Kings players, wherein they take the boldness, and p^rsumption in a rude, and dishonorable fashion to represent on the Stage the persons of his ma^tie, the Kinge of Spaine, the Conde de Gondomar, the Bishop of Spalato etc.

Conway therefore instructed the Council to call before them 'aswell the Poett, that made the comedie, as the Comedians that acted it, And vpon examinacon of them to comit them, or such of them, as yo[u] shall find most faultie, vnto prison'.[70] Although contemporary accounts make it clear that the White King represented James, the official response to the production appears to have focused on the players' impersonation of Gondomar and their representation of the Spanish King, which as Conway notes was against 'a commandmant, and restraint giuen against the rep[r]sentinge of anie modern Christian Kings in those Stage plays'.[71] The fact that James was also implicitly represented and not in wholly flattering terms is something which the court and the king do not seem to have acknowledged, although some contemporaries did, including Sir John Holles who noted how the play shows the Black Knight (Gondomar) as having 'sett y[e] Kings affayrs as a clock, backward, & forward, made him belieue, & vn=belieue as stood best wth his busines'.[72]

On 18 August a warrant was duly issued for the arrest of Middleton and the players, and they were forbidden to play. On 21 August the Privy Council reported on its actions to Secretary Conway, noting that they had called before them 'some of the principall Actors' to demand what authority they had for their performance of *A Game at Chess*. The players presented them with 'a booke being an orriginall and perfect coppie thereof (as they affirmed) seene and allowed by S[r] Henry Herbert knight M[r] of the Reuells, vnder his owne hand and subscribed in the last Page of the said booke' and the players claimed to have 'added or varied ... nothing at all' from the allowed text, which Herbert (licensed, 12 June 1624).[73] The councillors concluded their interview with the players by forbidding them to perform the play or any other 'vntill his Ma[ts] pleasure be further knowne' and by obliging them to enter into a bond for their reappearance. That the king (and/or his appointees) might judge the play for themselves they forwarded the allowed text to Conway.[74]

Significantly, the players had been able to demonstrate that the play had been licensed for performance by the Master of Revels, Sir Henry Herbert, as was customary. If the actors were telling the truth about not adapting the allowed text (and they might not be) they had not breached the licensing laws. This may help to explain why their punishment was not in the end severe or of long duration. On 27 August Secretary Conway reported that the king did not wish to 'punish the innocent, or vtterly ruine the Companie';[75] and William Herbert, Earl of Pembroke wrote to the president of the Council to request (on the king's behalf) that the players therefore be allowed to resume playing.[76] Middleton may have spent some time in prison but he, too, seems to have escaped severe penalty and there is no evidence that Sir Henry Herbert who licensed the play was punished in any way.[77]

The fact that Sir Henry Herbert licensed the play has perplexed many modern scholars. Indeed, the play is arguably the most famous example of what Janet Clare calls 'non-censorship' in the period.[78] Herbert's allowed text of the play does not appear to have survived but a number of other contemporary manuscript copies have, along with three early printed quartos.[79] What is thought to be the earliest of these textual witnesses for the play – the Archdale Manuscript (Folger MS.v a.231) – which is dated 13 August 1624 by its scribe, Ralph Crane, differs in some respects from the later texts of the play (for example, it does not include the character of the Fat Bishop), but it is still unmistakably anti-Spanish and anti-Jesuit and features the Black Knight prominently. As Richard Dutton notes, this suggests that 'the general allegory, with its broad and indelicate depiction of Gondomar, was always part of Middleton's conception and must have been present in the version that Herbert saw', even if the lengths to which the players would go to impersonate the ex-Spanish Ambassador – with regards to staging, costuming and properties – were not apparent from the text alone.[80]

Herbert's licensing of the play, combined with the eventual leniency of the punishment meted out to those involved in the case, has led a number of modern scholars to wonder if (and in some cases to assume that) the players had special backing for the production. Andrew Gurr, for example, writes that there 'was certainly connivance at a high level over the staging' and argues that the 'prior involvement of Henry Herbert and perhaps his master the Lord Chamberlain along with other Privy Councillors is the only practical explanation why it was all carried off so painlessly'.[81] Such patronage theories have a long history. As early as 1930 Dover Wilson wondered if the play might have been patronized by the Duke of Buckingham and Prince Charles, serving as 'a pawn in the game of foreign policy which' they 'were in 1624 playing against the Spanish ambassador', but other scholars have challenged this theory, noting that the play appears to incorporate subtle satire of Buckingham at least, as when Middleton has the White Duke feign that he is inclined to lust or 'infirmity of blood, flesh-frailty' (5.3.122), a weakness to which Buckingham was reputedly given.[82] Margot Heinemann makes the case instead for William Herbert, Earl of Pembroke, as informal patron of the production. Herbert was opposed to the Spanish match and had been the dedicatee of a number of anti-Spanish works in 1623 and early 1624. He was also well acquainted with the King's players: he not only intervened to help them on various occasions in his capacity as Lord Chamberlain (see p. 179), but he patronized at least one other production by the troupe, sponsoring a court 'performance of "*Rule a Wife and Have a Wife*, for the ladies, by the King's Company"' (2 November 1624).[83] That the King's Men considered him and his brother as allies is reflected in their dedication of the Shakespeare First Folio (1623) to them, rather than their patron. If Herbert was indeed the sponsor of *A Game at Chess* the fact that the Master of the Revels, Sir Henry Herbert, was Pembroke's cousin and probably owed his appointment to his more influential kinsman might explain why the play was licensed despite its potentially controversial engagement with recent political history.

Thomas Cogswell, another well-known scholar of the play and an influential historian of seventeenth-century England shares Heinemann's assumption that 'the production of a public entertainment which reviled the monarch and diplomats of an ostensibly friendly state must have had encouragement and protection of a powerful court faction', but he challenges the notion that the play satirizes Buckingham, arguing rather that it celebrates his role in bringing Charles back from Spain unmarried and uncorrupted by Catholicism. Cogswell goes on to consider whether 'the necessary encouragement and protection for Middleton and the King's Men came from the same broad-based "patriot" coalition that had been so successful in the 1624 Parliament', noting that if this was the case 'we would not have to decide between Pembroke and Buckingham; instead such a scenario would have allowed both of them to work together under the direction of Prince Charles'.[84]

The common assumption in modern times that the King's Men's performance of A Game at Chess was sponsored informally by one or more court patrons might seem to derive from the current preoccupation with conspiracy theories but at least some contemporaries drew similar conclusions. In his letter to Lord Somerset, Sir John Holles concluded his eye-witness account of a performance with the observation that 'surely y^{es} gamsters must haue a good retrayte (retreat), else dared y^{ei} not to charge thus Princes actions, & ministers, nay their intents: ... a foule iniury to Spayn, ... no great honor to England'.[85] Another contemporary, John Woolley, went further (20 August 1624), speculating that the play was licensed with the approval 'from the higher powers I mean the P.[rince] and D.[uke] if not from the K.[ing] for they were all loth to haue it forbidden, and by report laught hartely at it'.[86]

There is, however, no direct evidence that anyone supported or had any part in the play's composition and performance, besides Middleton and the King's Men, as several recent scholars have pointed out.[87] Neither is the existence of one or more secret patrons necessary to explain how the play came to be performed. Although it would not have been completely unprecedented for contemporary patrons to commission public propagandist drama, evidence of such commissions is rare and scholars such as Paul Yachnin have challenged the notion that the ruling classes used drama 'to influence the attitudes of the public'.[88] At the same time, in performing an anti-Spanish drama which presented the Spanish and Jesuits as desirous of 'universal monarchy' (1.1.52), politically and spiritually respectively, and Jesuits as dangerous, would-be seducers with a 'burning' desire to corrupt Protestants (2.1.21), Thomas Middleton and the King's Men were, to some extent, simply reflecting widespread views and anxieties in England in 1624 and using the same kind of imagery as did the authors of contemporary anti-Spanish tracts and libels.[89] It may have been an occasion therefore when the King's Men were thinking about the tastes of their theatre-going patrons (and their purses) rather than their own views or those of their official patron. As Mary Blackstone notes, 'sometimes players decided to be businessmen first and King's servants second'.[90] In this context, one can see the potential appeal of a polemical play like *A Game at Chess*: a play which 'purposefully appealed to the anti-Spanish mood of 1624, was calculated to deliver a quick profit for the players'.[91] Trevor Howard-Hill reaches much this conclusion, arguing that there 'is no certain evidence that *A Game* is anything other than it seems to be, a commercial play written and performed to take advantage of propitious public sentiment'.[92]

The pervasiveness of the anti-Spanish, anti-Jesuit views implicit in the play is demonstrated by the records of the parliament that had taken place earlier in 1624 during which we find MPs describing the conduct and intentions of the Spanish in terms very similar to those used in the play and politicians worrying in the same fashion about the seduction of Protestants and the threat posed to the nation by the Spanish. In the House of Commons, Sir M. Fleetwood cast the Spanish in the role of dissemblers and deceivers, asserting on 1 March 1624 that 'We have suffered by the State of *Spayne*, pretending a Marriage, but intending the Gain of the *Palatinate*, *Bohemia*, &c. not the Match'; and we find Sir Francis Seymour figuring the religious threat posed by Spanish Catholics in terms of seduction, complaining of:

'Many hundreds seduced to Idolatry by the *Spanish* agents. –
Attempted the Prince and Duke'. [93]

Middleton and the King's Men were not the only writers
and players turning to the Spanish business for inspiration
either. It may not have been performed but Jonson had written
a masque for performance at court on Twelfth Night that year,
in which the King's Men are likely to have been involved as
performers, which alludes allegorically to Charles's Spanish
trip: *Neptune's Triumph for the Return of Albion* (1624).
The masque casts Charles as Albion, Neptune's 'dear and
precious pawn' – a phrase suggestive of the chess imagery
Middleton adopts – who returns to the sea god and his home
after journeying through Celtiberia where 'arts were used to
make him stay'. Jonson alludes to Buckingham's part in the
journey to Spain, too, observing that Neptune gave Albion
'his powerfull manager of horse' to protect him on his travels
– a reference to Buckingham's role as James's Master of the
Horse.[94] Despite the controversy and trouble that ensued, the
King's Men commissioned another play concerned with Spain
that year, getting into trouble in late 1624 when they staged
The Spanish Viceroy (now lost) without Sir Henry Herbert's
permission.[95]

In this cultural and theatrical context one might argue, as
does Trevor Howard-Hill, that

> the mystery of Herbert's licence is no mystery at all. After
> the Master of the Revels had finished with Middleton's
> script, there was nothing in it that would give offence to
> any loyal, right-thinking Englishman – at *that* point in
> national history.[96]

Although it is possible that figures such as Buckingham,
Charles and Pembroke sympathized with the play's satire
of the Spanish and that Pembroke played a retrospective
part in protecting the players after the fact, there is no
reason to assume that any of them actively commissioned
the production. On the contrary, rather than assuming that

the players and play were subservient to the agenda of courtiers one could, as Thomas Postlewait suggests, read the production as revealing 'the politics of subversion', with the players deliberately adopting a radical but popular stance in defiance of their royal master and his officials.[97]

In many respects what is most significant about the case is the fact that the King's Men chose to perform a play so clearly at odds with the views of their official patron. Andrew Gurr describes it as the 'most famous of the company's displays of non-allegiance to their royal patron', and it is perhaps as an example of the growing distance between patron and players and of the increased importance of the paying patrons who attended the theatres that *A Game at Chess* is most revealing, reflecting what seems to have been a growing trend across the late sixteenth and early seventeenth century theatre world.[98] The willingness of the King's Men to stage a play that challenged the position of the king so profoundly (whether or not it was done for commercial reasons) is perhaps a telling sign, too, of James's growing political isolation and of what was to prove an increasing cultural readiness to dispute royal policy and the authority of patrons in and beyond the theatre in early Stuart England.

The Late Lancashire Witches

On 16 August 1634 letter-writer Nathaniel Tomkyns reported to Sir Robert Phelips news of the latest theatrical hit in London: 'Here hath bin lately a new comedie at the globe called *The Witches of Lancasheer*, acted by reason of ye great concourse of people 3 dayes together'.[99] The play Tomkyns saw was performed by the King's Men and is that known today as *The Late Lancashire Witches* by Richard Brome and Thomas Heywood. The play tells the story of a group of Lancashire witches and the magic that they practise upon a variety of local people before being eventually exposed and arrested. In writing about witchcraft and magic Brome and Heywood were doing nothing new; many plays had already been written on these subjects in the Elizabethan and early Stuart eras. What made their play unusual, and contributed to its success in drawing audiences, was the fact that it was topical. Like *A Game at Chess*, it was based on real individuals and an on-going trial, as Tomkyns (the only eye-witness) reports:

> The subiect was of the slights and passages done or supposd to be done by the<se> witches sent from thence hither and other witches and their familiars; ... And though there be not in it (to my vnderstanding) any poeticall Genius, or art, or language, or iudgement to state o^r tenet of witches (wch I expected.) $_\wedge$ or application to vertue but full of ribaldrie and of things improbable and impossible; yet in respect of the newnesse of y^e subiect (the witches being still visible and in prison here) and in regard it consisteth from the beginning to the ende of odd passages and fopperies to provoke laughter, and is mixed with diuers songs and dances, it passeth for a merrie and ex^{c}ellent new play.[100]

The 'witches' Tomkyns alludes to had been brought to London in June 1634 after the judges who sat on their original trial in Lancaster (24 March 1634) were reluctant to pass sentence on them. There were four women in total: Frances Dicconson, Jennet Hargreaves, Margaret Johnson and Mary Spencer. All four feature in the play. The case first began in late 1633 when a ten-year old boy, Edmund Robinson, accused several local women of being witches. Robinson was formally interrogated on 10 February 1634. By the time of the trial 21 people were charged with witchcraft. Only one person had confessed to being a witch: Margaret Johnson (2 March 1634). Having failed to sentence the prisoners 'all but one of' whom 'were found guilty' the judges referred the case to the crown.[101] On 16 May the king duly directed the Privy Council to summon 'some of the principall and most notorious offenders' to London for further questioning.[102] Before doing so the Council directed Bishop John Bridgeman of Chester to examine seven of the chief suspects. When he visited the jail in Lancaster he was only able to examine three of the prisoners, three others having died and one being seriously ill (13 June): depositions were taken from Margaret Johnson, Mary Spencer and Frances Dicconson. Shortly thereafter the three women were summoned to London, along with Jennet Hargreaves, following her recovery from illness. Their chief accuser Edmund Robinson was also brought to London for questioning with his father. We know that the women were in the capital by early July as a group of surgeons reported to the Privy Council on 2 July after searching the women for secret or 'unnatural' marks on their bodies; they had not found any such marks.[103] Those with doubts about the veracity of the case against the women were to find their concerns confirmed when, on 10 July, Robinson confessed that he had invented all the accusations and stories of witchcraft that he had reported.[104] Nonetheless the women continued to be held in prison and were still there when the play was eventually performed, probably opening between 11 and 13 August.[105]

That the story of the Lancashire women and their trial for witchcraft was the subject of considerable interest is suggested by the fact that their case was being discussed by contemporaries even before the women and their accuser arrived in London. On 16 May 1634 Sir William Pelham wrote to Sir Edward Conway that the 'greatest news from the country is of a huge pack of witches which are lately discovered in Lancashire'.[106] This same interest probably also explains why their story reportedly 'circulated in many forms', including 'letters, circulated manuscripts of the depositions and confessions at the original trial' and 'ballads'.[107] According to contemporary minister John Webster, the women themselves became an object of fascination, with people reportedly paying money to see them at the Fleet Prison in London.[108]

In this context it is not hard to see why an acting company such as the King's Men should have considered performing a play inspired by their case. Like the women's jailers, they presumably hoped to profit from Londoners' curiosity about the women. They were not the only players who hoped to do so either, as is revealed by a petition the company made to the Lord Chamberlain, Philip Herbert (20 July 1634), 'complaining of intermingleing some passages of witches in old playes to yᵉ pʳiudice of their designed Comedy of the Lancashire witches, & desiring a prohibition of any other till theirs bee allowed & Acted'.[109] By implication, Brome's and Heywood's play had already been conceived and possibly completed by this time.

More intriguing is the fact that Brome and Heywood appear to have had access to documents from the trial, following them in considerable detail in places in their play, as Herbert Berry demonstrates in his pioneering essay on *The Late Lancashire Witches*.[110] Thus, the scene in which the miller's boy finds two greyhounds that turn into 'my gammer *Dickison*' and an unknown boy appears to borrow directly from Edmund Robinson's first deposition (10 February 1633) in which he claimed that two greyhounds transformed before his eyes so that 'in stead of the black Grayhound one Dickensons Wife stood up, a Neighbour whom this informer knoweth. And instead of the brown one a little Boy, whom this informer knoweth not'.[111] Similarly, the scene in which Brome's and Heywood's witches magically pull in food for a banquet (IV.i. 1436–94) echoes Robinson's account of a witches' feast he claimed to have witnessed.[112] The playwrights' borrowings are not confined to the testimony of Robinson either. Mal Spenser's trick of moving a pail magically (II.i. 977–82) draws upon the charges against Mary Spencer; and the naming of Granny Johnson's familiar as 'Mamilion' (V.i. 2628) and her description of his first appearance, 'Gentleman like, but blacke blacke points and all' (V.i. 2646), closely follows the testimony of Margaret Johnson, who reported that 'Mamilion' first appeared to her as 'a Man in blacke Attire trussed wᵗʰ blacke pointes'.[113]

Although the names of the witches might have been easy to discover it is unlikely that Brome and Heywood would have been able to rely on hearsay for such detailed information from the legal documents relating to the women's case. If the writers had access to copies of at least some of the legal depositions (as it seems they did), how did they obtain them? The depositions of Robinson, Johnson and Spenser were taken in Lancashire, but were forwarded to the Privy Council. Herbert Berry argues that the only people who would have had immediate access to the manuscripts would have been members of the Privy Council and he concludes that one or more of its members must have been responsible for passing copies of the testimonies to Brome and Heywood and/or the King's players and that the same member(s) may in fact have sponsored the play, proposing Philip Herbert as the most likely candidate for this role as informal patron. He finds the explanation for why Herbert might have been interested in sponsoring such a play in the politics of the Privy Council in 1634 and a possible quarrel about the case between the Archbishop of Canterbury, William Laud (who was openly sceptical about witchcraft) and those who opposed him and his current Church reforms such as Herbert.[114] Commissioning a play which challenged Laudian scepticism about witchcraft afforded a potential 'opportunity for Pembroke to bring down a notch the most powerful official on the King's Council who would have opted for leniency in treating the Lancashire women'.[115]

Further support for Berry's case might be found in Herbert's well-known connections with the King's players and the theatre (see p. 179). The fact that the King's Men appear to have had no problems getting *The Late Lancashire Witches* licensed might make sense if Herbert sponsored the play, the Master of the Revels Sir Henry Herbert being his cousin. In the context of such circumstantial evidence, it is perhaps not surprising that so many critics have accepted Berry's case, including Andrew Gurr. In his recent study of the royal troupe he states unequivocally that the company 'worked for ... Philip', when they put on the play, and follows Berry in interpreting it as being 'designed to boost his opposition in the Privy Council to the king's chief agent on the Council, Archbishop Laud'.

For Gurr the play is thus 'the result' and an example of the troupe's 'subservience to the Lord Chamberlain'.[116] However, there is no explicit evidence that the play was commissioned by an informal patron.

Another problem with the theory that Herbert and/or others on the Privy Council sponsored the play as a way of lobbying against Laud is the fact that the play's handling of the witches is not without ambiguity. Although the case against the women is ultimately shown to be real it is 'difficult', as Paul Whitfield White points out, for 'anyone who reads' *The Late Lancashire Witches* or Tomkyns's eye-witness account 'to believe this play succeeds as a very effective piece of religious stage propaganda', not least because so much of the play's treatment of witchcraft is comic. As Whitfield White notes, 'the comedy' arguably 'encourages spectators to view the supernatural actions of the witches with some skepticism'.[117] The representation of the witches and their practices is not wholly condemnatory either, not least because their activities are mostly disorderly, rather than deadly, being equated with traditional forms of revelry, charivari and what Heather Hirschfield characterizes as 'festive inversion': when they are together the witches feast, dance, sport and turn the world 'upside downe' (1.1.402), so that, as Hirschfield observes, 'the coven's activities seem not so much illegal as recreational'.[118] Nonetheless, an explanation for how the players or playwrights obtained the case materials is needed. It may be that Berry is right and that the players were supplied with the documents and then commissioned Heywood and Brome to write *The Late Lancashire Witches*. Having been charged with such a commission, Heywood might have seemed an obvious author to approach being 'a noted witch-lorist' as well as an experienced dramatist, while Brome had enjoyed recent success with another play about the north (*The Northern Lass*).[119] The pair may have known each other, too, collaborating on at least one other topical play, possibly around the same time.[120]

The theory that the King's Men and/or Heywood and Brome were commissioned to produce *The Late Lancashire*

Witches assumes a subservient relationship between patrons and players, as is reflected in Andrew Gurr's reading of the case. Traditionally, this *was* the usual, expected relationship between elite patrons and players but the growing financial independence of acting companies combined with the weakening of the patronage system in the Caroline era meant that players were not necessarily subject to their royal or aristocratic patrons in the same way. Brome's and Heywood's comic treatment of the witches' case could thus be an example of writers and players resisting (or only partly responding to) a patron's request, if the play was indeed commissioned. At the very least, the play's light-hearted treatment of witchcraft would seem to challenge the assumption 'that the playwrights followed single-mindedly the interests of a noble sponsor', as Hirschfeld observes. This is a point Berry concedes when he notes that 'whatever the play's instigation and however grim some of its statements could be made to seem on stage, the King's Men played it as its writers saw to it they could – for the fun and not the message'.[121]

There is, however, another possible explanation for the troupe's acquisition of documents from the case: the writers and/or players might have solicited the preparation of copies themselves. Although theoretically such documents were not meant to be shared, the fact that transcriptions of the testimonies of Robinson and Margaret Johnson survive in several contemporary manuscripts suggests that copies did circulate unofficially at the time, as sometimes happened with other topical, unlicensed documents. Brome and Heywood and/or the King's Men might have sought out such copies, using them as their starting point for a play that aimed to draw in paying patrons. If this was the case, they achieved their aim. Despite the fact that the production took place during the summer holidays, the play ran for three consecutive days and drew a large cross-section of society, as Tomkyns reported, describing how he 'found' in the audience 'a greater apparance of fine folke gent[men] and gent[weomen] then j thought had bin in town in the vacation'.[122] Whether inspired by elite patrons or the players and playwrights, the play's success was arguably marked by its power to open the purses of the acting companies' now most crucial patron: theatre-goers. The power of topical plays to draw large audiences arguably provides a sufficient reason for the King's Men to have bought or commissioned *The Late Lancashire Witches*. Although we cannot rule out the intervention of one or more noble patrons (including Philip Herbert) such covert patronage for the play is neither necessary nor the only possible explanation for the King's Men's procurement of court documents relating to the 'witches' or their eventual performance of *The Late Lancashire Witches* and we should be wary of inferring the sponsorship of elite patrons in such cases in the absence of direct evidence for it. Indeed, although the play's existence could be a testimony to the power of informal dramatic patrons in the Caroline era it is as, if not more, likely to be a tribute to the growing power of the actors' theatrical patrons and their taste for topical drama in the 1630s.

EPILOGUE

Acting Companies and Their Plays in Shakespeare's London has explored some of the competing factors which informed the writing, performance and publication of plays in Renaissance England. This has included investigating how the ways in which playwrights wrote and the kinds of plays that they produced were shaped by the conventions and fashions associated with contemporary literary and theatrical culture and by their pragmatic awareness of the staging resources likely to be available to players. Playwrights occasionally wrote plays with specific theatres in mind, but most of the plays written for the English Renaissance stage were designed to be portable. Borne out of a theatrical tradition in which players were accustomed to playing in a variety of venues on tour, plays continued to be designed to be versatile, generally requiring no more than a small stock of costumes and properties and a playing space with a couple of entry and exit points. The adaptability of the plays and their comparatively simple staging demands were an important part of the players' success, not only allowing acting companies to perform almost anywhere in London and beyond, and for plays to be transferred between companies and theatres, but playing a role in the continuing theatrical viability of English Renaissance dramas in subsequent eras, including our own.

Chapter 4 showed how playwrights were similarly concerned with versatility when it came to audiences, generally writing plays designed to have as wide an appeal as possible. Although there came to be a distinction between the social make-up of the indoor and outdoor playhouses (because of the higher entry costs at the former) and contemporaries sometimes caricatured the open-air playhouses as more old-fashioned, direct evidence for any huge gulf between audience tastes or between the repertories on offer at the two types of playhouse is slim. Likewise, although elite patronage of drama played a key part in fostering and protecting the development of acting companies in late Medieval and Tudor England and players and their playwrights occasionally sought to cater for patrons' interests, there is little evidence of patrons commissioning or directly influencing their players' plays.

The key factor shaping the working practices and plays of most playwrights was their relationship with contemporary acting companies. Indeed, *Acting Companies* suggests that without an understanding of the period's troupes and playwrights' relations with them, we cannot fully understand how English Renaissance plays came into being, not least because players and theatrical personnel contributed to the readying and revision of those plays for performance and print. Since the Romantic era we have been accustomed to focus on the individual artist but this study suggests that we need to think, too, about the companies for which dramatists wrote and with whose members they collaborated, if we want to better understand their plays and the drama of the English Renaissance stage. This is not to suggest that playwrights were simply the servants of the playing companies who employed them any more than they were just the products of their culture. As *Acting Companies* makes clear, the needs of playing companies were an important contingency to which playwrights were necessarily alert and for which most sought to cater, at least to some degree, but playwrights enjoyed considerable independence too. Some acting companies, like the Queen's Men and the Children of the King's Revels, may have fostered a company 'house' style for their plays but this appears to have been atypical: most acting companies opted for eclectic, largely similar, repertories. At the same time, the demands posed by the professional stage and its players were not necessarily an obstacle to creative expression, but rather a potential source of artistic stimulation, as playwrights sought to rise to the challenge of making the most of players' talents and of pleasing them and their audiences, as well as themselves. In this sense the 'style' of Renaissance dramas was always borne out of the inter-play between the individual playwright's talents and preferences and the wishes of the dramatists they worked alongside, the players they worked for and their mutual audiences in and beyond the London playhouses. For this reason I would argue that better understanding the diversity of people who worked in, and contributed to, the English Renaissance theatre world and paying more attention in the future to the acting companies at its heart is central to a fuller appreciation of the plays of its dramatists. Hopefully, *Acting Companies*, like the studies upon which it builds, will help to foster such research and the fresh insights it promises into playwriting and production in this exciting and important era in English theatre.

NOTES

Introduction

1   Gerald Eades Bentley, 'Shakespeare and the Blackfriars
    Theatre', *SS* 1 (1948), 38–50 (38).

2   Scott McMillin and Sally-Beth MacLean, *The Queen's Men
    and Their Plays* (Cambridge, 1998), xi, xii.

3   See REED, http://www.reed.utoronto.ca/index.html (accessed
    25.05.13).

4   Tom Rutter, 'Introduction: The Repertory-based Approach',
    ET 13:2 (2010), 121–31 (123, 124).

5   Lucy Munro, *Children of the Queen's Revels: A Jacobean
    Theatre Repertory* (Cambridge, 2005), 3.

6   Grace Ioppolo, *Dramatists and Their Manuscripts in the Age
    of Shakespeare, Jonson, Middleton and Heywood: Authority,
    Authorship and the Playhouse* (London, 2006; repr. 2007), 4.

7   Andrew Gurr, *The Shakespearian Playing Companies* (Oxford,
    1996), 10.

8   Mary Bly, *Queer Virgins and Virgin Queans on the Early
    Modern Stage* (Oxford, 2000), 32, 32–3.

9   Munro, 5.

10 Roslyn L. Knutson, 'The Start of Something Big' in
    *Locating the Queen's Men 1583–1603: Material Practices
    and Conditions of Playing*, Helen Ostovich, Holger Schott
    Syme and Andrew Griffin (eds) (Farnham, 2009), 99–108 (99,
    100).

11 Mary Bly, 'Review of *Children of the Queen's Revels: A
    Jacobean Repertory* by Lucy Munro', *MRDE* 22 (2009),
    242–8 (245, 247).

12 Jeffrey Knapp, 'What is a Co-Author?', *Representations* 89

(2005), 1–29 (6); Gabriel Egan, 'What is not Collaborative about Early Modern Drama in Performance and Print?' *SS* 66 (forthcoming, 2013).

13   Bly, 'Review', 245.

14   Scott McMillin, 'Reading the Elizabethan Acting Companies', *ET* 4:1 (2001), 111–15 (111).

15   Andrew Gurr, *The Shakespeare Company, 1594–1642* (Cambridge, 2004), 129.

16   Rutter, 126.

17   David Nicol, 'The Repertory of Prince Charles's (I) Company, 1608–1625', *ET* 9:2 (2006), 57–72 (57).

18   Rutter, 129–30, 129.

19   David Scott Kastan, *Shakespeare After Theory* (London, 1999), 38; David Scott Kastan, '"To think these trifles some-thing": Shakespearean Playbooks and the Claims of Authorship', *SSt* 36 (2008), 37–48 (37–8).

Chapter 1

1   John Marston, *Histrio-Mastix* (London, 1610), 1.1. (sig.B). There are no line numbers in this edition.

2   Andrew Gurr, *The Shakespearian Playing Companies* (Oxford, 1996), 222.

3   Ibid., 339, 347.

4   John H. Astington, *Actors and Acting in Shakespeare's Time: The Art of Stage Playing* (Cambridge, 2010), 56.

5   Gurr, *Companies*, 348.

6   Ibid., 348, 350.

7   Michael Shapiro, *Children of the Revels: The Boy Companies of Shakespeare's Time and Their Plays* (New York, 1977), 229.

8   See Richard Dutton, 'The Revels Office and the Boy Companies, 1600–1613: New Perspectives', *ELR* 32:2 (2002), 324–51 (338, 344).

9   See Dutton, 339; Gurr, *Companies*, 356.

10 Dutton, 341.

11 See Gurr, *Companies*, 363, 365.

12 Andrew Gurr, *The Shakespearean Stage, 1574–1642*, 3rd edn (Cambridge, 2005), 63.

13 Astington, *Actors*, 56.

14 Gurr, *Companies*, 434, 423, 424.

15 Cited in Astington, *Actors*, 95–6.

16 Andrew Gurr, *The Shakespeare Company, 1594–1642* (Cambridge, 2004), 13; G. E. Bentley, 'The Troubles of a Caroline Acting Company: Prince Charles's Company', *HLQ* 41:3 (1978), 217–49 (222).

17 R. W. Ingram, ed., *REED: Coventry* (Toronto, 1981), 394; John Wasson, ed., *REED: Devon* (Toronto, 1986), 267.

18 See David Bradley, *From Text to Performance in the Elizabethan Theatre: Preparing the Play for the Stage* (Cambridge, 1992), 47.

19 G. E. Bentley, *The Profession of Player in Shakespeare's Time 1590–1642* (Princeton, NJ, 1984), 235.

20 William Ingram, 'The Economics of Playing' in *A Companion to Renaissance Drama*, ed. Arthur F. Kinney (Oxford, 2004), 313–27 (319).

21 Gurr, *Companies*, 94.

22 Walter W. Greg, ed., *Henslowe Papers* (London, 1907), 64.

23 Gurr, *Shakespeare Company*, 13; Andrew Gurr, *Shakespeare's Opposites: The Admiral's Company 1594–1625* (Cambridge, 2009; repr. 2012), 33.

24 See S. P. Cerasano, 'The "Business" of Shareholding, the Fortune Playhouse, and Francis Grace's Will', *MRDE* 2 (1985), 231–51 (239); Bentley, 'Troubles', 222.

25 Tom Rutter, 'Adult Companies 1603–1613' in *The Oxford Handbook of Early Modern Theatre*, ed. Richard Dutton (Oxford, 2009; repr. 2011), 72–87 (77).

26 See Gurr, *Companies*, 99; Gurr, *Shakespeare Company*, 108.

27 Paul L. Hughes and James F. Larkin (eds), *Tudor Royal*

Proclamations: The Later Tudors (1588–1603), III (New Haven, CT, 1969), 22–5.

28 E. K. Chambers, *The Elizabethan Stage* (Oxford, 1923; repr. 1961), I, 370.

29 Bentley, *Profession*, 66.

30 Gosson cited in Chambers, I, 348. R. A. Foakes, ed., *Henslowe's Diary*, 2nd edn (Cambridge, 2002), 268–9.

31 David Mateer, 'Edward Alleyn, Richard Perkins and the Rivalry between the Swan and Rose Playhouses', *RES* 60 (2009), 61–77.

32 David Kathman, 'Players, Livery Companies, and Apprentices' in *The Oxford Handbook of Early Modern Theatre*, ed. Richard Dutton (Oxford, 2009; repr. 2011), 413–28 (419); David Kathman, 'Grocers, Goldsmiths, and Drapers: Freemen and Apprentices in the Elizabethan Theater', *SQ* 55:1 (2004), 1–49 (8).

33 Bentley, 'Troubles', 224.

34 Bernard Beckerman, 'Philip Henslowe' in *The Theatrical Manager in England and America: Player of a Perilous Game*, ed. Joseph W. Donohue Jr (Princeton, NJ, 1971), 19–62 (60).

35 See Mary Bly, *Queer Virgins and Virgin Queans on the Early Modern Stage* (Oxford, 2000), 36.

36 Ingram, 'Economics', 314.

37 Stephen Gosson, *Plays Confuted in Fiue Actions* (London, 1582), sig.G6v.

38 Astington, *Actors*, 89, 184.

39 Gurr, *Companies* 402.

40 Bentley, 'Troubles', 225.

41 Gurr, *Stage*, 41–9; Bart van Es, *Shakespeare in Company* (Oxford, 2013), 105.

42 See Roslyn L. Knutson, *Playing Companies and Commerce in Shakespeare's Time* (Cambridge, 2001), 10; Foakes, *Diary*, 21.

43 See Siobhan Keenan, *Travelling Players in Shakespeare's England* (Basingstoke, 2002), 10.

44 See London, Dulwich College, MSS 1, f.97 (Article 69) and f.130 (Article 100), http://henslowe-alleyn.org.uk (accessed 21.02.13).

45 Barbara D. Palmer, 'Early Modern Mobility: Players, Payments, and Patrons', *SQ* 56:3 (2005), 259–305 (278); Knutson, *Playing*, 10.

46 Scott McMillin and Sally-Beth MacLean, *The Queen's Men and Their Plays* (Cambridge, 1998), xii, 125.

47 Roslyn L. Knutson, 'Playing Companies and Repertory' in *A Companion to Renaissance Drama*, ed. Arthur F. Kinney (Oxford, 2004), 180–92 (190).

48 Paul L. Hughes and James F. Larkin (eds), *Tudor Royal Proclamations: The Later Tudors (1553–1587)*, II (London, 1969), 115–16.

49 Hughes and Larkin, II, 350–2; *The Statutes of the Realm, Volume 4: Part 1, 1547–1585* (Buffalo, NY, 1993), 591–2.

50 See Gurr, *Companies*, 187.

51 William Ingram, 'The "Evolution" of the Elizabethan Playing Company' in *The Development of Shakespeare's Theater*, ed. John H. Astington (New York, 1992), 13–28 (26).

52 See W. R. Streitberger, 'Adult Companies to 1583' in *The Oxford Handbook of Early Modern Theatre*, ed. Richard Dutton (Oxford, 2009; repr. 2011), 19–38 (37, 36).

53 Gurr, *Companies*, 198; McMillin and MacLean, 41.

54 McMillin and MacLean, 2.

55 Ibid., 67, 44, 169.

56 Gurr, *Companies*, 65.

57 See, for example, Roslyn L. Knutson, 'Adult Playing Companies, 1593–1603' in *The Oxford Handbook of Early Modern Theatre*, ed. Richard Dutton (Oxford, 2009; repr. 2011), 56–71 (60).

58 See Gurr, *Stage*, 42, 139–40, 43; Gurr, *Companies*, 67, 68–9.

59 Following Prince Henry's death, patronage of his players passed to Frederick V the Elector Palatine (Lord Palsgrave), later husband of Lady Elizabeth. Gurr, *Companies*, 248.

60 Ibid., 137.

61   Ibid., 429.

62   Bentley, 'Troubles', 235, 236.

63   See Keenan, 183.

64   See Gurr, *Companies*, 51, 49–50.

65   Cited in Chambers, I, 246–7.

66   Gurr, *Companies*, 398.

67   See Lucy Munro, *Children of the Queen's Revels: A Jacobean Theatre Repertory* (Cambridge, 2005), 185.

68   Astington, *Actors*, 189, 197, 212, 219, 189.

69   Roberta Florence Brinkley, *Nathan Field: The Actor-Playwright* (Hamden, CT, 1973), 29–30.

70   Gerald Eades Bentley, *The Jacobean and Caroline Stage* (Oxford, 1941), I, 126.

71   E. K. Chambers, *The Elizabethan Stage* (Oxford, 1923; repr. 1945), IV, 126–7.

72   In Glynne Wickham, Herbert Berry and William Ingram, eds, *English Professional Theatre, 1530–1660* (Cambridge, 2000), 218, 219.

73   R. A. Foakes, 'Playhouses and Players' in *The Cambridge Companion to English Renaissance Drama*, A. R. Braunmuller and Michael Hattaway (eds), 2nd edn (Cambridge, 2003), 1–52 (30).

74   See Thomas Middleton, *A Chaste Maid in Cheapside*, 2nd edn, ed. Alan Brissenden (London, 2007).

75   Cited in Munro, 185, 186.

76   See Wickham, Berry and Ingram, 219.

77   Brandon Centerwall, 'A Greatly Exaggerated Demise: The Remaking of the Children of Paul's as the Duke of York's Men (1608)', *ET* 9:1 (2006), 85–107 (96).

78   See Ingram, *Coventry*, 394.

79   See Gurr, *Companies*, 413 and the events listed for Lady Elizabeth's players on the *REED: Patrons and Performances Website*, http://www.link.library.utoronto.ca/reed/index.cfm (accessed 14.02.13).

80   See Kathman, 'Grocers', 13.

81   See Munro, 134.

82   Chambers, IV, 129.

83   In Wickham, Berry and Ingram, 217, 218.

84   See Gurr, *Stage*, 153.

85   See Ben Jonson, *Bartholomew Fair*, 2nd edn, G. R. Hibbard and Alexander Leggatt (eds) (London, 2007), 5.3.73.

86   See Wickham, Berry and Ingram, 219.

87   See Gurr, *Companies*, 70, 395.

88   For a transcription of the contract, see Greg, 124; for the claim that Henslowe wanted the troupe to pay Dawes, see Wickham, Berry and Ingram, 219.

89   See Dulwich College, MSS 1, f.98 (Article 70), f.106 (Article 78), f.112 (Article 84), f.121 (Article 92), f.127 (Article 97), http://henslowe-alleyn.org.uk (accessed 21.02.13).

90   Gurr, *Companies*, 357.

91   In Wickham, Berry and Ingram, 220.

92   Gurr, *Companies*, 120.

93   See S. P. Cerasano, 'Competition for the King's Men?: Alleyn's Blackfriars Venture', *MRDE* 4 (1989), 173–86 (179–80, 173–4).

94   In Brinkley, 33.

95   Bentley, *Jacobean*, I, 176.

96   Brinkley, 34.

97   See Gurr, *Companies*, 401.

98   See David Galloway, ed., *REED: Norwich* (Toronto, 1984), 151–2.

99   See James J. Marino, 'Adult Playing Companies, 1613–1625' in *The Oxford Handbook of Early Modern Theatre*, ed. Richard Dutton (Oxford, 2009; repr. 2011), 88–103 (101).

100 In Bentley, *Jacobean*, I, 180.

101 See Gurr, *Companies*, 413–15.

102 Galloway, 162, 161.

103 Marino, 102.

104 Ibid., 99.

105 In N. W. Bawcutt, *The Control and Censorship of Caroline Drama: The Records of Sir Henry Herbert Master of the Revels 1623–73* (Oxford, 1996), 136.

106 Astington, *Actors*, 190, 218, 194, 199, 215–16, 222.

107 See Gurr, *Companies*, 407.

108 See Bawcutt, 136, 137, 141, 143, 145, 147, 149, 151, 155, 156, 157, 161.

109 See Galloway, 181.

110 Massinger's *The Bondman* and Shirley's *Love Tricks* include scenes which potentially call for as many as 20 players to be on stage at once. See Philip Massinger, *The Bondman* (London, 1638), 5.3; James Shirley, *The Schoole of Complement* (London, 1631), 5.1.

111 Gurr, *Stage*, 162.

112 Philip Massinger, *The Renegado*, ed. Michael Neill (London, 2010), 1.3 and 4.3; [Thomas Dekker, John Ford,] Thomas Middleton and William Rowley, *The Spanish Gipsie* (London, 1653), 1, ff.B2v, F2.

113 Gurr, *Companies*, 407.

114 Bentley, *Jacobean*, I, 187.

115 Gurr, *Companies*, 440.

116 Bentley, *Jacobean*, I, 188–9; Gurr, *Companies*, 446.

117 David George, ed., *REED: Lancashire* (Toronto, 1991), 200, 360.

118 See Gurr, *Companies*, 433–4, 436, 447, 448.

119 Kathleen E. McLuskie, 'Materiality and the Market: The Lady Elizabeth's Men and the Challenge of Theatre History' in *The Oxford Handbook of Early Modern Theatre*, ed. Richard Dutton (Oxford, 2009; repr. 2011), 429–40 (433).

Chapter 2

1   London, Dulwich College, MSS 1, f.130 (Article 100),
    http://henslowe-alleyn.org.uk (accessed 05.05.13).

2   Gerald Eades Bentley, *The Profession of Dramatist in
    Shakespeare's Time* (Princeton, NJ, 1971), 25, 12, 26.

3   See R. Mark Benbow, 'Dutton and Goffe versus Broughton: a
    Disputed Contract for Plays in the 1570s', *REED: Newsletter*
    2 (1981), 3–9.

4   See, for example, Jeffrey Masten, *Textual Intercourse:
    Collaboration, Authorship, and Sexualities in Renaissance
    Drama* (Cambridge, 1997), 14.

5   Bentley, 199.

6   See Jeffery Knapp, 'What is a Co-Author?', *Representations* 89
    (2005), 1–29 (8).

7   R. A. Foakes, ed., *Henslowe's Diary*, 2nd edn (Cambridge,
    2002), 105, 199.

8   See Ann Haaker, 'The Plague, the Theater, and the Poet',
    Renaissance Drama I (1968), 283–306 (297, 298).

9   Eleanor Collins, 'Richard Brome's Contract and the
    Relationship of Dramatist to Company in the Early Modern
    Period', *ET* 10:2 (2007), 116–28.

10 Dulwich College, MSS 1, f.114 (Article 85) and f.115 (Article
    86), http://henslowe-alleyn.org.uk (accessed 05.05.13).

11 *The Defence of Conny Catching* (London, 1592), sig.C3r-v.

12 Cited in Haaker, 301, 299.

13 Dulwich College, MSS 1, f.102 (Article 74) and f.127 (Article
    97), http://henslowe-alleyn.org.uk (accessed 05.05.13).

14 See James P. Bednarz, *Shakespeare and the Poet's War* (New
    York, 2001).

15 Andrew Gurr, *Shakespeare's Opposites: The Admiral's
    Company 1594–1625* (Cambridge, 2009), 106.

16 Gordon McMullan, *The Politics of Unease in the Plays of
    John Fletcher* (Amherst, MA, 1994), 133.

17 Grace Ioppolo, 'The Transmission of an English Renaissance

Play-Text' in *A Companion to Renaissance Drama*, ed. Arthur
F. Kinney (Oxford, 2004), 163–79 (164).

18   Dulwich College, MSS 1, f.109 (Article 81),
     http://henslowe-alleyn.org.uk (accessed 05.05.13).

19   For a possible example, see Foakes, *Diary*, 126.

20   See Haaker, 297.

21   See Scott McMillin, 'Professional Playwrighting' in *A
     Companion to Shakespeare*, ed. David Scott Kastan (Oxford,
     1999; repr. 2004), 225–38 (227, 228).

22   On plot scenarios, see Tiffany Stern, *Documents of
     Performance in Early Modern England* (Cambridge, 2009;
     repr. 2012), 8–35.

23   Dulwich College, MSS 1, f.46 (Article 32), http://henslowe-
     alleyn.org.uk (accessed 05.05.13).

24   For an example, see Foakes, *Diary*, 88.

25   In Bentley, 233.

26   See Foakes, *Diary*, 90–2.

27   Cyrus Hoy, 'Massinger as Collaborator: The Plays with
     Fletcher and Others' in *Philip Massinger: A Critical
     Reassessment*, ed. Douglas Howard (Cambridge, 1985), 51–82
     (52).

28   Dulwich College, MSS 1, f.106 (Article 78),
     http://henslowe-alleyn.org.uk (accessed 05.05.13).

29   See Anthony Munday, *Sir Thomas More*, ed. John Jowett
     (London, 2011), 180.

30   Dulwich College, MSS 1, f.115 (Article 86), f.98 (Article 70),
     http://henslowe-alleyn.org.uk (accessed 05.05.13).

31   Gerald Langbaine, *An Account of the English Dramatick
     Poets* (Oxford, 1691), 144.

32   See William B. Long, '"Precious Few": English Manuscript
     Playbooks' in *A Companion to Shakespeare*, ed. David Scott
     Kastan (Oxford, 1999), 414–33.

33   See Dulwich College, MSS 1, f.118 (Article 89),
     http://henslowe-alleyn.org.uk (accessed 05.05.13).

34   Walter W. Greg, *The Editorial Problem in Shakespeare*, 3rd

edn (Oxford, 1954), 31; Paul Werstine, 'The Continuing Importance of New Bibliographical Method', *SS* 62 (2009), 30–45 (35); Stern, 21.

35   Peter Thomson, 'Conventions of Playwriting' in *Shakespeare: An Oxford Guide*, Stanley Wells and Lena Cowen Orlin (eds) (Oxford, 2003), 44–54 (48).

36   Martin Wiggins, *Shakespeare and the Drama of his Time* (Oxford, 2000), 34, 64.

37   Andrew Gurr, *The Shakespeare Company, 1594–1642* (Cambridge, 2004), 135.

38   See Scott McMillin and Sally-Beth MacLean, *The Queen's Men and Their Plays* (Cambridge, 1998), xii.

39   Mary Bly, *Queer Virgins and Virgin Queans on the Early Modern Stage* (Oxford, 2000), 28, 36.

40   Roslyn L. Knutson, 'Playing Companies and Repertory', *A Companion to Renaissance Drama*, ed. Arthur F. Kinney (Oxford, 2004), 180–92 (190).

41   See Gurr, *Opposites*, 22; Gurr, *Company*, 135.

42   See Stern, 225; David Bradley, *From Text to Performance in the Elizabethan Theatre: Preparing the Play for the Stage* (Cambridge, 1992), 126.

43   On actors' parts, see Simon Palfrey and Tiffany Stern, *Shakespeare in Parts* (Oxford, 2007; repr. 2010).

44   See Dulwich College, MSS 1, ff.261–71 (Article 138), http://henslowe-alleyn.org.uk (accessed 05.05.13).

45   Stern, 243.

46   Alfred W. Pollard, *Shakespeare's Fight with the Pirates and the Problems of the Transmission of his Text*, revised edn (Cambridge, 1967; repr. 2010), 56–7, 63; William B. Long, 'Stage-directions: A Misinterpreted Factor in Determining Textual Provenance', *TEXT: Transactions of the Society for Textual Scholarship* 2 (1985), 121–37 (125).

47   Gabriel Egan, 'Precision, Consistency, and Completeness in Early-Modern Playbook Manuscripts: The Evidence from *Thomas of Woodstock* and *John a Kent and John a Cumber*', *The Library* 12 (2011) 376–91.

48 See BL, Egerton MS 2828, f.9v, f.8v, f.9 (© The British Library Board).

49 Quotations from the play are based on my transcriptions but I use the line numbers given in the Malone Society edition: Philip Massinger, *Believe As You List* (Malone Society Reprints, 1927), ed. Charles J. Sisson (Oxford, 1927).

50 See Leslie Thomson, 'A Quarto "Marked for Performance": Evidence of What?', *MRDE* 8 (1996), 176–210 (177).

51 For examples, see Long, 'Precious', 423, 425.

52 See, for example, T. H. Howard-Hill, 'Crane's 1619 "Promptbook" of *Barnavelt* and Theatrical Processes', *MP* 86:2 (1988), 146–70 (166).

53 Stern, 230.

54 In Janet Clare, *'Art made tongue-tied by authority': Elizabethan and Jacobean Dramatic Censorship*, 2nd edn (Manchester, 1999), 52.

55 London, BL, Additional MS 18653, f.16 and f.17v (© The British Library Board); John Fletcher and Philip Massinger, *The Tragedy of Sir John Van Olden Barnavelt* (Malone Society Reprints, 1979), ed. T. H. Howard-Hill (Oxford, 1980), ll.1557, 1685.

56 In N. W. Bawcutt, ed., *The Control and Censorship of Caroline Drama: The Records of Sir Henry Herbert, Master of the Revels, 1623–73* (Oxford, 1996), 182.

57 BL, Additional MS 18653, f.5v.

58 Gabriel Egan, 'Theatre in London' in *Shakespeare: An Oxford Guide*, Stanley Wells and Lena Cowen Orlin (eds) (Oxford, 2003), 20–31 (27).

59 Grace Ioppolo, *Dramatists and Their Manuscripts in the Age of Shakespeare, Jonson, Middleton and Heywood: Authority, Authorship and the Playhouse* (London, 2006; repr. 2007), 140.

60 Richard Dutton, *Mastering the Revels: The Regulation and Censorship of English Renaissance Drama* (Basingstoke, 1991), 248.

61 Carol A. Chillington, 'Playwrights at Work: Henslowe's, Not

Shakespeare's Book of *Sir Thomas More*', *ELR* 10 (1980), 439–79 (471).

62 William Shakespeare, *Richard II*, updated edn, ed. Andrew Gurr (Cambridge, 2003; repr. 2012), 9.

63 See, for example, Leeds Barroll, 'A New History for Shakespeare and his Time', *SQ* 39 (1988), 441–64 (449).

64 London, BL, Egerton MS 1994 (© The British Library Board). Quotations from the play are based on my transcriptions but I use the line numbers given in the Malone Society edition: *The Launching of the Mary* (Malone Society Reprints, 1933), ed. John Henry Walter (Oxford, 1933).

65 See Henry Glapthorne, *The Lady Mother* (Malone Society Reprints, 1958), ed. Arthur Brown (Oxford, 1959), viii–xi; Walter Mountfort, ix.

66 Ioppolo, *Dramatists*, 1.

67 See Howard-Hill, *Barnavelt*, vi–vii.

68 Andrew Gurr, 'Maximal and Minimal Texts: Shakespeare V. the Globe', *SS* 52 (1999), 68–87 (70).

69 Ben Jonson, *Every Man Out of His Humour*, ed. Randall Martin in *The Cambridge Edition of the Works of Ben Jonson*, David Bevington, Martin Butler and Ian Donaldson (eds), 7 vols (Cambridge, 2012), I, 249.

70 See Stern, 91.

71 See Foakes, *Diary*, 137, 203, 206.

72 See Ben Jonson, *Sejanus*, ed. Tom Cain in *The Cambridge Edition of the Works of Ben Jonson*, II, 215.

73 Howard-Hill, 'Crane's', 150.

74 John Kerrigan, 'Revision, Adaptation, and the Fool in *King Lear*' in *Division of the Kingdoms: Shakespeare's Two Versions of 'King Lear'*, Gary Taylor and Michael Warren (eds) (Oxford, 1983), 195–239 (196).

75 See Peter W. M. Blayney, 'The Publication of Playbooks' in *A New History of Early English Drama*, John D. Cox and David Scott Kastan (eds) (New York, 1997), 383–422 (384, 385, 389); Alan B. Farmer and Zachary Lesser, 'The Popularity of Playbooks Revisited', *SQ* 56:1 (2005), 1–32 (4, 16).

76   Ioppolo, 'Transmission', 176.

77   Thomas Heywood, *The English Traveller* (London, 1633), sig.
       A3r.

78   Blayney, 'Publication', 386.

79   Pollard, 48.

80   See, for example, Blayney, 'Publication', 404.

81   See Lukas Erne, *Shakespeare as Literary Dramatist*
       (Cambridge, 2003).

82   London, BL, Lansdowne MS 807, ff.29–56 (Thomas
       Middleton, *The Second Maiden's Tragedy*) (© The British
       Library Board). Quotations from the play are based on my
       transcriptions but I use the line references given in the Malone
       Society edition: *The Second Maiden's Tragedy* (Malone
       Society Reprints, 1909), ed. W. W. Greg (Oxford, 1909).
       Hereafter all references to the manuscript are cited in the text.
       On the play's attribution to Middleton, see Julia Briggs, ed.,
       The Lady's Tragedy in *Thomas Middleton: The Collected
       Works*, Gary Taylor and John Lavagnino (eds) (Oxford,
       2007), 833.

83   See Greg, *Second*, vi.

84   John Astington, *Actors and Acting in Shakespeare's Time: The
       Art of Stage Playing* (Cambridge, 2010), 213, 198–9.

85   Anne Lancashire, ed., *The Second Maiden's Tragedy*
       (Manchester, 1978), 283.

86   Ibid., 279.

87   In William Shakespeare, *King Lear*, ed. R. A. Foakes (London,
       1997), 111. All quotations from *Lear* are from this edition
       and are cited in the text hereafter.

88   See Peter W. M. Blayney, *The Texts of 'King Lear' and their
       Origins, Volume 1: Nicholas Okes and the First Quarto*
       (Cambridge, 1982), 148–9.

89   See Adele Davidson, *Shakespeare in Shorthand: the Textual
       Mystery of 'King Lear'* (Newark, NJ, 2009).

90   See Foakes, *Lear*, 120–1.

91   See Blayney, *Texts*, 186.

92   See Richard Knowles, 'The Evolution of the Texts of *Lear*'

in *'King Lear': New Critical Essays*, ed. Jeffrey Kahan (New York, 2008), 124–54 (142).

93 Ibid., 141.

94 Foakes, *Lear*, 130.

95 See *The Division of the Kingdoms: Shakespeare's Two Versions of 'King Lear'*, Gary Taylor and Michael Warren (eds) (Oxford, 1983).

96 Sidney Thomas, 'Shakespeare's Supposed Revision of *King Lear*', *SQ* 35:4 (1984), 506–11 (506).

97 See, for example, Steven Urkowitz, *Shakespeare's Revision of 'King Lear'* (Princeton, NJ, 1980).

98 Knowles, 140, 149.

99 Foakes, *Lear*, 137.

100 Kerrigan, 219; Bart van Es, *Shakespeare in Company* (Oxford, 2013), 186.

101 Foakes, *Lear*, 139–40.

102 Ibid., 146.

103 Michael Warren, 'The Diminution of Kent', *The Division of the Kingdoms: Shakespeare's Two Versions of 'King Lear'*, Gary Taylor and Michael Warren (eds) (Oxford, 1983), 59–73 (60, 64).

Chapter 3

1 Andrew Gurr and Mariko Ichikawa, *Staging in Shakespeare's Theatres* (Oxford, 2000; repr. 2012), 25.

2 Herbert Berry, 'Playhouses' in *A Companion to Renaissance Drama*, ed. Arthur F. Kinney (Oxford, 2004), 147–62 (148–60).

3 Ibid., 149.

4 See Andrew Gurr, *The Shakespearean Stage, 1574–1642*, 3rd edn (Cambridge, 2005), 155–6.

5 See Leeds Barroll, 'Shakespeare and the Second Blackfriars Theater', *SSt* 23 (2005), 156–70 (158, 164).

6 Andrew Gurr, 'London's Blackfriars Playhouse and the Chamberlain's Men' in *Inside Shakespeare: Essays on the Blackfriars Stage*, ed. Paul Menzer (Selinsgrove, PA, 2006), 17–30 (17).

7 Alan Somerset, 'The Blackfriars on Tour: Provincial Analogies' in *Inside Shakespeare: Essays on the Blackfriars Stage*, ed. Paul Menzer (Selinsgrove, PA, 2006), 80–5 (81).

8 Berry, 152.

9 For a reproduction, see Gurr, *Stage*, 133.

10 Ibid., 132, 123.

11 Bruce R. Smith, *The Acoustic World of Early Modern England* (Chicago, 1999), 209.

12 Berry, 160.

13 See R. B. Graves, *Lighting the Shakespearean Stage, 1567–1642* (Carbondale, IL, 1999), 125, 130.

14 Gurr, *Stage*, 177.

15 Andrew Gurr, *Shakespeare's Opposites: The Admiral's Company, 1594–1625* (Cambridge, 2009; repr. 2012), 55; Gurr, *Stage*, 103.

16 See Tiffany Stern, *Rehearsal from Shakespeare to Sheridan* (Oxford, 2003; repr. 2005), 54.

17 See N. W. Bawcutt, ed., *The Control and Censorship of Caroline Drama: The Records of Sir Henry Herbert, Master of the Revels 1623–73* (Oxford, 1996), 182.

18 Ibid., 183, 177.

19 Andrew Gurr, *The Shakespeare Company, 1594–1642* (Cambridge, 2004), 15; Stern, *Rehearsal*, 15.

20 See Rick Bowers, 'John Lowin: Actor-Manager of the King's Company, 1630–1642', *TS* 28:1 (1987), 15–35 (19).

21 T. J. King, *Casting Shakespeare's Plays: London Actors and their Roles, 1590–1642* (Cambridge, 1992), 18.

22 Ibid., 6.

23 See London, BL, Egerton MS 1994, ff.233, 235v; BL, Additional MS 10449, f.2 (© The British Library Board).

24 On 'parts', see Simon Palfrey and Tiffany Stern, *Shakespeare in Parts* (Oxford, 2007; repr. 2010).

25 See David Bradley, *From Text to Performance in the Elizabethan Theatre* (Cambridge, 1992), 35.

26 See Stern, *Rehearsal*, 10, 68.

27 Gurr, *Stage*, 210.

28 Peter Thomson, *Shakespeare's Theatre*, 2nd edn (London, 1992), 121.

29 Stern, *Rehearsal*, 64.

30 In Walter W. Greg, ed., *Henslowe Papers* (London, 1907), 124.

31 See Graves, 108.

32 See Tiffany Stern, *Documents of Performance in Early Modern England* (Cambridge, 2009; repr. 2012), 204, 231.

33 Gurr and Ichikawa, 42, 84.

34 See Andrew Gurr and Gabriel Egan, 'Prompting, Backstage Activity, and the Openings onto the Shakespearian Stage', *TN* 56 (2002), 138–42.

35 Ben Jonson, *Bartholomew Fair*, 2nd edn, G. R. Hibbard and Alexander Leggatt (eds) (London, 2007), Induction.25–6. Hereafter references to this play will be cited in the text.

36 S. P. Cerasano, 'Must the Devil Appear?: Audiences, Actors, Stage Business' in *A Companion to Renaissance Drama*, ed. Arthur F. Kinney (Oxford, 2004), 193–211 (202).

37 B. L. Joseph, *Elizabethan Acting* (London, 1951); Bernard Beckerman, *Shakespeare at the Globe, 1599–1609* (New York, 1962; repr. 1966), 132.

38 Gurr, *Shakespeare Company*, 16.

39 Marvin Rosenberg, 'Elizabethan Actors: Men or Marionettes?' *PMLA* 69:4 (1954), 915–27 (922).

40 Richard Flecknoe, 'A Short Discourse of the English Stage' in *Loves Kingdom, A Pastoral Trage-Comedy* (London, 1664), no page numbers.

41 *The Second Part of the Return from Parnassus* in *The*

Three Parnassus Plays, ed. J. B. Leishman (London, 1949), 4.3.1757–61.

42   Gerald Eades Bentley, 'Shakespeare and the Blackfriars Theatre', *SS* 1 (1948), 38–50 (47–8, 49).

43   See, for example, Tiffany Stern, *Making Shakespeare: From Stage to Page* (London, 2004; repr. 2005), 32.

44   John Astington, 'Playing the Man: Acting at the Red Bull and the Fortune', *ET* 9 (2006), 130–43 (130).

45   Andrew Gurr, *Playgoing in Shakespeare's London*, 3rd edn (Cambridge, 2004; repr. 2005), 215.

46   Thomas Goffe, *The Careless Shepherdess* (London, 1656), no page numbers.

47   Gurr, *Playgoing*, 215.

48   Edmund Gayton, *Pleasant Notes upon Don Quixot* (London, 1654), 24.

49   John Tatham, *Knavery in All Trades: Or, The Coffee-House* (London, 1664), sig.E; Thomas Rawlins, *The Rebellion* (London, 1640), 5.1., sig.I2.

50   See Andrew Gurr, 'Playing in Amphitheatres and Playing in Hall Theatres', *Elizabethan Theatre* 13 (1994), 27–62 (58).

51   Flecknoe, no page numbers.

52   T. J. King, *Shakespearean Staging, 1599–1642* (Cambridge, MA, 1971), 2.

53   R. A. Foakes, ed., *Henslowe's Diary*, 2nd edn (Cambridge, 2002), 99, 103.

54   See Greg, 124.

55   London, Dulwich College, MSS 1, f.44 (Article 30), http://henslowe-alleyn.org.uk (accessed 11.12.12).

56   Foakes, 292, 321, 322.

57   Jean MacIntyre and Garrett P. J. Epp, '"Cloathes worth all the rest": Costumes and Properties' in *A New History of Early English Drama*, John D. Cox and David Scott Kastan (eds) (New York, 1997), 269–85 (278).

58   See Gurr, *Stage*, 194; MacIntyre and Epp, 279.

59   On the significance of costumes, see Robert I. Lublin,

Costuming the Shakespearean Stage: Visual Codes of Representation in Early Modern Theatre and Culture (Farnham, 2011).

60   Christopher Marlowe, *Tamburlaine*, ed. J. W. Harper (London, 1992), 1.2.42. Hereafter references to this play will be cited in the text.

61   Foakes, 319–20.

62   Ibid., 319, 320.

63   Ibid., 318.

64   Andrea R. Stevens, '"Assisted by a Barber": The Court Apothecary, Special Effects, and *The Gypsies Metamorphosed*', *TN* 61:1 (2007), 2–11 (3).

65   See Gurr, *Stage*, 182–4.

66   Ben Jonson, *The Alchemist*, 3rd edn, ed. Elizabeth Cook (London, 2010), 1.1.17. Hereafter references to this play will be cited in the text.

67   Ian Donaldson, *Jonson's Magic Houses: Essays in Interpretation* (Oxford, 1997), 94.

68   Martin Butler, 'Jonson's London and its Theatres' in *The Cambridge Companion to Ben Jonson*, Richard Harp and Stanley Stewart (eds) (Cambridge, 2000), 15–29 (26).

69   Donaldson, *Jonson's*, 83–4.

70   See Siobhan Keenan, *Renaissance Literature* (Edinburgh, 2008), 80.

71   Richard Fotheringham, 'The Doubling of Roles on the Jacobean Stage', *TRI* 10 (1985), 18–32 (22, 28).

72   Ben Jonson, *The Workes of Beniamin Jonson* (London, 1616), 678.

73   James A. Riddell, 'Some Actors in Ben Jonson's Plays', *SSt* 5 (1969), 285–98 (289).

74   R. L. Smallwood, '"Here, in the Friars": Immediacy and Theatricality in *The Alchemist*', *RES* 32:136 (1981), 142–60 (151).

75   See John Astington, *Actors and Acting in Shakespeare's Time: The Art of Stage Playing* (Cambridge, 2010), 195, 197.

76 Irwin Smith, *Shakespeare's Blackfriars Playhouse: Its History and Design* (London, 1966), 323; Andrew Gurr, 'The Bare Island', *SS* 47 (1994), 29–43 (38–9).

77 John Marston, *The Malcontent*, ed. George K. Hunter (Manchester, 1975; repr. 1999), Induction.78–90.

78 Foakes, 317.

79 See Gurr, *Company*, 294.

80 See David Cook and F. P. Wilson (eds), 'Dramatic Records in the Declared Accounts of the Treasurer of the Chamber, 1558–1642', *Malone Society Collections* 6 (1961) (Oxford, 1962), 60.

81 In Gurr, *Stage*, 153.

82 Andrew Gurr, *The Shakespearian Playing Companies* (Oxford, 1996), 398.

83 Keith Sturgess, *Jacobean Private Theatre* (London, 1987), 170.

84 Leah Marcus, *The Politics of Mirth: Jonson, Herrick, Milton, Marvell and the Defence of Old Holiday Pastimes* (Chicago, 1986; repr. 1989), 49.

85 R. B. Parker, 'The Themes and Staging of *Bartholomew Fair*', *UTQ* 39 (1970), 293–309 (293).

86 Gabriel Egan, 'The Use of Booths in the Original Staging of Jonson's *Bartholomew Fair*', *Cahiers Elisabethains* 53 (1998), 43–52 (49).

87 Alison A. Chapman, 'Flaying Bartholomew: Jonson's Hagiographic Parody', *MP* 101:4 (2004), 511–41 (513, 526).

88 Parker, 302–3.

89 Jonas Barish, *Ben Jonson and the Language of Prose Comedy* (New York, 1960; repr. 1970), 232.

90 Parker, 308–9.

91 See Glynne Wickham, Herbert Berry and William Ingram (eds), *English Professional Theatre, 1530–1660* (Cambridge, 2000), 217, 219.

92 Sturgess, 180.

93 W. R. Streitberger, ed., 'Jacobean and Caroline Revels

Accounts, 1603–1642', *Malone Society Collections* 13 (Oxford, 1986), 70.

94   Egan, 44.

95   Parker, 298–9.

96   Ian Donaldson, *The World Upside-Down: Comedy from Jonson to Fielding* (Oxford, 1974), 53; Parker, 294.

97   Clifford Davidson, 'Judgment, Iconoclasm, and Anti-theatricalism in Jonson's *Bartholomew Fair*', *Papers on Language and Literature* 25:4 (1989), 349–63 (351).

98   Parker, 295.

99   Ibid., 291.

Chapter 4

1   'The Printer to the Reader' in J. C., *The Two Merry Milkmaids* (1620), ed. G. Harold Metz (New York, 1979), ll.38–40.

2   I use the terms 'audience', 'spectators' and 'playgoers' interchangeably to describe Shakespearean playgoers. Contemporaries usually used one of the first two terms. See Andrew Gurr, *Playgoing in Shakespeare's London*, 3rd edn (Cambridge, 2005), 107.

3   Andrew Gurr, *The Shakespearean Stage, 1574–1642*, 3rd edn (Cambridge, 2005), 213.

4   Andrew Gurr, *Playgoing in Shakespeare's London*, 2nd edn (Cambridge, 1997), xv.

5   Alfred Harbage, *Shakespeare's Audience* (New York, 1941), 90, 162.

6   Alfred Harbage, *Shakespeare and the Rival Traditions* (New York, 1952), xii.

7   Ann Jennalie Cook, *The Privileged Playgoers of Shakespeare's London, 1576–1642* (Princeton, NJ, 1981), 8, 219–20, 224–5, 272.

8   Martin Butler, *Theatre and Crisis, 1632–42* (Cambridge, 1984), 294, 300, 100, 282, 304.

9   Andrew Gurr, *The Shakespearian Playing Companies* (Oxford, 1996), 150; Gurr, *Playgoing*, 2nd edn, 4.

10 Gurr, *Playgoing*, 3rd edn, 196–7.

11 Ibid., 90.

12 Ibid., 92, 196; Gurr, *Stage*, 231.

13 Harbage, *Audience*, 137; Cook, *Privileged*, 7.

14 Butler, 305.

15 Jeremy Lopez, *Theatrical Conventions and Audience Response in Early Modern Drama* (Cambridge, 2003), 7.

16 Gurr, *Playgoing*, 3rd edn, 6.

17 Ibid., 69.

18 See Gurr, *Stage*, 213; Gurr, *Playgoing*, 3rd edn, 26, 32.

19 See Ann Jennalie Cook, 'Audiences: Investigation, Interpretation, Invention' in *A New History of Early English Drama*, John D. Cox and David Scott Kastan (eds) (New York, 1997), 305–20 (314).

20 Translated in Edward M. Wilson and Olga Turner, 'The Spanish Protest Against *A Game at Chesse*', *MLR* 44 (1949, repr. 1963), 476–82 (480).

21 Arthur Kinney, *Shakespeare by Stages: An Historical Introduction* (Oxford, 2003), 75–6.

22 Harbage, *Audience*, 55, 60, 59.

23 In Gurr, *Playgoing*, 3rd edn, 257.

24 In John Orrell, 'The London Stage in the Florentine Correspondence, 1604–1618', *TRI* 3 (1977–8), 157–76 (171).

25 See Leslie Thomson, 'Playgoers on the Outdoor Stages of Early Modern London', *TN* 64:1 (2010), 3–11.

26 See Gurr, *Playgoing*, 3rd edn, 232.

27 Gurr, *Stage*, 157–8.

28 See Charles Whitney, *Early Responses to Renaissance Drama* (Cambridge, 2006), 186.

29 See Charles Whitney, '"Usually in the Werking Daies": Playgoing Journeymen, Apprentices and Servants in Guild

Records, 1582–92', *SQ* 50:4 (1999), 433–58 (435); Whitney, *Early*, 169–85.

30 Gurr, *Playgoing*, 3rd edn, 225, 227, 231, 234, 238, 224.

31 Ibid., 229, 238, 241, 226, 231, 232, 236, 243, 230, 235, 236.

32 Ibid., 226, 231, 236.

33 Cited in Linda Levy Peck, 'The Caroline Audience: Evidence from Hatfield House', *SQ* 51:4 (2000), 474–7 (474, 477).

34 Cited in Gurr, *Playgoing*, 3rd edn, 67. For a possible explanation of the accident, see Charles Edelman, '"Shoot him all at once": Gunfire at the Playhouse, 1587', *TN* 57 (2003), 78–81.

35 Gurr, *Playgoing*, 3rd edn, 244, 231, 246, 231, 234, 240, 244.

36 James Wright, *Historia Histrionica: An Historical Account of the English Stage* (London, 1679), 5.

37 Alexander Gill, cited in *Ben Jonson: The Critical Heritage*, ed. D. H. Craig (London, 1999; repr. 2005), 137; John Tatham, *The Fancies Theater* (London, 1640), sig.H2v–H3r, ll.11–12.

38 Richard Rowland, '(Gentle)men Behaving Badly: Aggression, Anxiety, and Repertory in the Playhouses of Early Modern London', *MRDE* 25 (2012), 17–41 (29).

39 Gurr, *Playgoing*, 3rd edn, 226, 227, 230, 234, 235, 239, 242.

40 Ibid., 234.

41 Ibid., 230, 239, 230, 233.

42 Ibid., 70, 77.

43 Ben Jonson, 'To the worthy Author M. John Fletcher' in John Fletcher, *The Faithful Shepherdess*, ed. Florence Ada Kirk (New York, 1980), 6, 7; Thomas Goffe, *The Careless Shepherdess* (London, 1656); Richard Brome, *The Court Beggar*, Quarto Text (1653), ed. M. O'Connor, *Richard Brome Online*, http://www.hrionline.ac.uk/brome (accessed 30.01.13), Epilogue.2855. Hereafter references to Goffe's play will be cited in the text.

44 Gurr, *Playgoing*, 3rd edn, 233; Ben Jonson, *The Magnetic Lady*, ed. Helen Ostovich in *The Cambridge Edition of the Works of Ben Jonson*, David Bevington, Martin Butler and Ian Donaldson (eds), 7 vols (Cambridge, 2012), VI, Induction.23–4.

45   Lopez, 8.

46   John Astington, 'Playing the Man: Acting at the Red Bull and the Fortune', *ET* 9 (2006), 30–43 (38).

47   Andrew Gurr, 'Playing in Amphitheatres and Playing in Hall Theatres', *Elizabethan Theatre* 13 (1994), 27–62 (52–3); Gurr, *Playgoing*, 3rd edn, 208.

48   See, for example, Gurr, *Companies*, 389–90.

49   Richard Levin, 'Women in the Renaissance Theatre Audience', *SQ* 40:2 (1989), 165–74 (171).

50   David Kathman, 'Kirke, John (fl.1629–43)', *ODNB* online edn, http://www.oxforddnb.com (accessed 02.02.12).

51   Butler, 220, 235, 135.

52   John Lyly, *Midas* in *Gallathea and Midas*, ed. Anne Begor Lancashire (London, 1969; repr. 1970), Prologue.11–12. Hereafter references to this play will be cited in the text.

53   Anglophile Eutheo, *A Second and Third Blast of Retrait from Plaies and Theaters* (London, 1580), 100, 53–4.

54   See Gurr, *Stage*, 78.

55   Cook, 'Audiences', 312.

56   Ibid., 313.

57   Thomas Heywood, *An Apology for Actors* (London, 1612), sig.G.

58   James M. Gibson, ed., *REED: Kent – Diocese of Canterbury*, 3 vols (London, 2002), II, 920.

59   See Gurr, *Playgoing*, 3rd edn, 225, 232.

60   John Loftis, ed., *The Memoirs of Anne, Lady Halkett and Ann, Lady Fanshawe* (Oxford, 1979), 11.

61   Mary Blackstone and Cameron Louis, 'Towards "A Full and Understanding Auditory": New Evidence of Playgoers at the First Globe Theatre', *MLR* 90 (1995), 556–71 (561–2).

62   See Gurr, *Playgoing*, 3rd edn, 52, 300.

63   Francis Beaumont, *The Knight of the Burning Pestle*, 2nd edn, ed. Michael Hattaway (London, 2002), 9–10. Hereafter references to this play will be cited in the text.

64 Stephen Gosson, *The Trumpet of Warre* (London, 1598), sig. C8v.

65 See Levin, 170.

66 Edmund Gayton, *Pleasant Notes upon Don Quixot* (London, 1654), 140, 3.

67 Ben Jonson, *Every Man Out of His Humour*, ed. Randall Martin in *The Cambridge Edition of the Works of Ben Jonson*, I, Induction.159–61.

68 Ben Jonson, 'Dedication' in *The New Inn*, ed. Julie Sanders in *The Cambridge Edition of the Works of Ben Jonson*, VI, ll.6–7.

69 Thomas Dekker, *The Guls Horne-booke* (London, 1609), 28.

70 Cook, 'Audiences', 311.

71 Michael Neill, '"Wits most accomplished Senate": The Audience of the Caroline Private Theaters', *SEL*, 18 (1978), 341–60 (345).

72 Gayton, 271.

73 Tiffany Stern, *Documents of Performance in Early Modern England* (Cambridge, 2009; repr. 2012), 36, 86, 92.

74 Ben Jonson, *The Staple of News*, ed. Joseph Loewenstein in *The Cambridge Edition of the Works of Ben Jonson*, VI, Prologue.7–8.

75 Ben Jonson, *Bartholomew Fair*, 2nd edn, G. R. Hibbard and Alexander Leggatt (eds) (London, 2007), Induction.66–147.

76 See Ben Jonson, 'Dedicatory Epistle', *Volpone*, ed. Richard Dutton in *The Cambridge Edition of the Works of Ben Jonson*, III, ll.49–53.

77 Tiffany Stern, 'Sermons, Plays and Note-takers: *Hamlet* Q1 as a "Noted" Text', *SS* 66 (2013), 1–23.

78 Charles Whitney, 'Appropriate This', *Borrowers and Lenders: The Journal of Shakespeare and Appropriation* 3:2 (2008), http://www.borrowers.uga.edu (1) (accessed 23.01.13).

79 Whitney, *Early*, 2.

80 See E. K. Chambers, *William Shakespeare: A Study of Facts*

and Problems, 2 vols (Oxford, 1930), II, 337–41; Gurr, *Playgoing*, 3rd edn, 134–6.

81   Cited in Chambers, II, 340.

82   Nottingham, University of Nottingham Library, MS Ne C 15, 1405, f.4.

83   Taunton, Somerset Heritage Centre, DD/PH/212/12.

84   Ibid.

85   Chambers, II, 337–41. The date and location of *Cymbeline*'s production is not given; it is likely to have been 1611 at the Globe as well.

86   S. P. Cerasano, 'Philip Henslowe, Simon Forman, and the Theatrical Community of the 1590s', *SQ* 44:2 (1993), 145–58 (150, 157–8).

87   Whitney, *Early*, 149.

88   Ibid., 149.

89   See Chambers, 338.

90   Ibid., 339.

91   Whitney, *Early*, 155.

92   In Chambers, 340.

93   See Whitney, *Early*, 154.

94   In Chambers, 341.

95   Whitney, *Early*, 8, 149–50.

96   J. W., *The Valiant Scot*, ed. George F. Byers (New York, 1980), 65.

97   J. W., *The Valiant Scot* (London, 1637; repr. Marston Gate, 2011), Act 1, sig.A3v, sig.B3; Act 2, sig.D2. Hereafter references to this edition of the play are cited in the text. It does not include scene or line numbers. References give the act number and, where available, the page signature.

98   Byers, 59–60.

99   John Kerrigan, *Archipelagic English: Literature, History, and Politics, 1603–1707* (Oxford, 2008), 92, 153.

100 Ibid., 92.

101 *Vox Borealis Or The Northern Discoverie* (London, 1641), sig.B2-2v.

102 See G. E. Bentley, *The Jacobean and Caroline Stage*, 7 vols (Oxford, 1941–68), I (1941), 277.

103 Ibid., 270.

104 Gurr, *Companies*, 447. I must thank Gabriel Egan for the point about the religious topicality of Kirke's play.

105 *Vox Borealis*, sig.B2v.

106 See Butler, 135.

107 *Vox Borealis*, sig.B2v.

108 Butler, 236.

109 Ibid., 234.

110 Richard Brome, *A Jovial Crew: Or, The Merry Beggars*, Quarto Text (1652), ed. E. Lowe, *Richard Brome Online*, http://www.hrionline.ac.uk/brome (accessed 30.01.13), 2.1.1102. Hereafter references to the play will be cited in the text.

111 Bentley, 324.

112 Gurr, *Stage*, 162.

113 R. J. Kaufman, *Richard Brome. Caroline Playwright* (New York, 1961), 169.

114 Julie Sanders, 'Beggars' Commonwealths and the Pre-Civil War Stage: Suckling's *The Goblins*, Brome's *A Jovial Crew*, and Shirley's *The Sisters*', MLR 97:1 (2002), 1–14 (9).

115 Ira Clark, *Professional Playwrights: Massinger, Ford, Shirley, & Brome* (Lexington, KT, 1992), 161.

116 Rosemary Gaby, 'Of Vagabonds and Commonwealths: *Beggars' Bush*, *A Jovial Crew*, and *The Sisters*', SEL 34 (1994), 401–24 (409).

117 Garrett A. Sullivan Jr, *The Drama of Landscape: Land, Property, and Social Relations on the Early Modern Stage* (Stanford, CA, 1998), 159.

118 Butler, 270.

119 See Warren Chernaik, 'Stanley, Thomas (1625–1678)', *ODNB* online edn, http://www.oxforddnb.com (accessed 31.01.12).

Chapter 5

1   John Marston, *Histrio-Mastix* (London, 1610), 1.1. (sig.B).
    There are no line numbers in this edition.

2   In E. K. Chambers, *The Elizabethan Stage* (Oxford, 1923;
    repr. 1961), IV, 237.

3   See Suzanne R. Westfall, *Patrons and Performance: Early
    Tudor Household Revels* (Oxford, 1990), 11.

4   London, Dulwich College, MSS 1, f.19 (Article 14), http://
    www.henslowe-alleyn.org.uk (accessed 11.06.12).

5   In E. K. Chambers, *The Elizabethan Stage* (Oxford, 1923;
    repr. 1961), II, 86.

6   Anglophile Eutheo, *A Second and Third Blast of Retrait from
    Plaies and Theaters* (London, 1580), 76.

7   Mary A. Blackstone, 'Lancashire, Shakespeare and the
    Construction of Cultural Neighbourhoods in Sixteenth-
    Century England' in *Region, Religion and Patronage:
    Lancastrian Shakespeare*, Richard Dutton, Alison Findlay and
    Richard Wilson (eds) (Manchester, 2003), 186–204 (196).

8   Scott McMillin and Sally-Beth MacLean, *The Queen's Men
    and Their Plays* (Cambridge, 1998), 23.

9   Ibid., 23, 17.

10 Leeds Barroll, 'Shakespeare, Noble Patrons, and the Pleasures
    of "Common" Playing' in *Shakespeare and Theatrical
    Patronage in Early Modern England*, Paul Whitfield
    White and Suzanne R. Westfall (eds) (Cambridge, 2002),
    90–121 (92).

11 David George, 'The Playhouse at Prescot and the 1592–94
    Plague' in *Region, Religion and Patronage: Lancastrian
    Shakespeare*, Richard Dutton, Alison Findlay and Richard
    Wilson (eds) (Manchester, 2003), 227–42 (233); Peter
    Thomson, *Shakespeare's Professional Career* (Cambridge,
    1992), 44; Mary C. Erler, ed., *REED: Ecclesiastical London*
    (Toronto, 2008), 278.

12 See, for example, David Bergeron, 'Women as Patrons of
    English Renaissance Drama' in *Patronage in the Renaissance*,

Guy Fitch Lytle and Stephen Orgel (eds) (Princeton, NJ, 1981), 274–90.

13 See Andrew Gurr, *The Shakespearian Playing Companies* (Oxford, 1996), 74.

14 See Mary Edmond, 'Pembroke's Men', *RES* 25:98 (1974), 129–36 (130).

15 See Gurr, *Companies*, 265.

16 Barroll, 108–9.

17 Sally-Beth MacLean, 'Tracking Leicester's Men: the Patronage of a Performance Troupe' in *Shakespeare and Theatrical Patronage in Early Modern England*, Paul Whitfield White and Suzanne R. Westfall (eds) (Cambridge, 2002), 246–71 (260).

18 Audrey Douglas and Peter Greenfield (eds), *REED: Cumberland, Westmorland, Gloucestershire* (Toronto, 1986), 307.

19 Peter H. Greenfield, 'Professional Players at Gloucester: Conditions of Provincial Performing', *Elizabethan Theatre* 10 (1988), 73–92 (80).

20 Eutheo, 75–6.

21 *The Statutes of the Realm, Volume 4: Part 1, 1547–1585* (Buffalo, NY, 1993), 591–2.

22 In Chambers, II, 86.

23 Mary A. Blackstone, 'Patrons and Elizabethan Dramatic Companies', *Elizabethan Theatre* 10 (1988), 112–32 (115).

24 See Gurr, *Companies*, 113–14, 137.

25 See McMillin and MacLean, 27; Gurr, *Companies*, 64.

26 Andrew Gurr, *Shakespeare's Opposites: The Admiral's Company, 1594–1625* (Cambridge, 2009; repr. 2012), 11.

27 See Sally-Beth MacLean, 'The Politics of Patronage: Dramatic Records in Robert Dudley's Household Books', *SQ* 44:2 (1993), 175–82 (179, 181).

28 London, Lambeth Palace Library, MS 3196, f.29.

29 Paul L. Hughes and James F. Larkin (eds), *Tudor Royal Proclamations: The Later Tudors (1553–1587)* (New Haven, CT, 1969), II, 115–16; William Ingram, *The Business of*

Playing: The Beginnings of Adult Professional Theater in Elizabethan London (Ithaca, NY, 1992), 89.

30 See Glynne Wickham, Herbert Berry, William Ingram (eds), *English Professional Theatre, 1530–1660* (Cambridge, 2000), 206.

31 London, TNA, SP 12/163/44:1 (Mr Potter's Information against Sir Walter Waller, November 1583).

32 TNA, SP 12/160/48 (Letter from Sir Walter Waller to Sir Francis Walsingham, 20 May 1583).

33 Ibid.

34 For a fuller account of the case, see Peter Roberts, 'Elizabethan Players and Minstrels and the Legislation of 1572 against Retainers and Vagabonds' in *Religion, Culture and Society in Early Modern Britain: Essays in Honour of Patrick Collinson*, Anthony Fletcher and Peter Roberts (eds) (Cambridge, 1994), 29–55.

35 See Gurr, *Companies*, 262.

36 Westfall, *Patrons*, 151.

37 See Paul Whitfield White, *Theatre and Reformation: Protestantism, Patronage and Playing in Tudor England* (Cambridge, 1993), 62–6; McMillin and MacLean, 166.

38 Paul Whitfield White, 'Patronage, Protestantism, and Stage Propaganda in Early Elizabethan England', *YES* 21 (1991), 39–52 (41); Gurr, *Companies*, 33.

39 Andrew Gurr, *The Shakespeare Company, 1594–1642* (Cambridge, 2004), 173.

40 Eleanor Rosenberg, *Leicester: Patron of Letters* (New York, 1955), 301, 302–3.

41 In C. L. Kingsford and William A. Shaw (eds), *Historical Manuscripts Commission: Report on the Manuscripts of Lord De L'Isle & Dudley, preserved at Penshurst Place* (London, 1934), II, 415.

42 In Michael Brennan, *Literary Patronage in the English Renaissance: The Pembroke Family* (London, 1998), 140, 105.

43 Peter Davison, 'Commerce and Patronage: the Lord

Chamberlain's Men's Tour of 1597' in *Shakespeare Performed: Essays in Honor of R. A. Foakes*, ed. Grace Ioppolo (Newark, NJ, 2000), 56–71 (63).

44 London, BL, Egerton MS 2592, f.81 (letter from William Herbert, Earl of Pembroke to James Hay, Earl of Carlisle, 20 May 1619) (© The British Library Board).

45 MacLean, 'Tracking', 262.

46 Barroll, 99, 100.

47 Suzanne Westfall, '"The useless dearness of the diamond": Patronage Theatre and Households' in *Region, Religion and Patronage: Lancastrian Shakespeare*, Richard Dutton, Alison Findlay and Richard Wilson (eds) (Manchester, 2003), 32–49 (33).

48 See Gurr, *Companies*, 417, 418.

49 Margot Heinemann, 'Rebel Lords, Popular Playwrights, and Political Culture: Notes on the Jacobean Patronage of the Earl of Southampton', *YES* 21 (1991), 63–86 (70).

50 Blackstone, 'Patrons', 125.

51 Ibid., 123.

52 Werner Gundersheimer, 'Patronage in the Renaissance: An Exploratory Approach' in *Patronage in the Renaissance*, Guy Fitch Lytle and Stephen Orgel (eds) (Princeton, NJ, 1981), 3–23 (23).

53 John Stephens, *Satyrical Essayes Characters and Others* (London, 1615), 246.

54 Suzanne R. Westfall, '"The useless dearness of the diamond": Theories of Patronage Theatre' in *Shakespeare and Theatrical Patronage in Early Modern England*, Paul Whitfield White and Suzanne R. Westfall (eds) (Cambridge, 2002), 13–42 (20).

55 Westfall, 'Patronage Theatre and Households', 45.

56 Heinemann, 'Rebel', 70.

57 Kathleen McLuskie, 'The Poets' Royal Exchange: Patronage and Commerce in Early Modern Drama', *YES* 21 (1991), 53–62 (54).

58 Trevor Howard-Hill suggests that the play ran from 5 to 14 August; other scholars deduce that the run was from

6 to 17 August. See Trevor Howard-Hill, 'The Unique Eye-Witness Report of Middleton's *A Game at Chess*', *RES* 42: 166 (1991), 168–78 (170); for the alternative view see, for example, Richard Dutton, *Mastering the Revels: The Regulation and Censorship of English Renaissance Drama* (Basingstoke, 1991), 237.

59 Don Carlos Coloma (10 August, 1624), translated in Edward M. Wilson and Olga Turner, 'The Spanish Protest Against *A Game at Chesse*', *MLR* 44 (1949; repr. 1963), 476–82 (480); Nottingham, University of Nottingham, MS Ne C 15, 1405, f.3v (letter from Sir John Holles to Robert Carr, Earl of Somerset, 11 August 1624); for a transcription, see Gurr, *Playgoing*, 134–5.

60 TNA, SP 14/171/66 (letter from John Chamberlain to Sir Dudley Carleton, 21 August 1624).

61 See Mary Anne Everett Green, ed., *Calendar of State Papers, Domestic Series of the reign of James I, 1623–1625* (London, 1859; repr. Nendeln, Liechtenstein, 1967), 329.

62 See Trevor Howard-Hill, *Middleton's "Vulgar Pasquin": Essays on 'A Game at Chess'* (Newark, NJ, 1995), 232.

63 See Margot Heinemann, *Puritanism and Theatre: Thomas Middleton and Opposition Drama under the Early Stuarts* (Cambridge, 1980; repr. 1982), 155–6.

64 Thomas Middleton, *A Game at Chess*, ed. T. H. Howard-Hill (Manchester, 2003; repr. 2009), 2.2.106–70; 2.2.58; 5.3.160. Hereafter references to this play are cited in the text.

65 See Jane Sherman, 'The Pawns' Allegory in Middleton's *A Game at Chesse*', *RES* 29:114 (1978), 147–59 (156).

66 TNA, SP 14/171/49 (letter from Sir Francis Nethersole to Sir Dudley Carleton, 14 August 1624); University of Nottingham, MS Ne C 15, 1405, f.4.

67 TNA, SP 14/171/66.

68 Translated in Wilson and Turner, 480.

69 Ibid., 481.

70 TNA, SP 14/171/39 (letter from Sir Edward Conway to the Privy Council, 12 August 1624).

71 Ibid.

72 University of Nottingham, MS Ne C 15, 1405, f.4.

73 TNA, SP 14/171/64 (letter from Sir Edward Conway to the Privy Council, 21 August 1624); N. W. Bawcutt, *The Control and Censorship of Caroline Drama: The Records of Sir Henry Herbert, Master of the Revels, 1623–73* (Oxford, 1996), 152.

74 TNA, SP 14/171/64.

75 TNA, SP 14/171/75 (letter from Sir Edward Conway to the Privy Council, 27 August 1624).

76 See *Thomas Middleton and Early Modern Textual Culture: A Companion to the Collected Works*, Gary Taylor and John Lavagnino (eds) (Oxford, 2007), 871.

77 See Bawcutt, 66.

78 Janet Clare, *'Art made tongue-tied by authority': Elizabethan and Jacobean Dramatic Censorship*, 2nd edn (Manchester, 1999), 219.

79 See Trevor Howard-Hill, 'Political Interpretations of Middleton's *A Game at Chess*', YES 21 (1991), 274–85 (274).

80 Dutton, 239.

81 Gurr, *Companies*, 143, 144.

82 John Dover Wilson, 'Review of *A Game at Chesse* by Thomas Middleton. Ed. R. C. Bald', *The Library*, 4th series, 11 (1930), 105–16 (111).

83 In Brennan, 139.

84 Thomas Cogswell, 'Thomas Middleton and the Court, 1624: *A Game at Chess* in Context', HLQ 47 (1984), 273–88 (275, 284, 281).

85 University of Nottingham, MS Ne C 15, 1405, f.5.

86 In Bawcutt, 153.

87 See, for example, Bawcutt, 65; Dutton, 245; Howard-Hill, *Middleton's "Vulgar Pasquin"*, 105.

88 Paul Yachnin, '*A Game at Chess*: Thomas Middleton's "Praise of Folly"', MLQ 48 (1987), 107–23 (111).

89 On the equation of Catholicism with lechery in English Protestant culture, see Jerzy Limon, *Dangerous Matter:*

English Drama and Politics in 1623/24 (Cambridge, 1986), 127.

90 Blackstone, 'Patrons', 129.

91 Thomas Postlewait, 'Theater Events and Their Political Contexts: A Problem in the Writing of Theater History' in *Critical Theory and Performance*, revised edn, Janelle G. Reinelt and Joseph P. Roach (eds) (Ann Arbor, MI, 2007), 198–222 (212).

92 Howard-Hill, *"Vulgar"*, 105.

93 *Journal of the House of Commons, Vol. 1: 1547–1629* (1802), *British History Online* (1 March 1624), http://www.british-history.ac.uk (accessed 11.06.12).

94 Ben Jonson, *Neptune's Triumph for the Return of Albion*, ed. Martin Butler in *The Cambridge Edition of the Works of Ben Jonson*, David Bevington, Martin Butler and Ian Donaldson (eds), 7 vols (Cambridge, 2012), ll.280, 96, 89.

95 See Dutton, 236.

96 Howard-Hill, *"Vulgar"*, 108–9.

97 Postlewait, 203.

98 Gurr, *Company*, 177.

99 Taunton, Somerset Heritage Centre, DD/PH/212/12, f.2; for a transcription, see Gurr, *Playgoing*, 136.

100 Somerset Heritage Centre, DD/PH/212/12, ff.2-2v.

101 Herbert Berry, 'The Globe Bewitched and El Hombre Fiel', *MRDE* 1 (1984), 211–30 (215).

102 In Berry, 215.

103 See John Bruce, ed., *Calendar of State Papers: Domestic Series of the Reign of Charles I, 1634–1635* (Nendeln, Liechtenstein, 1967), 129.

104 TNA, SP 16/271, f.57 (Examination of Edmund Robinson, 10 July 1634).

105 See Berry, 214.

106 In Bruce, 26.

107 Diane Purkiss, *The Witch in History: Early Modern and Twentieth-Century Representations* (London, 1996), 233.

108 John Webster, *The Displaying of Supposed Witchcraft* (London, 1677), 346.

109 In Bawcutt, 189.

110 Berry, 216–18.

111 Robinson, cited in Webster, 347; Richard Brome and Thomas Heywood, *The Late Lancashire Witches*, Quarto Text (1634), ed. H. Ostovich, *Richard Brome Online*, http://www.hrionline. ac.uk/brome (accessed 15.05.12), II.i.900. Hereafter references to this play are cited in the text.

112 In Webster, 347.

113 TNA, SP 16/269, f.85:Iv (Examination of Mary Spencer, 13 June 1634), f.85:I (Examination of Margaret Johnson, 13 June 1634).

114 Berry, 219, 221–3, 223.

115 Paul Whitfield White, *Drama and Religion in English Provincial Society, 1485–1660* (Cambridge, 2008), 186.

116 Gurr, *Company*, 140–1, 177.

117 Whitfield White, *Drama*, 186, 187.

118 Heather Hirschfield, 'Collaborating across Generations: Thomas Heywood, Richard Brome, and the Production of *The Late Lancashire Witches*', *Journal of Medieval and Early Modern Studies*, 30:2 (2000), 339–74 (356, 364).

119 See Whitfield White, 183; Hirschfield, 355.

120 Hirschfield, 349.

121 Hirschfield, 367; Berry, 221.

122 Somerset Heritage Centre, DD/PH/212/12, f.2.

BIBLIOGRAPHY

Manuscripts are held in archives in London, unless otherwise stated.

Primary

Manuscripts

BL, Additional MS 10449
BL, Egerton MS 2592, f.81
Dulwich College, MSS 1
Lambeth Palace Library, MS 3196, f.29
TNA, SP 12/160/48
TNA, SP 12/163/44:1
TNA, SP 14/171/39, 49, 64, 66, 75
TNA, SP 16/269, f.85:1
TNA, SP 16/271, f.57
Nottingham, University of Nottingham, MS Ne C 15, 1405, ff.3–5
Taunton, Somerset Heritage Centre, DD/PH/212/12
Anonymous, *The Two Noble Ladies*, BL, Egerton MS 1994, ff.224–44
Fletcher, John and Philip Massinger, *The Tragedy of Sir John Van Olden Barnavelt*, BL, Additional MS 18653
Glapthorne, Henry, *The Lady Mother*, BL, Egerton MS 1994, ff.186–211
Heywood, Thomas, *The Captives*, BL, Egerton MS 1994, ff.52–73
Massinger, Philip, *Believe As You List*, BL, Egerton MS 2828
Middleton, Thomas, *The Second Maiden's Tragedy*, BL, Lansdowne MS 807, ff.29–56
Mountfort, Walter, *The Launching of the Mary*, BL, Egerton MS 1994, ff.317–49

Printed

Beaumont, Francis, *The Knight of the Burning Pestle*, 2nd edn, ed. Michael Hattaway (London, 2002)

Brome, Richard, *The Court Beggar*, Quarto Text (1653), ed. M. O'Connor, *Richard Brome Online*, http://www.hrionline. ac.uk/brome (accessed 30.01.13)

—*A Joviall Crew: Or, The Merry Beggars*, Quarto Text (1652), ed. E. Lowe, *Richard Brome Online*, http://www.hrionline.ac.uk/ brome (accessed 30.01.13)

Brome, Richard and Thomas Heywood, *The Late Lancashire Witches*, Quarto Text (1634), ed. H. Ostovich, *Richard Brome Online*, http://www.hrionline.ac.uk/brome (accessed 15.06.12)

C. J., *The Two Merry Milkmaids* (1620), ed. G. Harold Metz (New York, 1979)

Cook, David and F. P. Wilson (eds), 'Dramatic Records in the Declared Accounts of the Treasurer of the Chamber, 1558–1642', *Malone Society Collections* 6 (1961) (Oxford, 1962)

The Defence of Conny Catching (London, 1592)

Dekker, Thomas, *The Guls Horne-booke* (London, 1609)

[Dekker, Thomas, John Ford,] Thomas Middleton and William Rowley, *The Spanish Gipsie* (London, 1653)

Douglas, Audrey and Peter Greenfield (eds), *REED: Cumberland, Westmorland, Gloucestershire* (Toronto, 1986)

Erler, Mary C., ed., *REED: Ecclesiastical London* (Toronto, 2008)

Eutheo, Anglophile, *A Second and Third Blast of Retrait from Plaies and Theaters* (London, 1580)

Flecknoe, Richard, 'A Short Discourse of the English Stage' in *Loves Kingdom, A Pastoral Trage-Comedy* (London, 1664)

Fletcher, John, *The Faithful Shepherdess*, ed. Florence Ada Kirk (New York, 1980)

Fletcher, John and Philip Massinger, *The Tragedy of Sir John Van Olden Barnavelt* (Malone Society Reprints, 1979), ed. T. H. Howard-Hill (Oxford, 1980)

Galloway, David, ed., *REED: Norwich* (Toronto, 1984)

Gayton, Edmund, *Pleasant Notes upon Don Quixot* (London, 1654)

George, David, ed., *REED: Lancashire* (Toronto, 1991)

Gibson, James M., ed., *REED: Kent: Diocese of Canterbury*, 3 vols (London, 2002)

Glapthorne, Henry, *The Lady Mother* (Malone Society Reprints, 1958), ed. Arthur Brown (Oxford, 1959)

Goffe, Thomas, *The Careless Shepherdess* (London, 1656)

Gosson, Stephen, *Playes Confuted in Fiue Actions* (London, 1582)

—*The Trumpet of Warre* (London, 1598)

Halkett, Lady Anne, *The Memoirs of Anne, Lady Halkett and Ann, Lady Fanshawe*, ed. John Loftis (Oxford, 1979)

Heywood, Thomas, *An Apology for Actors* (London, 1612)

—*The English Traveller* (London, 1633)

Hughes, Paul L. and James F. Larkin (eds), *Tudor Royal Proclamations: The Later Tudors (1553–1587)*, II (London, 1969)

—*Tudor Royal Proclamations: The Later Tudors (1588–1603)*, III (New Haven, CT, 1969)

Ingram, R. W., ed., *REED: Coventry* (Toronto, 1981)

Jonson, Ben, *The Alchemist*, 3rd edn, ed. Elizabeth Cook (London, 2010)

—*Bartholomew Fair*, 2nd edn, G. R. Hibbard and Alexander Leggatt (eds) (London, 2007)

—*The Cambridge Edition of the Works of Ben Jonson*, David Bevington, Martin Butler and Ian Donaldson (eds), 7 vols (Cambridge, 2012)

—*The Workes of Beniamin Jonson* (London, 1616)

Journal of the House of Commons, Vol. 1: 1547–1629 (1802), *British History Online*, http://www.british-history.ac.uk (accessed 11.06.12).

J. W., *The Valiant Scot* (London, 1637; repr. Marston Gate, 2011)

— *The Valiant Scot*, ed. George F. Byers (New York, 1980)

Langbaine, Gerald, *An Account of the English Dramatick Poets* (Oxford, 1691)

Leishman, J. B., ed., *The Second Part of the Return from Parnassus* in *The Three Parnassus Plays* (London, 1949)

Lyly, John, *Midas* in *Gallathea and Midas*, ed. Anne Begor Lancashire (London, 1969; repr. 1970)

Marlowe, Christopher, *Tamburlaine*, ed. J. W. Harper (London, 1992)

Marston, John, *Histrio-Mastix* (London, 1610)

—*The Malcontent*, ed. George K. Hunter (Manchester, 1975; repr. 1999)

Massinger, Philip, *Believe As You List* (Malone Society Reprints, 1927), ed. Charles J. Sisson (Oxford, 1927)

—*The Bond-Man* (London, 1638)

—*The Renegado*, ed. Michael Neill (London, 2010)

Middleton, Thomas, *A Chaste Maid in Cheapside*, 2nd edn, ed. Alan Brissenden (London, 2007)

—*The Collected Works*, Gary Taylor and John Lavagnino (eds) (Oxford, 2007)

—*A Game at Chess*, ed. T. H. Howard-Hill (Manchester, 2003; repr. 2009)

—*The Second Maiden's Tragedy*, ed. Anne Lancashire (Manchester, 1978)

—*The Second Maiden's Tragedy* (Malone Society Reprints, 1909), ed. W. W. Greg (Oxford, 1909)

Middleton, Thomas and William Rowley, *The Changeling*, 2nd edn, ed. Joost Daalder (London, 1990)

[Mountfort, Walter] *The Launching of the Mary* (Malone Society Reprints, 1933), ed. John Henry Walter (Oxford, 1933)

Munday, Anthony et al., *Sir Thomas More*, ed. John Jowett (London, 2011)

Rawlins, Thomas, *The Rebellion* (London, 1640)

Shakespeare, William, *King Lear*, ed. R. A. Foakes (London, 1997)

—*Mr William Shakespeares Comedies, Histories, & Tragedies* (London, 1623)

—*Richard II*, updated edn, ed. Andrew Gurr (Cambridge, 2003; repr. 2012)

—*Shakespeare: Complete Works*, revised edn, Richard Proudfoot, Ann Thompson and David Scott Kastan (eds) (London, 2011)

Shirley, James, *The Schoole of Complement* (London, 1631)

The Statutes of the Realm, Volume 4: Part 1, 1547–1585 (Buffalo, NY, 1993)

Stephens, John, *Satyrical Essayes Characters and Others* (London, 1615)

Streitberger, W. R., ed., 'Jacobean and Caroline Revels Accounts, 1603–1642', *Malone Society Collections* 13 (Oxford, 1986)

Tatham, John, *The Fancies Theater* (London, 1640)

—*Knavery in All Trades: Or, The Coffee-House* (London, 1664)

—*Vox Borealis, or The Northern Discoverie* (London, 1641)

Wasson, John, ed., *REED: Devon* (Toronto, 1986)

Webster, John, *The Displaying of Supposed Witchcraft* (London, 1677)

Wickham, Glynne, Herbert Berry and William Ingram (eds), *English Professional Theatre, 1530–1660* (Cambridge, 2000)

Wright, James, *Historia Histrionica: An Historical Account of the English Stage* (London, 1679)

Secondary

Astington, John H., *Actors and Acting in Shakespeare's Time: The Art of Stage Playing* (Cambridge, 2010)

—'Playing the Man: Acting at the Red Bull and the Fortune', *ET* 9 (2006), 130–43

Barish, Jonas, *Ben Jonson and the Language of Prose Comedy* (New York, 1960; repr. 1970)

Barroll, Leeds, 'A New History for Shakespeare and his Time', *SQ* 39 (1988), 441–64

—'Shakespeare and the Second Blackfriars Theater', *SSt* 23 (2005), 156–70

—'Shakespeare, Noble Patrons, and the Pleasures of "Common" Playing' in *Shakespeare and Theatrical Patronage in Early Modern England*, Paul Whitfield White and Suzanne R. Westfall (eds) (Cambridge, 2002), 90–121

Bawcutt, N. W., *The Control and Censorship of Caroline Drama: The Records of Sir Henry Herbert Master of the Revels 1623–73* (Oxford, 1996)

Beckerman, Bernard, 'Philip Henslowe' in *The Theatrical Manager in England and America: Player of a Perilous Game*, ed. Joseph W. Donohue Jr (Princeton, NJ, 1971), 19–62

—*Shakespeare at the Globe, 1599–1609* (New York, 1962; repr. 1966)

Bednarz, James P., *Shakespeare and the Poet's War* (New York, 2001)

Benbow, R. Mark, 'Dutton and Goffe versus Broughton: A Disputed Contract for Plays in the 1570s', *REED: Newsletter* 2 (1981), 3–9

Bentley, Gerald Eades, *The Jacobean and Caroline Stage*, 7 vols (Oxford, 1941–68)

—*The Profession of Dramatist in Shakespeare's Time* (Princeton, NJ, 1971)

—*The Profession of Player in Shakespeare's Time 1590–1642* (Princeton, NJ, 1984)

—'Shakespeare and the Blackfriars Theatre', *SS* 1 (1948), 38–50

—'The Troubles of a Caroline Acting Company: Prince Charles's Company', *HLQ* 41:3 (1978), 217–49

Bergeron, David M., 'Women as Patrons of English Renaissance Drama' in *Patronage in the Renaissance*, Guy Fitch Lytle and Stephen Orgel (eds) (Princeton, NJ, 1981), 274–90

Berry, Herbert, 'The Globe Bewitched and El Hombre Fiel', *MRDE* 1 (1984), 211–30

—'Playhouses' in *A Companion to Renaissance Drama*, ed. Arthur F. Kinney (Oxford, 2004), 147–62

Blackstone, Mary A., 'Lancashire, Shakespeare and the Construction of Cultural Neighbourhoods in Sixteenth-century England' in *Region, Religion and Patronage: Lancastrian Shakespeare*, Richard Dutton, Alison Findlay and Richard Wilson (eds) (Manchester, 2003), 186–204

—'Patrons and Elizabethan Dramatic Companies', *Elizabethan Theatre* 10 (1988), 112–32

Blackstone, Mary and Cameron Louis, 'Towards "A Full and Understanding Auditory": New Evidence of Playgoers at the First Globe Theatre', *MLR* 90 (1995), 556–71

Blayney, Peter W. M., 'The Publication of Playbooks' in *A New History of Early English Drama*, John D. Cox and David Scott Kastan (eds) (New York, 1997), 383–422

—*The Texts of 'King Lear' and their Origins, Volume 1: Nicholas Okes and the First Quarto* (Cambridge, 1982)

Bly, Mary, *Queer Virgins and Virgin Queans on the Early Modern Stage* (Oxford, 2000)

—'Review of *Children of the Queen's Revels: A Jacobean Repertory* by Lucy Munro', *MRDE* 22 (2009), 242–8

Bowers, Rick, 'John Lowin: Actor-Manager of the King's Company, 1630–1642', *Theatre Survey* 28:1 (1987), 15–35

Bradley, David, *From Text to Performance in the Elizabethan Theatre: Preparing the Play for the Stage* (Cambridge, 1992)

Brennan, Michael, *Literary Patronage in the English Renaissance: The Pembroke Family* (London, 1998)

Brinkley, Roberta Florence, *Nathan Field: The Actor-Playwright* (Hamden, 1973)

Bruce, John, ed., *Calendar of State Papers, Domestic Series of the*

Reign of Charles I, 1634–1635 (London, 1859; repr. Nendeln, Liechtenstein, 1967)

Butler, Martin, 'Jonson's London and its Theatres' in *The Cambridge Companion to Ben Jonson*, Richard Harp and Stanley Stewart (eds) (Cambridge, 2000), 15–29

—*Theatre and Crisis, 1632–42* (Cambridge, 1984)

Centerwall, Brandon, 'A Greatly Exaggerated Demise: The Remaking of the Children of Paul's as the Duke of York's Men (1608)', *ET* 9:1 (2006), 85–107

Cerasano, S. P., 'The "Business" of Shareholding, the Fortune Playhouse, and Francis Grace's Will', *MRDE* 2 (1985), 231–51

—'Competition for the King's Men?: Alleyn's Blackfriars Venture', *MRDE* 4 (1989), 173–86

—'Must the Devil Appear?: Audiences, Actors, Stage Business' in *A Companion to Renaissance Drama*, ed. Arthur F. Kinney (Oxford, 2004), 193–211

—'Philip Henslowe, Simon Forman, and the Theatrical Community of the 1590s', *SQ* 44:2 (1993), 145–58

Chambers, E. K., *The Elizabethan Stage*, 4 vols (Oxford, 1923), I and II (repr. 1961), IV (repr. 1945)

—*William Shakespeare: A Study of Facts and Problems*, 2 vols (Oxford, 1930)

Chapman, Alison A., 'Flaying Bartholomew: Jonson's Hagiographic Parody', *MP* 101:4 (2004), 511–41

Chernaik, Warren, 'Stanley, Thomas (1625–1678)', *ODNB* online edn, http://www.oxforddnb.com (accessed 31.01.12).

Chillington, Carol A., 'Playwrights at Work: Henslowe's, Not Shakespeare's *Book of Sir Thomas More*', *ELR* 10 (1980), 439–79

Clare, Janet, *'Art made tongue-tied by authority': Elizabethan and Jacobean Dramatic Censorship*, 2nd edn (Manchester, 1999)

Clark, Ira, *Professional Playwrights, Massinger, Ford, Shirley, & Brome* (Lexington, MA, 1992)

Cogswell, Thomas, 'Thomas Middleton and the Court, 1624: *A Game at Chess* in Context', *HLQ* 47 (1984), 273–88

Collins, Eleanor, 'Richard Brome's Contract and the Relationship of Dramatist to Company in the Early Modern Period', *ET* 10:2 (2007), 116–28

Cook, Ann Jennalie, 'Audiences: Investigation, Interpretation, Invention' in *A New History of Early English Drama*, John D. Cox and David Scott Kastan (eds) (New York, 1997), 305–20.

—*The Privileged Playgoers of Shakespeare's London, 1576–1642* (Princeton, NJ, 1981)

Craig, D. H., ed., *Ben Jonson: The Critical Heritage* (London, 1999; repr. 2005)

Davidson, Adele, *Shakespeare in Shorthand: the Textual Mystery of 'King Lear'* (Newark, NJ, 2009)

Davidson, Clifford, 'Judgment, Iconoclasm, and Anti-theatricalism in Jonson's *Bartholomew Fair*', *Papers on Language and Literature* 25:4 (1989), 349–63

Davison, Peter, 'Commerce and Patronage: The Lord Chamberlain's Men's Tour of 1597' in *Shakespeare Performed: Essays in Honor of R. A. Foakes*, ed. Grace Ioppolo (Newark, NJ, 2000), 56–71

Donaldson, Ian, *Jonson's Magic Houses: Essays in Interpretation* (Oxford, 1997)

—*The World Upside-Down: Comedy from Jonson to Fielding* (Oxford, 1974)

Dutton, Richard, *Mastering the Revels: The Regulation and Censorship of English Renaissance Drama* (Basingstoke, 1991)

—'The Revels Office and the Boy Companies, 1600–1613: New Perspectives', *ELR* 32:2 (2002), 324–51

Edelman, Charles, '"Shoot him all at once": Gunfire at the Playhouse, 1587', *TN* 57 (2003), 78–81

Edmond, Mary, 'Pembroke's Men', *RES* 25:98 (1974), 129–36

Egan, Gabriel, 'Precision, Consistency, and Completeness in Early-Modern Playbook Manuscripts: The Evidence from *Thomas of Woodstock* and *John a Kent and John a Cumber*', *The Library* 12 (2011) 376–91

—'Theatre in London' in *Shakespeare: An Oxford Guide*, Stanley Wells and Lena Cowen Orlin (eds) (Oxford, 2003), 20–31

—'What is not Collaborative about Early Modern Drama in Performance and Print?' *SS* 66 (forthcoming, 2013)

—'The Use of Booths in the Original Staging of Jonson's *Bartholomew Fair*', *Cahiers Elisabethains* 53 (1998), 43–52

Erne, Lukas, *Shakespeare as Literary Dramatist* (Cambridge, 2003)

Farmer, Alan B. and Zachary Lesser, 'The Popularity of Playbooks Revisited', *SQ* 56:1 (2005), 1–32

Foakes, R. A., ed., *Henslowe's Diary*, 2nd edn (Cambridge, 2002)

—'Playhouses and Players' in *The Cambridge Companion to English Renaissance Drama*, A. R. Braunmuller and Michael Hattaway (eds), 2nd edn (Cambridge, 2003), 1–52

Fotheringham, Richard, 'The Doubling of Roles on the Jacobean Stage', *TRI* 10 (1985), 18–32

Gaby, Rosemary, 'Of Vagabonds and Commonwealths: *Beggars' Bush*, *A Jovial Crew*, and *The Sisters*', *SEL* 34 (1994), 401–24

George, David, 'The Playhouse at Prescot and the 1592–94 Plague' in *Region, Religion and Patronage: Lancastrian Shakespeare*, Richard Dutton, Alison Findlay and Richard Wilson (eds) (Manchester, 2003), 227–42

Graves, R. B., *Lighting the Shakespearean Stage, 1567–1642* (Carbondale, IL, 1999)

Green, Mary Anne Everett, ed., *Calendar of State Papers, Domestic Series of the Reign of James I, 1623–1625* (London, 1859; repr. Nendeln, Liechtenstein, 1967)

Greenfield, Peter H., 'Professional Players at Gloucester: Conditions of Provincial Performing', *Elizabethan Theatre* 10 (1988), 73–92

Greg, W. W., *The Editorial Problem in Shakespeare*, 3rd edn (Oxford, 1954)

—ed., *Henslowe Papers* (London, 1907)

Gundersheimer, Werner, 'Patronage in the Renaissance: An Exploratory Approach' in *Patronage in the Renaissance*, Guy Fitch Lytle and Stephen (eds) Orgel (Princeton, NJ, 1981), 3–23

Gurr, Andrew, 'The Bare Island', *SS* 47 (1994), 29–43

—'London's Blackfriars Playhouse and the Chamberlain's Men' in *Inside Shakespeare: Essays on the Blackfriars Stage*, ed. Paul Menzer (Selinsgrove, 2006), 17–30

—'Maximal and Minimal Texts: Shakespeare V. the Globe', *SS* 52 (1999), 68–87

—*Playgoing in Shakespeare's London*, 2nd edn (Cambridge, 1997), 3rd edn (Cambridge, 2004)

—'Playing in Amphitheatres and Playing in Hall Theatres', *Elizabethan Theatre* 13 (1994), 27–62

—*The Shakespeare Company, 1594–1642* (Cambridge, 2004)

—*The Shakespearean Stage, 1574–1642*, 3rd edn (Cambridge, 2005)

—*Shakespeare's Opposites: The Admiral's Company 1594–1625* (Cambridge, 2009; repr. 2012)

—*The Shakespearian Playing Companies* (Oxford, 1996)

Gurr, Andrew and Gabriel Egan, 'Prompting, Backstage Activity, and the Openings onto the Shakespearian Stage', *TN* 56 (2002), 138–42

Gurr, Andrew and Mariko Ichikawa, *Staging in Shakespeare's Theatres* (Oxford, 2000; repr. 2012)

Haaker, Ann, 'The Plague, the Theater, and the Poet', *Renaissance Drama* I (1968), 283–306

Harbage, Alfred, *Shakespeare and the Rival Traditions* (New York, 1952)

—*Shakespeare's Audience* (New York, 1941)

Heinemann, Margot, *Puritanism and Theatre: Thomas Middleton and Opposition Drama under the Early Stuarts* (Cambridge, 1980; repr. 1982)

—'Rebel Lords, Popular Playwrights, and Political Culture: Notes on the Jacobean Patronage of the Earl of Southampton', *YES* 21 (1991), 63–86

Hirschfield, Heather, 'Collaborating across Generations: Thomas Heywood, Richard Brome, and the Production of *The Late Lancashire Witches*', *Journal of Medieval and Early Modern Studies* 30:2 (2000), 339–74

Howard-Hill, Trevor, 'Crane's 1619 "Promptbook" of *Barnavelt* and Theatrical Processes', *MP* 86:2 (1988), 146–70

—*Middleton's "Vulgar Pasquin": Essays on 'A Game at Chess'* (Newark, NJ, 1995)

—'Political Interpretations of Middleton's *A Game at Chess*', *YES* 21 (1991), 274–85

—'The Unique Eye-Witness Report of Middleton's *A Game at Chess*', *RES* 42:166 (1991), 168–78

Hoy, Cyrus, 'Massinger as Collaborator: The Plays with Fletcher and Others' in *Philip Massinger: A Critical Reassessment*, ed. Douglas Howard (Cambridge, 1985), 51–82

Ingram, William, *The Business of Playing: The Beginnings of Adult Professional Theater in Elizabethan London* (Ithaca, NY, 1992)

—'The Economics of Playing' in *A Companion to Renaissance Drama*, ed. Arthur F. Kinney (Oxford, 2004), 313–27

—'The "Evolution" of the Elizabethan Playing Company' in *The Development of Shakespeare's Theater*, ed. John H. Astington (New York, 1992), 13–28

Ioppolo, Grace, *Dramatists and Their Manuscripts in the Age of Shakespeare, Jonson, Middleton and Heywood: Authority, Authorship and the Playhouse* (London, 2006; repr. 2007)

—'The Transmission of an English Renaissance Play-Text' in

A Companion to Renaissance Drama, ed. Arthur F. Kinney (Oxford, 2004), 163–79

Joseph, B. L., *Elizabethan Acting* (London, 1951)

Kahan, Jeffrey, ed., *'King Lear': New Critical Essays* (New York, 2008)

Kastan, David Scott, *Shakespeare After Theory* (London, 1999)

—'"To think these trifles some-thing": Shakespearean Playbooks and the Claims of Authorship', *SSt* 36 (2008), 37–48

Kathman, David, 'Grocers, Goldsmiths, and Drapers: Freemen and Apprentices in the Elizabethan Theater', *SQ* 55:1 (2004), 1–49

—'Kirke, John (fl. 1629–1643)', *ODNB* online edn, http://www.oxforddnb.com (accessed 02.02.12).

—'Players, Livery Companies, and Apprentices' in *The Oxford Handbook of Early Modern Theatre*, ed. Richard Dutton (Oxford, 2009; repr. 2011), 413–28

Kaufmann, R. J., *Richard Brome. Caroline Playwright* (New York, 1961)

Keenan, Siobhan, *Renaissance Literature* (Edinburgh, 2008)

—*Travelling Players in Shakespeare's England* (Basingstoke, 2002)

Kerrigan, John, *Archipelagic English: Literature, History, and Politics, 1603–1707* (Oxford, 2008)

—'Revision, Adaptation, and the Fool in *King Lear*' in *Division of the Kingdoms: Shakespeare's Two Versions of 'King Lear'*, Gary Taylor and Michael Warren (eds) (Oxford, 1983), 195–239

King, T. J., *Casting Shakespeare's Plays: London Actors and their Roles, 1590–1642* (Cambridge, 1992)

—*Shakespearean Staging, 1599–1642* (Cambridge, MA, 1971)

Kingsford, C. L. and William A. Shaw (eds), *Historical Manuscripts Commission: Report on the Manuscripts of Lord De L'Isle & Dudley, preserved at Penshurst Place* (London, 1934) *Volume II*

Kinney, Arthur, *Shakespeare by Stages: An Historical Introduction* (Oxford, 2003)

Knapp, Jeffrey, 'What is a Co-Author?', *Representations* 89 (2005), 1–29

Knowles, Richard, 'The Evolution of the Texts of *Lear*' in *'King Lear': New Critical Essays*, ed. Jeffrey Kahan (New York, 2008), 124–54

Knutson, Roslyn L., 'Adult Playing Companies, 1593–1603' in *The Oxford Handbook of Early Modern Theatre*, ed. Richard Dutton (Oxford, 2009; repr. 2011), 56–71

—*Playing Companies and Commerce in Shakespeare's Time*
(Cambridge, 2001)

—'Playing Companies and Repertory' in *A Companion to
Renaissance Drama*, ed. Arthur F. Kinney (Oxford, 2004),
180–92

—*The Repertory of Shakespeare's Company, 1594–1613*
(Fayetteville, NC, 1991)

—'The Start of Something Big' in *Locating the Queen's Men
1583–1603: Material Practices and Conditions of Playing*,
Helen Ostovich, Holger Schott Syme and Andrew Griffin (eds)
(Farnham, 2009), 99–108

Levin, Richard, 'Women in the Renaissance Theatre Audience', *SQ*
40:2 (1989), 165–74

Limon, Jerzy, *Dangerous Matter: English Drama and Politics in
1623/24* (Cambridge, 1986)

Long, William B., '"Precious Few": English Manuscript Playbooks'
in *A Companion to Shakespeare*, ed. David Scott Kastan
(Oxford, 1999), 414–33

—'Stage-directions: A Misinterpreted Factor in Determining Textual
Provenance', *TEXT: Transactions of the Society for Textual
Scholarship* 2 (1985), 121–37

Lopez, Jeremy, *Theatrical Conventions and Audience Response in
Early Modern Drama* (Cambridge, 2003)

Lublin, Robert I., *Costuming the Shakespearean Stage* (Farnham,
2011)

MacIntyre, Jean and Garrett P. J. Epp, '"Cloathes worth all the
rest": Costumes and Properties' in *A New History of Early
English Drama*, John D. Cox and David Scott Kastan (eds)
(New York, 1997), 269–85.

MacLean, Sally-Beth, 'Players on Tour: New Evidence from Records
of Early English Drama', *Elizabethan Theatre* 10 (1988), 55–72

—'The Politics of Patronage: Dramatic Records in Robert Dudley's
Household Books', *SQ* 44:2 (1993), 175–82

—'Tracking Leicester's Men: The Patronage of a Performance
Troupe' in *Shakespeare and Theatrical Patronage in Early
Modern England*, Paul Whitfield White and Suzanne R. Westfall
(eds) (Cambridge, 2002), 246–71

Marcus, Leah, *The Politics of Mirth: Jonson, Herrick, Milton,
Marvell and the Defence of Old Holiday Pastimes* (Chicago,
1986; repr. 1989)

Marino, James J., 'Adult Playing Companies, 1613–1625' in *The Oxford Handbook of Early Modern Theatre*, ed. Richard Dutton (Oxford, 2009; repr. 2011), 88–103

Masten, Jeffrey, *Textual Intercourse: Collaboration, Authorship, and Sexualities in Renaissance Drama* (Cambridge, 1997)

Mateer, David, 'Edward Alleyn, Richard Perkins and the Rivalry between the Swan and Rose Playhouses', *RES* 60 (2009), 61–77

McLuskie, Kathleen E., 'Materiality and the Market: The Lady Elizabeth's Men and the Challenge of Theatre History' in *The Oxford Handbook of Early Modern Theatre*, ed. Richard Dutton (Oxford, 2009; repr. 2011), 429–40

—'The Poets' Royal Exchange: Patronage and Commerce in Early Modern Drama', *YES* 21 (1991), 53–62

McMillin, Scott, 'Professional Playwrighting' in *A Companion to Shakespeare*, ed. David Scott Kastan (Oxford, 1999; repr. 2004), 225–38

—'Reading the Elizabethan Acting Companies', *ET* 4:1 (2001), 111–15

McMillin, Scott and Sally-Beth MacLean, *The Queen's Men and Their Plays* (Cambridge, 1998)

McMullan, Gordon, *The Politics of Unease in the Plays of John Fletcher* (Amherst, MA, 1994)

Munro, Lucy, *Children of the Queen's Revels: A Jacobean Theatre Repertory* (Cambridge, 2005)

Neill, Michael, '"Wits most accomplished Senate": The Audience of the Caroline Private Theaters', *SEL* 18 (1978), 341–60

Nicol, David, 'The Repertory of Prince Charles's (I) Company, 1608–1625', *ET* 9:2 (2006), 57–72

Orrell, John, 'The London Stage in the Florentine Correspondence, 1604–1618', *TRI* 3 (1977–8), 157–76

Palfrey, Simon and Tiffany Stern, *Shakespeare in Parts* (Oxford, 2007; repr. 2010)

Palmer, Barbara D., 'Early Modern Mobility: Players, Payments, and Patrons', *SQ* 56:3 (2005), 259–305.

Parker, R. B., 'The Themes and Staging of *Bartholomew Fair*', *UTQ* 39 (1970), 293–309

Peck, Linda Levy, 'The Caroline Audience: Evidence from Hatfield House', *SQ* 51:4 (2000), 474–7

Pollard, Alfred W., *Shakespeare's Fight with the Pirates and the Problems of the Transmission of his Text*, revised edn (Cambridge, 1967; repr. 2010)

Postlewait, Thomas, 'Theater Events and Their Political Contexts: A Problem in the Writing of Theater History' in *Critical Theory and Performance*, revised edn, Janelle G. Reinelt and Joseph P. Roach (eds) (Ann Arbor, MI, 2007), 198–222

Purkiss, Diane, *The Witch in History: Early Modern and Twentieth-Century Representations* (London, 1996)

Riddell, James A., 'Some Actors in Ben Jonson's Plays', *SS* 5 (1969), 285–98

Roberts, Peter, 'Elizabethan Players and Minstrels and the Legislation of 1572 against Retainers and Vagabonds' in *Religion, Culture and Society in Early Modern Britain: Essays in Honour of Patrick Collinson*, Anthony Fletcher and Peter Roberts (eds) (Cambridge, 1994), 29–55

Rosenberg, Eleanor, *Leicester: Patron of Letters* (New York, 1955)

Rosenberg, Marvin, 'Elizabethan Actors: Men or Marionettes?' *PMLA* 69:4 (1954), 915–27

Rowland, Richard, '(Gentle)men Behaving Badly: Aggression, Anxiety, and Repertory in the Playhouses of Early Modern London', *MRDE* 25 (2012), 17–41

Rutter, Tom, 'Adult Companies 1603–1613' in *The Oxford Handbook of Early Modern Theatre*, ed. Richard Dutton (Oxford, 2009; repr. 2011), 72–87

—'Introduction: The Repertory-based Approach', *ET* 13:2 (2010), 121–31

Sanders, Julie, 'Beggars' Commonwealths and the Pre-Civil War Stage: Suckling's *The Goblins*, Brome's *A Jovial Crew*, and Shirley's *The Sisters*', *MLR* 97:1 (2002), 1–14

Shapiro, Michael, *Children of the Revels: The Boy Companies of Shakespeare's Time and Their Plays* (New York, 1977)

Sherman, Jane, 'The Pawns' Allegory in Middleton's *A Game at Chesse*', *RES* 29: 114 (1978), 147–59

Smallwood, R. L., '"Here, in the Friars": Immediacy and Theatricality in *The Alchemist*', *RES* 32:136 (1981), 142–60

Smith, Bruce R., *The Acoustic World of Early Modern England* (Chicago, 1999)

Smith, Irwin, *Shakespeare's Blackfriars Playhouse: Its History and its Design* (London, 1966)

Somerset, Alan, 'The Blackfriars on Tour: Provincial Analogies' in

Inside Shakespeare: Essays on the Blackfriars Stage, ed. Paul Menzer (Selinsgrove, 2006), 80–5

Stern, Tiffany, *Documents of Performance in Early Modern England* (Cambridge, 2009; repr. 2012)

—*Making Shakespeare: From Stage to Page* (2004; repr. 2005)

—*Rehearsal from Shakespeare to Sheridan* (Oxford, 2003; repr. 2005)

—'Sermons, Plays and Note-takers: *Hamlet* Q1 as a "Noted" Text', *SS* 66 (2013), 1–23

Stevens, Andrea R., '"Assisted by a Barber": The Court Apothecary, Special Effects, and *The Gypsies Metamorphosed*', *TN* 61:1 (2007), 2–11

Streitberger, W. R., 'Adult Companies to 1583' in *The Oxford Handbook of Early Modern Theatre*, ed. Richard Dutton (Oxford, 2009; repr. 2011), 19–38

Sturgess, Keith, *Jacobean Private Theatre* (London, 1987)

Sullivan Jr., Garrett A., *The Drama of Landscape: Land, Property, and Social Relations on the Early Modern Stage* (Stanford, CT, 1998)

Taylor, Gary and John Lavagnino (eds), *Thomas Middleton and Early Modern Textual Culture: A Companion to the Collected Works* (Oxford: 2007)

Taylor, Gary, and Michael Warren (eds), *The Division of the Kingdoms: Shakespeare's Two Versions of 'King Lear'* (Oxford, 1983)

Thomas, Sidney, 'Shakespeare's Supposed Revision of *King Lear*', *SQ* 35:4 (1984), 506–11

Thomson, Leslie, 'Playgoers on the Outdoor Stages of Early Modern London', *TN* 64:1 (2010), 3–11

—'A Quarto "Marked for Performance": Evidence of What?', *MRDE* 8 (1996), 176–210

Thomson, Peter, 'Conventions of Playwriting', in *Shakespeare: An Oxford Guide*, Stanley Wells and Lena Cowen Orlin (eds) (Oxford, 2003), 44–54

—*Shakespeare's Professional Career* (Cambridge, 1992)

—*Shakespeare's Theatre*, 2nd edn (London, 1992)

Urkowitz, Steven, *Shakespeare's Revision of 'King Lear'* (Princeton, NJ, 1980)

van Es, Bart, *Shakespeare in Company* (Oxford, 2013)

Warren, Michael, 'The Diminution of Kent' in *The Division of the*

Kingdoms: Shakespeare's Two Versions of 'King Lear', Gary
Taylor and Michael Warren (eds) (Oxford, 1983), 59–73

Werstine, Paul, 'The Continuing Importance of New Bibliographical
Method', *SS* 62 (2009), 30–45

Westfall, Suzanne R., *Patrons and Performance: Early Tudor
Household Revels* (Oxford, 1990)

—'"The useless dearness of the diamond": Patronage Theatre and
Households' in *Region, Religion and Patronage: Lancastrian
Shakespeare*, Richard Dutton, Alison Findlay and Richard
Wilson (eds) (Manchester, 2003), 32–49

—'"The useless dearness of the diamond": Theories of Patronage
Theatre' in *Shakespeare and Theatrical Patronage in Early
Modern England*, Paul Whitfield White and Suzanne R. Westfall
(eds) (Cambridge, 2002), 13–42

White, Paul Whitfield, *Drama and Religion in English Provincial
Society, 1485–1660* (Cambridge, 2008)

—'Patronage, Protestantism, and Stage Propaganda in Early
Elizabethan England', *YES* 21 (1991), 39–52

—*Theatre and Reformation: Protestantism, Patronage and Playing
in Tudor England* (Cambridge, 1993)

Whitney, Charles, 'Appropriate This', *Borrowers and Lenders:
The Journal of Shakespeare and Appropriation* 3:2 (2008),
http://www.borrowers.uga.edu (accessed 23.01.13)

—*Early Responses to Renaissance Drama* (Cambridge, 2006)

—'"Usually in the Werking Daies": Playgoing Journeymen,
Apprentices, and Servants in Guild Records, 1582–92', *SQ* 50:4
(1999), 433–58

Wiggins, Martin, *Shakespeare and the Drama of his Time* (Oxford,
2000)

Wilson, Edward M. and Olga Turner, 'The Spanish Protest against
A Game at Chesse', *MLR* 44 (1949; repr. 1963), 476–82

Wilson, John Dover, 'Review of *A Game at Chesse* by Thomas
Middleton. Ed. R. C. Bald', *The Library*, 4th series, 11 (1930),
105–16

Yachnin, Paul, '*A Game at Chess*: Thomas Middleton's "Praise of
Folly"', *MLQ* 48 (1987), 107–23

INDEX